Praise for *Emotionomics*

"Dan Hill's book is a revelation. Marketers have clearly overemphasized the power of rational over emotional factors in their ads, packaging, product design, and sales presentations. We all know that emotions count but we lacked the vocabulary and tools for capturing and quantifying emotional appeals and impacts. Read this book so that your next marketing campaign creates high emotional buy-in."

Philip Kotler, S C Johnson Distinguished Professor of International Marketing Kellogg School of Management, Northwestern University

"*Emotionomics* leads the global business mindset into a new paradigm – one that demands and rewards sensory and emotional connections between the 21st-century corporate entity and its consumers. Dan Hill's expertise guides business in securing the bonds of empathy that will drive commercial growth over the coming years."

Martin Lindstrom, author of BRAND sense *and* BRANDchild

"Dan Hill's new book is the most penetrating and playful application of the latest research in the psychology of emotions, human interaction, neuroscience and endocrinology to sales and marketing. Read it – you'll never think about your brand the same again!"

Professor Richard Boyatzis, Departments of Organizational Behavior and Psychology Case Western Reserve University, co-author of Primal Leadership *and* Resonant Leadership

"Dan Hill tantalizes us to the very end! He travels along familiar paths to what we are afraid to know and yet knew all along. *Emotionomics* compels us to rethink all old assumptions. It captures the heart of capitalism! We must blend our aspirations and business imagination with our heartfelt intentions to truly engage those we serve. This is a 'must read' for all great leaders and great followers!"

Juli Ann Reynolds, President & CEO, Tom Peters Company

"*Emotionomics* is a powerful new work that pushes the limits of research into the emotional dynamics that connect brands with people. By using facial movements as an expression of the subconscious, *Emotionomics* captures powerful emotional responses and gives new insights into people's subconscious realities. This book is a must-read for marketers and designers, as it sheds new light on the ways brands can better fulfil consumers' unspoken desires."
Marc Gobé, author of Emotional Branding *and* Brandjam *and Chairman and CEO, Desgrippes Gobé*

"Dan Hill has cracked the code on how to get deep inside the hearts and minds of today's consumer. *Emotionomics* provides a 'radical' approach to the holy grail of business: find out what the customer really wants. He deftly blends the best of the old (rational appeal) with the radically new (emotional connection) to offer businesses an effective way to reframe their products and their marketing. The book itself is visually exciting, simply presented, and well designed. Halleluiah! The heart can no longer be marginalized if you really want to connect to your customer."
Robyn Waters, author of The Trendmaster's Guide *and* The Hummer and the Mini: Navigating the Contradictions of the New Trend Landscape

"Every aspiring experience stager must understand how to manipulate – and I mean that in the nicest possible way! – the emotions of its customers. Read *Emotionomics* to learn how to do so in a way they will perceive as authentic. How you market to your customers will never be the same."
B Joseph Pine II, co-author of The Experience Economy *and* Authenticity: What Consumers Really Want

"Emotions matter! Long gone are the days when it was enough to help your customers 'understand' what you sell, or grasp rationally what it can do for them. On today's increasingly competitive playing field, marketers missing emotional savvy won't be able to keep up. Happily, Dan Hill's compelling examples show how the findings can predict the future before you commit your budget. If you're looking to build the success rate of your marketing, communication or hiring decisions – and who isn't? – cancel your meetings until you've read *Emotionomics* cover to cover!"
Marti Barletta, author of Marketing to Women

"*Emotionomics* is a must-read book for all businesses aiming to create and maintain a dynamic, persistent and potent brand. Most brand owners fail to infuse emotional attributes to their brands. The dynamic of how emotions can be utilized to sell your brand is very well-outlined and described in the pages of this book. Fasten your seat belts and discover what you've missed in your organization and your brand, in order to be productive, creative and to engage with your target audience. The invaluable insights in this book are the keys to your success for your brands to flourish both locally and globally."

Said Aghil Baaghil, marketing strategist and author of Eccentric Marketing

"Being able to appeal to customers emotionally is *the* way to success in the marketplace. It is a profound transformation. It is not easy, but Dan Hill shows how to do it – in a convincing and fun way."

Rolf Jensen, author of The Dream Society

A profound, practical guide to navigating the emotional dynamics that determine a company's sales and productivity

Step closer to customers and employees, step ahead of competitors. How? First, by acknowledging the say/feel gap: the frequent disconnect between what people say versus how they feel and what they will actually do. Then by adopting a new approach to measure and manage emotions. Achieve success by ensuring that one's efforts avoid the say/feel gap into which most of the business world falls.

In the tradition of *Blink* and *Emotional Intelligence*, Dan Hill takes a concise, incisive look at how breakthroughs in brain science have mind-opening implications for how companies should be conducting business in the 21st century. Gone is the old consumer and worker model in which appeals to utilitarian benefits alone will carry the day. Instead, making a sensory–emotional connection through superior creativity and empathy becomes the key to winning over those on whom profitability depends.

What can bridge the say/feel gap, exposing the self-justifying rationalizations (intellectual alibis) that often mask people's true, intuitive gut reaction? It's facial coding, a research tool so powerful that both the CIA and FBI rely on it and so universal that, as Charles Darwin first realized, even a person born blind signals feelings to others using the same facial muscle movements.

As the originator and decade-long veteran of applying facial coding to business issues, Hill is uniquely qualified to quantify the extent of the say/feel gap and instruct companies on ways to maximize emotional buy-in. Advantage now depends on mastering the emotional dynamics that actually drive results. So to help readers survive and thrive in today's extraordinarily competitive environment, *Emotionomics* comes complete with:

- emotional strategies for success, using the Emotionomics Matrix™ as a guide;
- specific, tactical action plans ready to be enacted;
- real-life examples from leading companies;
- a top-line introduction of how to read faces;
- a vast supply of helpful, provocative and, at times, amusing insights about human nature.

Emotionomics

Emotionomics

Leveraging emotions for business success

Revised Edition

Dan Hill

KOGAN
PAGE

London and Philadelphia

First published in the United States in 2007 by Adams Business & Professional
Revised first edition published in Great Britain and the United States in 2008 by Kogan Page Limited

120 Pentonville Road
London N1 9JN
United Kingdom
www.koganpage.com

525 South 4th Street, #241
Philadelphia PA 19147
USA

© Dan Hill, 2007, 2008

ISBN 978 0 7494 5399 2

British Library Cataloguing-in-Publication Data

A CIP record for this book is available from the British Library.

Library of Congress Cataloging-in-Publication Data

Hill, Dan, 1959-
   Emotionomics : leveraging emotions for business success / Dan Hill. – Rev. ed.
      p. cm.
   Includes bibliographical references and index.
   ISBN 978-0-7494-5399-2
   1. Economics–Psychological aspects. 2. Decision making–Psychological aspects.
3. Emotions. I. Title.
   HB74.P8H55 2008
   658.001'9–dc22
                                          2008023377

Typeset by Saxon Graphics Ltd, Derby
Printed and bound in India by Replika Press Pvt Ltd

To Lucinda Williams for 'Song to a Poet'
and to Karen for everything else

Contents

Foreword

I met Dan Hill when he was a fellow panellist on a PBS show called *Mental Engineering*. You've probably never heard of it, but Bill Moyers called it 'the most interesting half hour of social commentary on television'.

On the show, they would screen commercials and the panel would analyse them for 'larger meanings'. I know that sounds kind of wide open, but the discussions often revealed political, sociological or psychological messages in the ads that you would never have thought about unless you were a panellist on a national television show and were worried about looking stupid and not having anything to say. The panel was usually composed of three highly educated intellectuals, such as Dan Hill, and some comic relief, usually a stand-up comedian who was on the road for a gig in Minneapolis, or sometimes me.

Most of the commercials were bad, even offensive. No surprise there. You've probably seen a few yourselves. Making fun of them was like shooting fish in a barrel. But Dan had a unique ability to identify the mistakes the advertisements – and the people that were paying for them – were making. He was insightful. He even had an answer to the big question: 'Why do all these intelligent people with all their sophisticated testing waste so much money on these horrible commercials?'

I'm fond of saying that I never worked a day in my life, and I think that most coal miners would agree that comedy writing, which is basically sitting in a room with a bunch of funny people while you crack jokes and eat catered food, isn't really work, but we did have testing. Just like in the real business world. Networks would use it to help decide what pilots to pick up, and just like with products and ads in the real business world, the testing process seemed wildly inaccurate. Every year it seemed that a truly funny pilot would test poorly and not get picked up, while a pilot that everyone hated would test 'through the roof', only to get on the air and be cancelled after one showing. Sometimes a pilot would test badly, get on the air through a miracle, such as a network executive trusting his own judgement, and would go on to become one of the finest, longest-running shows in the history of television. I think *Cheers*, a show I'm proud to have worked on, was one of those.

The show that will be in the first line of my obituary, *The Simpsons*, tested through the roof. The scores were so crazy high that the guy who was interpreting the data for us didn't really know how to deal with it. One of the characters was an infant named Maggie. She didn't do anything. She couldn't even talk. All she did was make a sucking noise on a pacifier. Still, her test score was a 97, which meant that test audiences liked her better than 97 per cent of all the characters from every pilot tested in the history of network television. Now normally, the network would have asked us to dump the rest of the cast, revamp the show, and make this amazing Maggie character the star of the series, but they didn't. Because, at 97 per cent, Maggie was still actually the lowest-testing character on the show. So they advised us not to do a lot of stories about Maggie.

It's an exception that proves the rule, I think. *The Simpsons* was not only good, but it contained a lot of the stuff – fast pace, vulgarity, broad cartoony performances – that allowed bad shows to get high scores. It was something so powerful the system couldn't screw it up.

Chocolate would probably have tested well, too. I doubt anyone would have tasted chocolate for the first time and wondered how such a God-awful tasting product ever got to market the way I did when I first tasted, for example, Tab energy drink. I'm sure anyone that watched *Emeril!*, the short-lived situation comedy starring chef Emeril LaGasse, wondered what NBC was thinking. Ever been to Disney's California Adventure?

It turns out that a lot of big companies are making a huge, fundamental mistake, and Dan Hill knows what it is. They don't know how to connect with their customers emotionally.

Dan also knows how they can, and it's all in this book.

As I said, I'm not a businessman, I don't work, but if I ever decided to give it a try, I think *Emotionomics* would be a very powerful weapon. For a recreational reader like me, it's fascinating and fun.

I've already worked the tidbit about the Red Bull can into the conversation at a couple of parties.

Sam Simon
co-creator of *The Simpsons*
writer, director and producer for *Cheers*, *Taxi* and *The Drew Carey Show*
Pacific Palisades, California

Sam Simon

The author

Acknowledgements

When I started on this book two years ago, I never expected it would be this much work. Many drafts later, I owe a tremendous debt of gratitude to all of the people who have compelled me to keep revising so that the book could best achieve its potential.

Three people in particular deserve my heartfelt thanks. The first is my dear friend, Joe Rich, whose insights, humour and profound caring helped me get to the human dimension of the business issues discussed here. Conversations with Joe aided me greatly in developing the content. Second is my wife, Karen Bernthal, who not only read and re-read chapters, offering wise advice, but also had patience as weekends and evenings went into this project. The third person is Andrew Langdell, who helped hone my prose and whose creative wit can be found in the visuals that so enhance this book. *Emotionomics* wouldn't exist without his talents and effort.

Readers and editors have emerged from numerous parts of my life. They include Judy Bell, Arlene Carroll, Jeff Christiansen, Joe Dylla, Eldon Hill, Holly Johnson, Jennifer Manion, Jack Murphy, Kim Saxton, Paul Schuster and Kathy Seamon.

Thanks also goes to the designer of the US edition, Jay Monroe of Soulo Communications, and to Milt Adams of Beaver's Pond Press for having the vision and generosity of spirit to create a viable alternative to how the publishing industry is normally run. Without Milt, the earlier version of this book wouldn't have been possible.

Finally, I appreciate the valuable input of staffers not already cited: people like Joe Bockman, Nancy Christensen, Kate Cook, Dominique DuCharme, Luke Elstad, Rhonda Farran, Nik Hengel, Todd Kringlie, Kim Wanten and others who have kept Sensory Logic moving along while I was distracted by getting this book finished.

To one and all, thank you.

Introduction

So why are you here?

For far too long, emotions have been concealed behind closed doors and ignored in favour of rationality and efficiency. But as businesses are forced to forge emotional connections in this age of commoditization, emotions are now front and centre.

Emotionomics opens this long-locked door and shows the importance of leveraging emotions in business.

Breakthroughs in brain science have revealed that people are primarily emotional decision makers. To help readers capitalize on those scientific findings, this book is twofold in nature. At a strategic level, the key point is that emotions matter. Emotions are central, not peripheral, to both marketplace and workplace behaviour. As a result, companies able to identify, quantify and thereby act on achieving emotional buy-in or acceptance from consumers and employees alike will enjoy a tremendous competitive advantage.

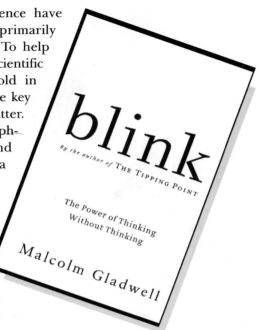

Meanwhile, at a tactical level this book showcases facial coding – the research tool highlighted in Malcolm Gladwell's bestseller, *Blink* (2005) – as a means of scientifically gauging emotional response. It's a powerful tool

Gladwell's *Blink* has brought to popular attention the degree to which people make quick, intuitive decisions and how facial coding can be used to reveal them.

my company, Sensory Logic, Inc, first brought to business applications a decade ago.

Taken together, both the theory and practice of combining psychology, biology and commerce, as shown in this book, can benefit three distinct groups of readers:

- The first group consists of business leaders, creatives (including notably those at advertising agencies and design firms) as well as anybody else in business who has long advocated for the importance of emotional buy-in in achieving business results. For them, this book is meant not only as affirmation or supporting evidence for their views, but also as a source of additional insights.
- Second, the book is meant to serve those readers who have been noticing the accelerating wealth of brain science and emotion-related articles in mainstream publications. For them, this book represents an opportunity to get up to speed on a topic they find interesting and sense is vital, but haven't had the time to investigate on their own.

● Last but not least, this book is also meant to serve those already in business or about to enter the business world who are looking for that extra edge. In marketplaces where differentiation is ever more crucial and yet harder to achieve, leveraging the centrality of emotions offers a new, largely untapped wealth of information. At the same time, in workplaces, using emotional intelligence to improve the company culture and interactive dynamics can provide a cost-free way to lift productivity.

Facing the rational/emotional split

What's most obviously left to be explained is the title of this book. *Emotionomics*, is a term I've coined to signal the role of emotions in economics. Its underlying significance, however, is to signal to the business community that measuring and managing emotions is the new strategic playing field on which companies must play well. After all, cost-cutting measures can only go so far. And technological advances will almost inevitably be me-too'ed over time. That leaves making a stronger emotional connection with customers and employees as the key to long-term, sustainable success.

In the end, the fact is that achieving a competitive advantage depends on both rational and emotional endorsement from the target market – and that the two are by no means synonymous. If they were, then perhaps words alone would be enough. But because people spin, deflect, hint or hold back from others and even from themselves, everybody's a facial coder. We all intuitively study faces to understand whether the rational explanation being given confirms or is at odds with the emotional response being communicated in any dialogue, presentation, or speech.

> A man makes a decision for two reasons – the good reason and the real reason.
> J P Morgan

In that sense, this book is moreover about lifting what is common, casual practice into a carefully honed business process. Facial coding is essential because ascertaining the truth can be difficult given that J P Morgan was right: the deeper reasons for our choices aren't the good, rational, defensible ones. In other words, there's a rational/emotional split in all of us, which we're often not consciously aware of, and which makes getting to emotions crucial. Without knowing what the other party really feels, it's hard to make progress.

The dilemma posed by the rational/emotional split J P Morgan noted is personal. Who among us doesn't want to appear more logical than we actually are? The effort to put up an appearance creates a huge gap between what we feel and what we say, and between what we say and what we actually do. If putting up appearances becomes a habit, we may even create a disconnect between what we think and what we feel.

The dilemma is also corporate-wide. Company after company espouses the ruling orthodoxy that feelings are messy, dangerous, inferior and perhaps even irrelevant to day-to-day business. So to one degree or another we end up downplaying the fact that emotions are central to life, and our business planning and outcomes suffer accordingly.

This book aims to help readers to understand emotions in terms of business opportunities. Not only do actions speak louder than words, emotions and the motivations linked to them drive those actions. Fortunately, there are ways to navigate and leverage feelings in order to enhance any company's effectiveness and ability to succeed.

Part One of this book will establish the scientific basis for the relevance of emotions and explain how they can now be measured to ensure optimal results. But to start laying the groundwork for why the business world should take emotions seriously, consider a couple of statistics, one from the marketplace and one from the workplace:

A *Journal of Advertising Research* study, involving 23,000 US consumers, 13 categories of goods and 240 advertising messages, concluded that 'emotions are twice as important as "facts" in the process by which people make buying decisions' (Morris et al, 2002).

Time magazine's cover story linking emotions and productivity involved a round-up of expert opinion, including the estimate that the emotional happiness present in employees can account for 10 to 25 per cent higher job performance (Thottam, 2005).

The paradigm shift awaiting business

Given statistics like these, one would think the business world would place emotions at the centre of decision making. It seems so obvious. What is business if not providing services or products by and for emotionally driven people? And yet emotional literacy is viewed as mystical, a force few companies have explored and even fewer have constructively managed to interject into their cultures.

Perhaps the root of this bias against emotion can be attributed to a 17th-century French philosopher. In 1667, René Descartes famously uttered, 'I think, therefore I am.' With those brief words the western world's love affair with rationality began.

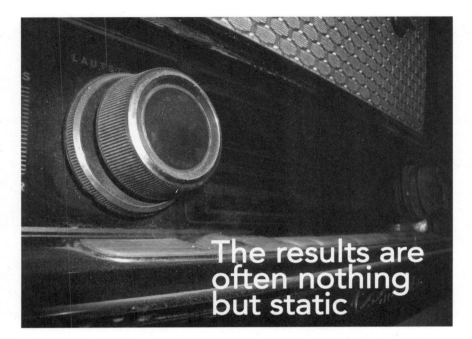

The results are often nothing but static. As we'll discuss in Chapter 1, the rational and emotional parts of the brain are distinct separate entities. So think-your-feelings research questions run the risk of being like trying to find an FM station using the AM dial.

Given this cultural legacy, we shouldn't be surprised that business is very adept at, and comfortable with, rational, utilitarian functionality. After all, that basis for evaluation can be measured. By contrast, emotions often go unacknowledged. Or if they are taken into account, emotions are typically accessed through what might be called 'think-your-feelings' survey methods that rely on people being able – and willing – to rationally assess and accurately report their emotional responses. In reality, however, people are frequently unable to do so.

From a business point of view, the reason for ignoring emotions has been that, according to the popular view, emotions can't be quantified, segmented and put into a spreadsheet. If emotions can't be measured, they can't be managed. If they can't be managed, they can't be planned for and have no viable role to play in commerce.

In human terms, however, we avoid emotions because we're uncomfortable with them. To evade personal conflict, people bypass talking about sadness, anger and frustration. It's easier to discuss financial yardsticks like returns on investment and to simply be sad, angry or frustrated. Even more simple is to avoid acknowledging the existence of feelings altogether.

At the root of this behaviour lies what French psychologist Claude Rapaille calls the rational or 'intellectual alibi'. By that he means we invoke the supporting 'good reason' J P Morgan cited to defend our responses. Thus we rationalize the emotion-based decisions we've already made in our hearts.

Without a method of learning how customers and employees are actually feeling, perhaps the business world has always had a valid point in ignoring emotions. The reluctance of business leaders to deal in a non-measurable medium makes some sense in that, without an accurate measuring tool, emotions can't be strategically anticipated or tactically handled well.

Nevertheless, companies ignore the role of emotions in business at their own peril. After all, emotions affect awareness, consideration, persuasion, recall and loyalty in the marketplace. They also apply to management issues such as performance and retention. The bottom line? It's impossible to escape the role emotional buy-in plays in achieving success.

In *One Size Fits One* (1999), Heil, Parker and Stephens look at why a variety of business initiatives launched during the last two decades didn't achieve all that they might have. In the section 'Putting a face on the faceless customer', they observe that companies simply tend:

> to overlook the essential fact that, at its heart, business is a human endeavor where individuals meet, talk, work, and otherwise try to help and benefit one another and that emotions were and are at least as much the currency of exchange, satisfaction, and loyalty as dollars. Messy, elusive, irrational, and difficult to quantify, the emotional component of the value equation has been ignored – and often for these very reasons.

A scientific solution

Fortunately, there is now a viable, actionable way to measure emotional responses. This scientific method is known as facial coding. Its roots lie in the observational work of Charles Darwin and it has become well known due to Malcolm Gladwell's extensive account of it in his previously mentioned best-seller *Blink: the power of thinking without thinking* (2005).

Facial coding enhances traditional research by ensuring the reliability of what subjects are reporting. Facial coding captures a person's emotional buy-in, while verbal input, including verbal responses and ratings, best reflects the person's rationalized intellectual alibi. When used together to gauge the degree of any target market's buy-in to a product or service, the combination will, if in sync and positive, confirm that the target market is on-board. But if the two sets of data conflict, then a business leader is always wiser to make decisions based on the results of emotional responses. That's because the rational 'facts' are malleable, unlike people's emotional gut reactions.

From its start in 1998, Sensory Logic has led the way in measuring emotional buy-in through the analysis of facial muscle activity. While we'll discuss facial coding in detail in Chapter 2, here's a teaser: the human tendency to express feelings through facial expressions is so stable, ubiquitous and uniform that even a person born blind has the same innate facial expressions as those who can see.

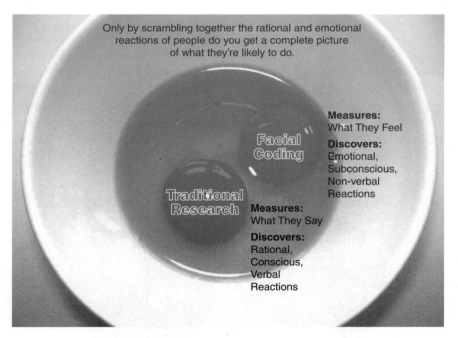

Only by scrambling together the rational and emotional reactions of people do you get a complete picture of what they're likely to do.

Facial Coding

Measures:
What They Feel

Discovers:
Emotional, Subconscious, Non-verbal Reactions

Traditional Research

Measures:
What They Say

Discovers:
Rational, Conscious, Verbal Reactions

Figure 0.1   The differences between traditional research and facial coding.
The danger of traditional research is that people try to look smart by engaging in intellectual filtering. By adding facial coding to the usual verbal input, companies can learn how people are responding on a more gut level basis through the correlation of facial expressions and relevant emotions, and thereby be better positioned for success.

Two studies with different outcomes

Case 1: Bad luck

A major mobile phone company creates a humorous TV spot in which an architect demolishes his scale model during a post-presentation melt-down. Unbeknownst to him, his current phone service causes him to miss a call telling him the clients have changed their minds; they now like the building. He finds out, but too late. It's a funny mishap of events. The ad agency's client found the concept amusing and approved production. Filming and editing were completed.

Then the events of 11 September 2001 happened. Enter Sensory Logic to conduct the field testing research, the last step necessary before the spot launched. The charts in Figure 0.2 depict the results of that research. The pie chart on the left shows the positive/negative breakdown of the verbal rating responses given by subjects participating in the test. Obviously, most people said they liked the commercial.

In contrast, the pie chart on the right reveals the results of research using facial coding. Based on the coding of individual emotional responses, the commercial was in serious trouble. Only a third of the subjects' emotional responses were positive. Most people said they liked the commercial, but our research revealed a large gap between what subjects said about the TV spot and what their facial expressions revealed about how they felt about it. Subjects claimed to like the commercial, but their emotional reactions told us they didn't.

Figure 0.2   Introducing the say/feel gap.
Even though over half the subjects gave a positive verbal response to the TV spot involving the architect, less than a third of the emotional response was positive – a nearly 50 per cent drop.

Given the contrasting data, the question becomes: which set of scores makes more sense? Is it the verbal ratings signalling acceptance or the emotional responses indicating resistance to a post 9/11 commercial involving the stylized, violent destruction of a building?

Case 2: Triumph

As Cargill, the largest private company in America, prepared to launch its consulting practice, Sensory Logic was asked to test the campaign's TV spots to gauge their strengths and identify any opportunities for improvement. In this case, the facial coding response was almost twice as positive as it was for the architecture spot – and in range of the strongest responses we've ever measured.

As a result, our role consisted of recommending that already strong commercials could benefit from slightly slower pacing and a little less imagery. In essence, we gave the client and its agency guidance on how to make winners even better. What was the outcome? For the best spot in the campaign, Cargill and its advertising agency, Martin/Williams, won the Creative Excellence in Business Advertising (CEBA) award.

This book's theme and scope

The key concept of this book is that rational reasons alone don't win people over. It's not enough for companies and their leaders to be on-message. In addition, they must be on-emotion, which means being able to connect with consumers and employees by knowing which emotions matter, how they matter and also when exactly they're being invoked.

In the end, a company's profitability depends on how the targeted market internalizes its emotional response to whatever experiences it has regarding that company. Consequently, a company's long-term viability depends on how it shapes, gauges and responds to people's feelings.

Besides sharing cutting-edge research about how, when and why people experience emotions, this book will share insights from a decade of tests. They involve almost every customer touch point – from products and services to branding and retail environments – as well as about workplace issues. In total, we're talking about a database of over 50,000 comparisons of verbal and non-verbal responses.

I believe that 'emotion' is where it's at.

Tom Peters

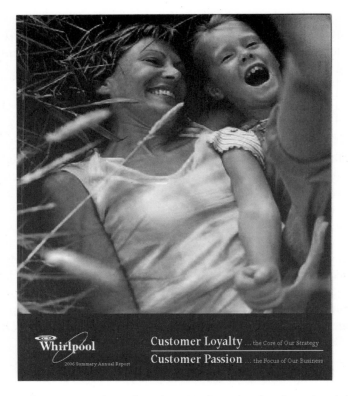

'The success of our strategy depends on knowing the rational and emotional drivers that build customer loyalty for a brand.' – Jeff Fettig, CEO of Whirlpool

Part One: Why emotions matter (Chapters 1–3)

Breakthroughs in brain science show us that emotions drive outcomes. Readers will develop an understanding of why and how the core emotions deciphered through facial coding are related to the core motivational drivers that lead to action. They will learn how to incorporate this knowledge into projects through a strategic model: the Emotionomics Matrix™.

Part Two: Marketplace applications (Chapters 4–8)

Branding is primarily emotional because it is primarily about trust. But branding is not the only arena in which emotional buy-in generates revenue. Readers will see that from designing an offer to promotion, sales, shopping sites and customer service, it's actually more important (and lucrative) to be on-emotion than on-message alone.

Part Three: Workplace applications (Chapters 9–10)

Given that only 29 per cent of employees report being engaged by their jobs, and 16 per cent are actively disengaged ('Feeling'), it's imperative to create greater emotional as well as intellectual commitment. Employees' feelings will inevitably impact the bottom line. These chapters cover the best means of bringing employees emotionally on board to lift productivity and increase retention.

Reader's guide and terminology

A fair amount of information will be new to many readers of this book. So I have decided to provide my sources of information both as a form of validation and for people eager to do additional, follow-up study. Those sources appear in parentheses in the text, with a complete listing to be found in the References.

Moreover, this book uses terminology readers may not be familiar with or may see in a new and different light. Some of it is a result of how my company, Sensory Logic, uniquely approaches business issues. At other times, it may be because of the science and psychology involved. To help get readers oriented, here are some of the key terms present in *Emotionomics*.

Appeal: The degree of positive or negative emotional response (based on facial coding).

Bridge of consideration: the gap a salesperson tries to get a prospect to cross, using both emotional and rational influence factors to convince the prospect that buying the offer is a safe, smart move.

Commodity trap: the problem of having the offer regarded by consumers as undistinguished, interchangeable or vulnerable to price pressures. The solution lies in being able to differentiate a product or service in terms of what it does for consumers on a sensory-emotional level, driven at times by superior functionality.

Emotional response rate: the measure of response or no response to a given stimulus. Lack of response indicates failure to break through the clutter.

Emotionomics matrix: an actionable model used in broadening strategic business planning to include not only rational but also the often neglected human factors of emotions and motivations. The model serves as a guide for connecting with the target market so that it cares and buys into the offer or course of action being proposed.

Facial coding: the analysis of people's emotional response to stimuli, including questions, which is achieved by studying the movement of facial muscles using the system developed by Dr Paul Ekman.

Feature-itis: a company's tendency to over-think and over-execute the design of a product, service or experience by including too many extraneous features.

Fiction: the strongest version of brand equity, which exists in the hearts of consumers based on a brand story they believe in so strongly that it drives preference without regard to utilitarian 'facts'. In contrast, nonfiction refers to marginal brand equity that relies not on how the brand makes consumers feel, but on what the branded offer does for them in more limited, functional terms.

Great chain of buying: everything for sale has a chain of longer or shorter length, based on the purchase cycle frequency, and heavier or lighter weight based on the emotional interest or significance with which the purchase is imbued.

Impact: the degree of intensity or enthusiasm in people's emotional response (based on facial coding).

Intellectual alibi: rational thoughts that are used to justify gut reaction after completion of the decision-making process.

Me-story: the recited story that spells out the consumer's underlying emotional reasons for seeking vindication through a customer service redress of a problem.

Message-itis: a company's tendency to attempt to persuade consumers by loading up its advertising with extra, rationally oriented messages that overly complicate the execution.

Offer: a product, service or experience deliberately created for the customer.

On-emotion: generating an emotional response in the target market that's appropriate to support one's business goal. Being on-emotion is at least as important as being on-message or on-strategy, both of which often fail to engage the heart and win people over.

Say/feel gap: the disconnect that frequently occurs between what people say and their actual feelings.

Script: the meaning behind every codeable emotion.

Sensory bandwidth: the ability to engage consumers with stimuli that play to their five senses of sight, sound, touch, taste and smell.

Part One

Why emotions matter

1 The new mental model

In an increasingly interdisciplinary world, breakthroughs in brain science have first challenged psychology, then economics, to rethink old assumptions underestimating the role of emotions.

1986
Joseph LeDoux discovers the role of the amygdala, the brain's 'hot button'

1990
President Bush declares 1990s the "Decade of the Brain"

Science

1995
Daniel Goleman's *Emotional Intelligence* sells almost five million copies

Psychology

1998 Dr Martin Seligman launches the positive psychology movement

Economics

2002 Daniel Kahneman wins a Nobel Prize for his work in behavioral economics

2005 Malcolm Gladwell's *Blink* challenges the traditional business decision making model

Overview

In business, we've traditionally been told to think with our heads and not with our hearts. Breakthroughs in brain science have now shown that this is impossible. Rather than being cast aside and hidden, emotions have begun to move from the margins to the centre of discourse in many fields. As illustrated by the puzzle-piece diagram, this chapter will focus on three key, interlocking developments:

- **Science**: the old mental model in which conscious, rational, verbally oriented thought was predominant has given way. Technology like fMRI brain scans has instead affirmed a new model in which our three-part brain (sensory, emotional and rational) is most influenced by the two oldest, non-rational parts. As a result, people's decision-making process is primarily quick, emotional and subconscious; in a word, it's intuitive. The bottom line is that people feel before they think. The implication for business? Looking for commitment from customers and employees based on rational messages alone won't be nearly as effective as communication that emphasizes emotional benefits.
- **Psychology**: the news that people's psyches have been 'hardwired' through evolution, linking us to cave men and women, could lead to the assumption that everything in human nature is set in stone and can't be changed. But psychologists are balancing that reality with a second neurological reality: as shown by the creation of new neurons throughout life (neurogenesis) and the existence of empathetically oriented brain receptors (mirror neurons), people have the ability to grow and adapt. The implication for business? The type of market-place and workplace experiences people have may rewire the brain. Therefore, the concept of building brand equity – accruing positive feelings – now extends to every company/customer interaction and outcome as well as to manager/employee relationships.
- **Economics**: long the preserve of rationality, this field is also experiencing a transition. As Nobel Laureate Daniel McFadden has said, the new movement of 'behavioural economics is where gravity is pulling the field'. What's the impetus? It's again the influence of brain science, which has undermined the old notion that people make logical choices. The implication for business? Value gets assigned emotionally, not rationally. Failure to account for emotions will lead to assumptions that could be seriously off-base regarding everything from pricing to productivity.

Now let's look more closely at developments in each of these three fields, starting with brain science.

Science: the meaning of a three-part brain

Synopsis: This section opens by detailing the order in which the three brains developed. Then it provides the general followed by the specific implications of that order in terms of how our three-part brain works and what its processing patterns mean to business.

Key take-aways

- Emotion drives reason more than reason drives emotion.
- The brain's hardwiring makes us more primitive than we might think.
- Feelings happen before thought, and they happen with great speed.
- Conscious thought is only a small portion of mental activity.
- Visual imagery and other non-verbal forms of communication predominate.

Our three brains

Emotion drives reason more than reason drives emotion

After the Second World War, the US government funded extensive brain research in an effort to aid the large number of GIs who had suffered head wounds. As a result, in 1949 Paul MacLean discovered that human beings really have a three-part brain whose complexity developed sequentially over time (Howard, 2000).

What is known as the original brain supports our senses. In fact, this part of the brain began as a small clump of tissue atop the spinal column, facilitating smell, which is still the most robust of people's five senses (Ackerman, 1990). Reptile brains didn't make it past this developmental point. In humans, this part of the brain is notable for engaging in pattern matching, automatically benchmarking current experience against previous encounters. This ability allows us to orient and gauge levels of safety and comfort.

The second part of the brain, the limbic system, is our emotional centre and evolved with the first mammals. It turns sensory perceptions into emotional and physical responses. It also interfaces with the newest brain, the rational brain, which forms the third part of the modern human brain. Thus one could say that the limbic system serves as our Grand Integrator, linking the sensory, emotional and rational parts of the brain. Its key activity is to assign gut-level value to the situations we encounter.

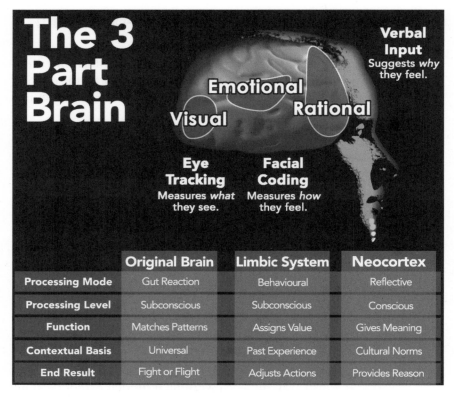

Figure 1.1   The three parts of the brain and their functions.
This illustration provides an overview of the location of each of the three parts of the
brain. The evolutionary function chart below it compares the parts to give a more
in-depth understanding of how each part processes, utilizes and responds to stimuli
(Ortony *et al*, 2004). The original brain has been estimated to be 500 million years
old, the limbic system 200 million years old, and the neocortex 100,000 years old
(Postma, 2005).

The neocortex was the last part of the brain to develop. As the rational
part, it often gets called the 'mind'. Its frontal lobes are the executive
centre of the brain, where complex data is processed. Social mammals
evolved this part of the brain. The size of the neocortex is directly propor-
tional to the size of the group they live in because having to track more
relationships requires more brain power (Baker, 2006). Given our
complex societal ties, humans have the largest neocortex on the planet.

That's the progression of development over the millennia. But calling it
a progression may incorrectly cause people to assume that since the
rational part of the brain came into existence last, its being new and
capable of more complex processing also means it dominates. In short,
rationality *wins*.

But in truth we aren't supremely rational creatures like Mr Spock or Data from *Star Trek*. To clarify matters, let's turn to prominent neuroscientist Joseph LeDoux. He notes that:

> emotions can flood consciousness ... because the wiring of the brain at this point in our evolutionary history is such that connections from the emotional systems to the cognitive systems are stronger than connections from the cognitive systems to the emotional systems (2003).

To reiterate: emotion drives reason more than reason drives emotion.

General implications of having a three-part brain

The brain's hardwiring makes us more primitive than we might think

In general terms, the fact that people have a hardwired, three-part brain has two major implications. The first major implication has already been introduced by LeDoux. It's that the older, sensory and emotional brains dominate our decision-making process. Emotions are central, not peripheral, because they drive reason more than vice versa. In essence, we're not nearly as rational as we would like to think we are.

The second major implication is that we're much more similar to our ancient ancestors than to the sophisticated consumers and workers we would like to think we are. Businesspeople who make their plans based on complex, intellectual assumptions about how targeted consumers or affected employees will behave are missing an opportunity to leverage recent breakthroughs in brain science. Our neuron-biological legacy means that emotions enjoy pre-emptive, first-mover advantage in every decision process.

The bottom line is that we're not very far removed from our cave-dwelling ancestors who – driven by the fight-or-flight impulse – were

Figure 1.2   Humanity's timeframe: the long shadow of our caveperson legacy.
Most of the advances we take for granted weren't even around 150 years ago. This chart shows the development of human society in generational terms. In short, a modern veneer of sophistication overlays a long history of rudimentary living (Toffler, 1970).

more concerned with escaping wild animal attacks than activities such as viewing abstract art, enjoying nouvelle cuisine, shopping or showering.

Specific implications of having a three-part brain

So far, we've addressed the two big general implications of having a three-part brain: emotions dominate and our ancient, hardwired nature casts a long shadow. Along with those general implications, however, there are also specific ones we're now ready to detail so that you can have a firmer grasp of how people's decision-making process really operates.

Feelings happen before thought, and they happen with great speed

Feelings come first. Feelings precede conscious thought. Since it's true that in evolutionary terms the rational brain literally grew out of the emotional brain and remains intricately tied to it, this order of influence makes sense. Indeed, the emotional part of the brain is larger than the rational part and so the entire brain processes more emotive than cognitive activity (Baker, 2006). Moreover, the degree to which signals run from the emotional brain to the rational brain outnumber those running the opposite direction by a ratio of ten to one (Hawkins and Blakeslee, 2004).

To emphasize the extent to which the rational brain isn't at the centre of determining what happens in life, consider the fact that only the sensory and emotional brain centres direct our muscle activity (Ortony *et al*, 2004). Thus by analogy the rational brain is a little bit like a logic lobbyist who tries to get the other two duly authorized parts of the brain to actually vote for his bill on the floor of Congress.

'The essential difference between emotion and reason is that emotion leads to action while reason leads to conclusions' – Dr Donald Calne

We take the low road, not the high one. The brain has both high-road and low-road response mechanisms (Goleman, 1995), and as in most aspects of life, the low road dominates. For example, the low road is the path we take in making impulse purchases as input gets filtered straight to the amygdala, the brain's hot button. In contrast, the high road takes longer to travel and isn't nearly as sovereign as it may seem to be. As a result, our rational responses get coloured by the low road's quicker emotional responses. Moreover, guess where the high road ends? Back at the amygdala to 'sign the cheque' we've already emotionally spent.

Recall is emotion-based. Let's start by introducing the parts of the brain that bring us recall. First, there's the hippocampus, our memory device. Next, the amygdala is not only the part of the brain associated with feelings of fear and aggression, it also plays a role in visual learning and memory. Not by chance, the hippocampus and the amygdala are both located in the emotional brain and in close proximity to one another. That's because memory formation happens in only two ways (LeDoux, 1994): a new memory can be established when a stimulus hits the amygdala and makes an emotional connection, and secondly, another similar stimulus may hit the amygdala and be easily assimilated since it resembles the previously established connection. What results is a network of recalled associations that gets started by an actual hot-button stimulus or even the memory of a hot-button stimulus. Everything we retain owes that outcome to its having gained an emotional toehold in our brain.

We have gut reactions in three seconds or less. In other words, our gut reactions happen very quickly (Gladwell, 2005). In fact, emotions process sensory input in only one-fifth the time our conscious, cognitive brain takes to assimilate that same input (Marcus, 2002). Quick emotional processing also happens with cascading impact. Our emotional reaction to a stimulus resounds more loudly in our brain than does our rational response, triggering the action to follow.

To put the long-term implications of this action in straight, scientific terms: neurons that fire together wire together (Banich, 2004). The experiences we have rewire the brain by fusing together neural networks. As a result, what we've already seen will predispose us to what we can see the next time around. That incumbent advantage makes the next action more intuitive and quicker to unfold because it leverages a network already in existence.

Conscious thought is only a small portion of mental activity

Conscious thought is the tip of the iceberg. Both the sensory and emotional brains operate subconsciously. In all, less than .0005 per cent of our mental activity qualifies as fully conscious. According to the latest estimates, the brain takes in 400 billion bytes of information per second, but only consciously processes 2,000 (*What*, 2004). The implication? We are much less aware than we prefer to believe. Likewise, the eye picks up 10,000,000 bytes of visual information per second but only 40 bytes per second become mental images; that's a ratio of 250,000 to one (Zimmermann, 1986; Medgadget.com, 2006).

Visual imagery and other non-verbal forms of communication predominate

'A picture is worth a thousand words.' Cliché, but true. In fact, it's a cliché because it's true. A battle between pictures and words is like one between Mike Tyson and Tiny Tim: the picture throws the bigger punch. Consider these illuminating facts:

- Two-thirds of the stimuli reaching the brain are visual (Zaltman, 1996).
- Over 50 per cent of the brain is devoted to processing visual images (Bates and Cleese, 2001).
- As a result, 80 per cent of learning is visually based (American Optometric Association, 1991).

Business people, take note. Humans are extremely visual: we think largely in images, not words. What consumers and employees can't actually see, or at the very least mentally envision based on how a topic gets explained, is most likely going to be lost on them.

Most communication is non-verbal in ambiguous situations. Every day, we find ourselves in situations where the other party's words and body language strike us as either ambiguous or conflicting. In those cases, what do we do? We tend to rely more on the non-verbals to evaluate the emotional state of the person speaking. Here are the exact statistics (Mahrabian, 1981):

- 55 per cent of communication comes through facial expressions.
- 38 per cent of communication gets accomplished by tone of voice.
- Only 7 per cent of communication relies on verbal exchange.

For anyone who wants to 'get back to basics,' remember that nothing is more basic than non-verbal communication. Human beings have existed for over 500,000 years, but we've had the benefit of language for less than a quarter of that time (Dunbar, 1996). Moreover, because the rational and sensory parts of the brain aren't adjacent neighbours, we're not very good at describing verbally the details our senses detect. Ironically, that's true despite the fact that our initial, gut-level perceptions are largely based on sensory impressions.

'Who are you going to believe, me or your own eyes?' Groucho Marx

In summary, here's what we've just covered:

- We feel first and last in the decision-making process, asking the amygdala to sign the cheque.
- We feel more quickly than we think.
- Even the formation of memories is emotionally based.
- Most of our mental activity also happens beyond our awareness, subconsciously.
- Mental activity is often initiated by visual, sensory impressions that lead to emotional responses which we mostly communicate non-verbally.

Psychology: balancing blind instinct with growth

Synopsis: As mental healthcare workers, psychologists parallel companies in seeking to make the people they serve happier. In doing so, they balance two aspects of human nature that also have broad relevance to business. The first applies especially to the marketplace, where people's 'blind' instincts influence how perceptions are emotionally evaluated. The second applies especially to the workplace, where the goal of working more effectively with staff can benefit from new brain science insights about people's capacity for growth.

Key take-aways

- We perceive matters in ways that emotionally protect and enhance our self-image.
- Two open-loop mental capacities facilitate our use of emotional intelligence in pursuit of happiness.

Emotions colour perceptions and inhibit change

We perceive matters in ways that emotionally protect and enhance our self-image

First, let's tackle the bad news: unbiased perception is not one of humanity's strong suits. The processing of 'facts' is, in essence, as much about the processing of one's emotions as it is the processing of whatever external dynamics a person happens to be experiencing. After all, genetically we're designed for self-preservation. Goals high on the list for human beings are feeling good about ourselves and accruing allies and partners drawn by our vitality (Wright, 1995).

As Robert Zajonc and other psychologists have noted, the perceptual process, and the reactions and judgments that flow from it, are emotionally encoded ('Preferences'). Feelings provide us with information. We usually ask ourselves, 'How do I feel about such and such?' Feelings also influence how we process information.

For instance, how do we 'choose' which brands to notice? Well, the first step in the perceptual process is that of screening, which often occurs subconsciously. We tend to screen out the unfamiliar (since paying attention to unfamiliar stimuli requires effort). Instead, we prefer to focus on what we already know and can relate to more easily. Then when looking at a TV commercial or the store shelf in front of us, for example, we classify and interpret brand choices based on perceptual reactions – or biases – that again are rooted in emotion.

Yes, at times people will analyse the 'facts' vigorously. But emotions are basic and more dominant. Remember: we feel before we think, and those reactions are subconscious, immediate and inescapable. That's why our reactions are often hard to verbalize. Our language skills reside in the rational brain, which may not get invoked because automatic reactions are primarily emotional in nature. As Zajonc (1980) notes, to say 'I decided in favour of X' often means nothing more or less than 'I liked X' – and that's good enough.

Why is instinctive preference good enough in life in general as well as in business specifically? The reason is that emotional judgements tend to be irrevocable because they implicate the self, revealing our biases. In terms of our basic emotional reactions, we're never wrong about what we like or dislike. So it's important for companies not just to sell objectively or to appeal to consumers only rationally. As Zajonc again notes, the factual reality of 'The cat is black' pales in contrast to the more intimate emotional reality of 'I don't like black cats.'

What's the last stage in perception? It's retrieval, which is mediated by our emotions yet again. We tend to store and recall more readily those experiences that fit most comfortably into our existing mental frameworks. Therefore, memory is driven by preferences rooted in being at ease with our choice. Consumers and employees alike often defend their choices or actions based on details they previously deemed rationally irrelevant. Why? The explanation is that emotions are self-justifying and, therefore, emotional reactions can become totally separated from content.

Therefore, remember that what we've already seen will predispose us to what we can see the next time around because of our emotional investment in what's familiar to us. This incumbent advantage has implications for branding (Chapter 4), offer design (Chapter 5) and advertising (Chapter 6) in particular. While a company may believe it has a technically or functionally superior offer, consumers' evaluations are in essence emotionally based. Objectivity doesn't exist because everything gets filtered and coloured by emotional responses. The bottom line is there's almost always more commercial gain to be made by going with, rather than against, what people have already emotionally internalized and accepted.

How emotions feed the brain and aid growth

Two open-loop mental capacities facilitate our use of emotional intelligence in pursuit of happiness

If people's innate tendency to control, even distort, perceptions to fit their emotionally encoded preconceptions constitutes the bad news (or at least a reality business needs to acknowledge and plan for this accordingly), what's the good news? It would have to be that people also have the capacity to learn, grow, adopt and adapt. While as much as two-thirds of the brain may be hardwired to reflect ancient survival lessons (Pinker, 2003), that leaves at least a third open and receptive to discovery.

For a long time, psychology has been oriented to erasing pain: treating neuroses, and in the process focusing on negative emotions. But as we're now about to see, in recent years the field has begun to shift, aided by two specific brain science discoveries and a growing respect for the power of positive feelings (as well as thinking).

The first of those two discoveries is neurogenesis (Lehrer, 2006; Boyatzis, 2006). That term refers to the creation of new neurons throughout life. It means we're not set for life; we have an ability to change. We have the means to achieve mental flexibility and thereby enhance our lives. Emotion plays a direct role here. That's because the natural brain chemistry that gets those neurons to fire and wire together is, as mentioned earlier, a function of emotional responses that resound more loudly in our brain than do our rational responses. In effect, we get new mental building blocks to utilize throughout life – and it's up to us to make the most of that opportunity to refresh ourselves.

Our ability not to simply repeat past behaviour is supported by the second recent discovery: the existence of mirror neurons (Goldberg, 2005). These neurons enable us to imitate and empathize with other people, thus reinforcing the importance of using our emotions to gather information in interpersonal situations.

Combined with neurogenesis, the crucial benefit of mirror neurons is that there exists a pair of open-loop mental capacities. Together, they have helped carry psychology into a new, more emotionally enriched era, past earlier movements such as behaviourism and cognitive psychology.

Gone is the hyper-rational view of humans evolving into *Star Trek*'s Mr Spock. An emphasis on emotions has emerged instead. Backed by the breakthroughs in brain science, psychology now recognizes two evaluation systems. The slower, thinking system is dominated by the faster, intuitive feeling system which must finally be given due respect.

Born of emotion's new-found prominence is the Positive Psychology movement. Its founder is Dr Martin Seligman (2002), who – like Walt Disney did – focuses on nothing less than creating happiness. His key formula is H = S + C + V (Happiness equals our genetic Set point, plus our Circumstances, plus what we Voluntarily change). How can we change our feelings? By changing external stimuli or by learning to perceive them differently, we're able to alter the left side of the equation.

Moreover, Positive Psychology in league with neurogenesis and mirror neurons points to the importance of another term, which Daniel Goleman made famous: emotional intelligence. In essence, emotional intelligence as practised by consumers, executives, managers and employees entails being in touch with one's feelings (not thinking them). It also means being able to understand them, deal with them, and profit by letting them inform and work in harmony with more rationally oriented insights.

The reason that the two brain science discoveries and the concepts of Positive Psychology and emotional intelligence all fit together is quite simple: people and companies in general can change their performance for the better. The new neural networks that neurogenesis enables can be

Figure 1.3   Reflecting on mirror neurons.
So named because they fire when performing an action or when watching that same action being performed, mirror neurons help us learn by mimicking others. Perhaps even more important is that mirror neurons help create emotional connections through empathy.

more constructive, more beneficial, by virtue of using mirror neurons. Meanwhile, emotional intelligence to pick up on improvements we want to incorporate. Positive Psychology, in turn, provides the impetus by encouraging us in the belief that greater happiness is possible.

The underlying key, however, remains emotions. In the fact that emotions drive us internally and are externally so contagiously shared between people lies the basis for why the brain's dual open-loop capacity can be put to work as an engine for growth. Without the spark of feelings, progress is drawing on limited, merely rational mental resources.

All of this – neurogenesis, mirror neurons, Positive Psychology and emotional intelligence – has tremendous implications for business. Let's start with the marketplace. As we'll discuss in Chapter 4, branding is in essence purely emotional and psychological. It pertains to beliefs and to the mental models or neural networks by which we form our associations about a company. Therefore, the type of marketplace experiences consumers have is crucial. They may rewire the brain, meaning that the concept of brand equity – accruing positive feelings – now extends to every company/customer interaction and outcome.

In other words, the connections and the conclusions we intuitively form regarding a company will follow from how our old and new neurons and mirror neurons all get encoded. From brand icons to advertising, offer design to retail and e-tail sites – and especially customer service – the sensory-emotional impressions and experiences that consumers take away from encountering a company really matter. That's because they will dictate whether the inherently emotional barometer of brand equity rises or falls.

Meanwhile, the implications of all of this for the workplace are, if anything, even stronger. As will be discussed in Chapters 9 and 10, the basis for success is getting employees emotionally engaged in their jobs. Neurogenesis is important in that regard because it means people don't have a fixed or even depleting mental capacity. Instead, they have the resources for growth and positive change. But that's true only so long as the mirror neurons that practise continuous monitoring detect signals within the workplace environment – including notably from leaders and managers – that give cause for the hope enshrined in the Positive Psychology movement.

As a result, the type of workplace experiences employees have may rewire the brain, meaning that the concept of brand equity also extends to creating constructive interactions and outcomes among co-workers. In turn, the concepts of emotional intelligence and Positive Psychology can provide a whole new way to handle workplace practices like hiring, training and providing feedback. The bottom line is that by nurturing employees' well-being and fulfilling on their desire for meaning, companies can establish a self-reinforcing cycle that will lead to higher productivity through genuine employee satisfaction.

Economics: plugging emotions into the equation

Synopsis: Like psychology, the field of economics has also been profoundly influenced by the break-throughs in brain science. As a result, emotions – not logic alone – have become the focus point of the new emerging practice of behavioural economics. As will be discussed here, the influence of emotions can be found in areas that range from big issues like achieving offer differentiation and value in a hyper-competitive global economy to everyday practices like the way in which people react to prices.

Key take-aways

- The best way to predict outcomes is to fully account for the vagaries of human nature.
- Delivering a unique emotional value proposition is the key to success.
- How consumers respond to price points is profoundly influenced by their emotions.

What behavioural economics can teach us

The best way to predict outcomes is to fully account for the vagaries of human nature

In 2002, Princeton University's Daniel Kahneman won the Nobel Prize in economics. His work is part of the emerging field of behavioural economics. Supported by neurobiology's recent findings, this new brand of economics is challenging the rationally oriented economic theories of yesteryear. After all, its basic premise is that people aren't very logical decision makers. Like others exploring this field, Dr Kahneman knows people are fallibly human and don't necessarily make very rational choices. Instead, forces like altruism, greed and revenge are likely to tip the decision balance as much as anything else.

Emerging from observations of human behaviour instead of from abstract theory, behavioural economics involves a handful of essential concepts. For the purposes of simplifying the discussion here, those concepts have been put into one of two realms: either categorization or loss aversion (Kahneman, 2005; Wahrman, Fusso and Serrins, 2003).

The first set of concepts has to do with the categorization tricks we engage in for emotional reasons. Besides taking mental shortcuts by labelling things so they fit easily into preconceived categories, we also get caught up in:

- **Framing**: making a choice more attractive by deliberately comparing it with inferior options.
- **Mental accounting**: placing artificial limits on the amounts we're willing to spend in certain categories.
- **Prospect theory**: judging pleasure based on a change in condition rather than on how happy we are.
- **Anchoring**: evaluating new information strictly in terms of what our baseline of knowledge happens to be.
- **Recency**: giving undue weight to recent experiences.

Mental accounting is based on the idea that consumers have a mental 'cheque' made out for how much they're willing to spend on an item.

The second set of concepts has to do with loss aversion. As neurologist LeDoux has concluded from his research, 'Negative emotions are linked to survival – and are much stronger' (2003). It's not surprising then that people feel more pain from loss than pleasure from profit. The result is loss aversion behaviour, for people will take more risks to avoid losses than they will to realize gains. Aspects of loss aversion include:

- **Familiarity**: having a bias toward the status quo.
- **New-risk premium**: inflating the cost of accepting new risks while casually discounting familiar risks.
- **Fear of regret**: suffering from having to admit a mistake.
- **Decision paralysis**: failing to make a decision when faced with lots of choices for fear of making the wrong one.

More obviously so than brain science or psychology, behavioural economics also has huge implications for business. What are they? From a marketplace perspective, companies have already taken into account *framing* (by using a good–better–best format), and they have used *recency* as the rationale for engaging in heavy bouts of advertising around major holidays (most notably the Christmas season).

Companies have not been nearly as good at coming to terms with mental accounting, which would require repositioning categories so that consumers lift artificially imposed expenditure limits. Nor have most companies made the effort to really understand the baseline knowledge people have of an offer in order to make *anchoring* work in their favour. But the most clear-cut shortcoming of almost all companies is the way in which their confusing product line extensions have ignored the lesson of *decision paralysis*.

As for the workplace, all leaders know they must grapple with the pref-erence for *familiarity* in trying to get employees to accept change. Meanwhile, leaders and managers alike struggle with the *fear of regret* – but may not always recognize the extent of the influence it's likely to have on worker motivation and behaviour.

Finally, the other two concepts introduced here can also be relevant to the workplace. For instance, leaders can cope with the *new-risk premium* by reminding employees of the dangers of staying with the status quo. Meanwhile, efforts must also be made to lessen the corrosive effect of the *prospect theory*. Employees given to jealousy based on their relative status within the company not only negate the happiness they can enjoy from their own success, they also plant the seeds for discord among colleagues.

The top rung of the hierarchy of value

Delivering a unique emotional value proposition is the key to success

As brain science has shown, and as behavioural economics is reflecting, people often don't make logical choices. Instead, they go with their gut reactions and justify them afterwards using intellectual alibis. Now companies may find that kind of decision-making process confusing, frus-trating, even objectionable. To protest against the hardwired nature of human nature isn't a productive business strategy. Far better is to acknowledge human nature and work with it accordingly.

To that end, consider Maslow's famous hierarchy of needs: the one in which basic needs like food and shelter must be met before higher needs ranging from the social to the spiritual kick in. Well, a similar hierarchy of value also exists – based on the scientific fact that value gets assigned emotionally, not rationally, given the role the emotional, middle brain plays in people's decision-making process.

At the lowest rung, you'll find a desire for security. The next step up is comfort. Finally, at the top rung is the pleasure consumers will pay the most for. Throughout this hierarchy of emotional value, rationality is a factor. For example, security comes in part from the offer working prop-erly, and comfort can involve the social utility of being able to defend the

Here's how the ladder of value stacks up when looked at from an emotional vantage point. At the bottom is the basic need for security. At the top is the desire for pleasure and the beauty and indulgence that comes with it.

purchase to friends and family. But rationality is never the decisive factor and it disappears almost entirely at the top rung.

There the game changes. Atop the highest rung – the place of sensory indulgence, thrilling aesthetic beauty and the sweet joy of being intimately immersed in an experience afforded by an offer – is where greater profitability, differentiation, even business survival increasingly reside nowadays. Let's explore why.

How come plugging emotions into the value equation, throughout the hierarchy but especially at the top rung, is so important to the performance of companies? To focus just on selling to consumers for the moment, the reason is that the best way to avoid having a commoditized offer in a world of product parity is by adding emotional value. It's no longer enough to have a unique selling proposition. Companies must develop a unique emotional proposition to get out of the commodity trap, which is easier than it may sound.

Consumers evaluate an offer – by which is meant a product, service or experience deliberately created for the customer – by internalizing it and assigning it emotional value. So add the right emotional cues to trigger a positive consumer encounter. Then consumers will intuitively form a strong connection to the offer deep in their emotional brain. Better yet, it will be a connection customized by their feelings about the offer and in which they will have invested emotionally, thereby creating a resilient barrier against entry by the competition.

Good designers are the new 'rock stars' of the business world, in part because of the way they infuse their work with emotional charge. As Richard Florida notes in *The Rise of the Creative Class* (2002), about 30 per cent of American workers are already engaged in feeling-fuelled creative endeavours. Their development of innovative new technology and other intellectual property causes a kind of organic growth that forklifts and computers alone can't produce.

Whether a company's focus is on the marketplace or workplace, adding emotion into its strategic planning and tactical executions adds value. Moreover, recognizing emotions reaps rewards. The way to maximize sales is to get consumers more emotionally devoted to what a company offers. The way to maximize productivity is to get employees and business partners more emotionally committed to delivering exceptional offers and support. But to do either one, a company must know how to identify the emotions of others, customers and co-workers alike.

The point being made in Figure 1.4 (opposite) is that the creative class authors like Florida and Daniel Pink have heralded constitutes the leading edge, the tip of the iceberg. Its substantial and growing presence points to where all companies in America and the world at large must increasingly go over time. Otherwise they can't fortify their offers and survive against the lowest-cost providers, regardless of whatever country those providers locate in at the moment – China today, somewhere else tomorrow.

In short, being strategic about plugging emotions into the mix is no longer optional. For companies that want to be winners, it's imperative – as Chapters 4 to 10 will discuss in depth.

The cost of emotions

How consumers respond to price points is profoundly influenced by their emotions

Granted, for the cautious or even sceptical reader not easily convinced that emotions truly affect what happens in business, everything that's been said so far might seem rather abstract or theoretical in nature. If you're that kind of person, you may be saying to yourself 'OK', or 'So what? Show me the money. Prove relevance.' For you, it isn't enough that the physical arrangement of the brain makes feelings both the starting point and end point in the transformation of responses into actions.

Phase III: The only way for humans to differentiate themselves and create value is through the creative right brain. Bohemians everywhere rejoice, but still don't work.

Phase II: The advent of the computer age means the logical left brain is no longer superior.

Phase I: Technology makes the human body a non-essential aspect. Labour is now done by machines which are cheaper, faster and always happy to be working overtime.

Figure 1.4   The phasing out of humans.

So in concluding this opening chapter of *Emotionomics*, let's go straight to the intersection of money and emotions. After all, in addressing logic, value and feelings, the assertion being made here is that failure to account for emotions will lead to assumptions that could be seriously off-base regarding everything from pricing to productivity.

Now it's time for some tangible evidence

As behavioural economists have observed, there's an awful lot of irrationality built into the way people actually make decisions. What supposedly remains constant and easy to predict is our responses to pricing, since everybody likes a bargain. Wal-Mart's famous promise, 'Lowest price always', would appear to serve as proof that, when it comes to price, emotion ceases to matter and everything becomes clear-cut.

Despite appearances, however, responding to pricing isn't simple. Instead, it's another perceptually influenced issue, just like every other aspect of business, because the value we assign to a potential purchase is so emotional. Consider a study, for example, that found that since prices ending in the number nine suggest bargains, a company was able to increase the price of its dresses from $34 to $39 while also increasing sales volume (Anderson and Simester, 2003).

As Sensory Logic confirmed in work for a manufacturer contemplating three different price points for a new product, the lowest price doesn't always win with consumers. Figure 1.5 shows a case in which people emotionally opted for the middle price. Why? The reason is that the subjects felt good about accepting a slightly higher price because they believed it meant the offer must be superior to cheaper alternatives.

Even more striking, consider the results of a study investigating the impact that sadness and disgust have on people's willingness to buy and sell at different prices (Lerner, Small and Loewenstein, 2004; Begley, 2004). After watching a movie clip designed to induce either sadness or disgust, the subjects were asked to consider buying or selling a highlighter pen.

As Figure 1.6 shows, members of the control group, who were not shown any movie clips, were, not surprisingly, given to selling high and buying low. In contrast, the subjects induced to feel disgust were eager to sell low and hesitant to pay anything to purchase something new because they expected to find it unacceptable. Meanwhile, those feeling sad were also inclined to sell low. But unlike their disgusted colleagues, those feeling sad were eager to improve their circumstances and paid by far the highest price for the pen.

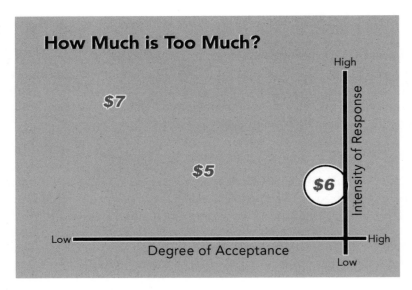

Figure 1.5 Price and quality implications.
Like the story of Goldilocks and her porridge, people found the middle price to be just right. It was high enough to denote quality but not overpricing. And it was low enough to be affordable without giving off an air of shoddiness.

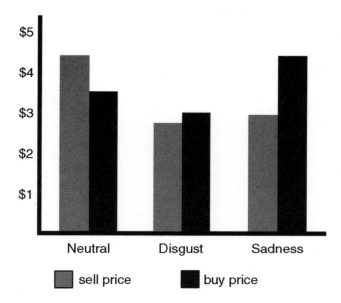

Figure 1.6   Talk about price sensitivity.
For anyone who thinks emotions don't effect actions, look at the results from a study
that induced emotional states in subjects and then had them make financial decisions.
Isn't it astounding (and somewhat intuitive) that how people feel affects what they do?
People who were made sad were much more likely to sell – or get rid of – an item they
associated with sadness.

The take-away here is that emotional states clearly create behaviour contrary
to rational thought. To understand how the world at large truly functions,
and business within it, understanding how emotions operate is crucial to
realizing success. To gain a practical, real-life window into emotions, let's
move on to Chapter 2, which discusses the facial coding tool that brings this
discussion of emotions into a measurable, manageable realm.

2 The science of facial coding

While many companies are struggling to acknowledge emotions, let alone reliably take them into account in their business strategies, others have secured insights and business advantages through the science of facial coding.

Overview

The primary goal of Chapter 1 was to establish how central emotions are to business. From a scientific perspective, however, it's equally important to note how important it is to move beyond a think-your-feelings to a feel-your-feelings approach to capturing emotional responses. That's because conscious, cognitively based verbal input alone is unlikely to be true to the quick, largely subconscious nature of emotions.

In Chapter 2, the goal is to explain facial coding – the only really viable tool currently available for the purpose of quantifying the impact specific emotions have on business. In particular, this chapter will focus on:

- **The challenge**: what problem is facial coding the solution to? The answer is that as the new model of a three-part brain made clear in Chapter 1, there are profound, scientific reasons why verbal input alone is inadequate. To overcome the challenge, however, requires first recognizing the extent of the problem, which gets summarized here before we introduce the solution. The implication for business? At present, almost all companies depend on rationally oriented input such as comments and ratings to help them make decisions. Facial coding provides a means of supplementing that data with insights based on the feelings that drive behaviour.
- **Origins and scope**: the roots of facial coding go back more than a century, most notably to Charles Darwin as well as a French anatomist named Guillaume Duchenne. Then, beginning in the 1960s, psychologist Paul Ekman and his colleague Wally Freisen codified their additional learnings as the Facial Action Coding System (FACS). A summary of facial coding's scope will be provided, including its biological basis and the seven core emotions that it gauges across cultures. The implication for business? Finally, a thorough, precise feel-your-feelings approach exists, enabling companies to know consumers' and employees' actual emotional responses to company initiatives and to plan accordingly. Moreover, computer vision research suggests that automated facial coding may soon be possible. Automation promises to allow faster coding and quicker results.
- **Deliverables**: since first bringing facial coding into the business realm a decade ago, my company, Sensory Logic, has built a set of unique deliverables. These charts (and the processes underlying them) make it possible to extract the maximum degree of utility from facial coding as a research tool. Deliverable formats will be shown, along with a pair of mini case studies that illustrate the tool's validity. The implication for business? Not only is facial coding a repeatable, actionable methodology,

it's also true that companies can use it to gain a more complete picture of people's responses across a wide range of applications, from offer design and advertising to personnel issues as well as other opportunities.

Now let's look more closely at the competitive advantage facial coding offers, starting with why it's needed in the first place.

The challenge: when words alone fail us

Synopsis: New scientific insights about human nature and how our decision-making process actually works require new research tools to quantify these new insights. Where the current set of tools reaches its inherent limits will be summarized first, followed by a more personal history of how people, including myself, have come to know about and use facial coding for their own purposes.

Key take-aways

- To access emotions requires going beyond rationally filtered verbal input.
- Facial coding is incredibly versatile in terms of applications.

Limitations confronting traditional methods

To access emotions requires going beyond rationally filtered verbal input

The degree to which people can't or won't indicate their preferences should be abundantly obvious based on the brain science, psychology and behavioural economics material covered in Chapter 1. But now let's bring it home to how research gets conducted. As Gerald Zaltman has noted in *How Customers Think* (2003), 'A great mismatch exists between the way consumers experience and think about their world and the methods marketers use to collect this information.'

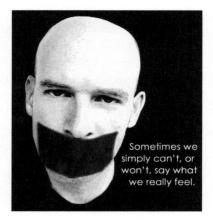

Sometimes we simply can't, or won't, say what we really feel.

Indeed, for every company the difficulty involved in trying to ascertain people's commitment levels to brands, offers, advertising and employers is great. The following few paragraphs show some reasons why the difficulty exists. Then the discussion will turn to how facial coding provides a solution by using an activity-oriented, scientific approach. Not only does facial coding avoid being invasive, it's also able to capture the subtle responses that indicate people's true inclinations in real time.

Here then are some key limitations confronting traditional research:

Words won't suffice

In many ways we live in a post-literate society. Book reading is down while TV watching stays sky high. One urban myth is that teenagers' vocabularies are shrinking with each new generation. While that might not be true, a credible report from an Oxford University professor estimates that up to 20 per cent of adults in the Western world are functionally illiterate (O'Shaughnessy, 2003). These are people who will have money to spend but are unlikely to give very articulate responses to questions about their choices. What's the other big factor limiting the effectiveness of words? It's the difficulty of crossing language barriers – an issue that continues to grow given both globalized marketing and greater mobility, leading to countries with increasingly diverse ethnic groups within their own borders.

Subjects may be going through the motions

Do marketing research recruiters really call on recurring 'professional subjects' when they can't meet quotas? Yes, despite screeners meant to avoid that problem (Leitch, 2004; Bernthal, 2006). These professional subjects may prove to be the most articulate, helpful subjects. But in receiving incentives as an ongoing revenue source, these subjects run the risk of being overly polite and given to saying 'yes' whether they mean it or not. Moreover, there's an additional segment of subjects who, despite the best efforts of good moderators or hosts, succumb to routine by giving indifferent, essentially unvarying answers or ratings to survey questions or don't even finish the surveys. Coverage in *Quirk's Marketing Research Review* (Mullet, 2003; Sack, 2003; Lauer, 2004) indicates that as much as 50 to 70 per cent of some online surveys are left incomplete. Moreover, too often someone else steps in for the original subject part-way through the test (a daughter taking over while the mother starts dinner, for example).

Subjects have a tendency to fall in line

A study quoted in *Advertising and the Mind of the Consumer* (Sutherland and Sylvester, 2000) found that 75 per cent of people in a given situation are willing to go against their own perceptions and give the responses they know or think others will give. This limitation often arises in focus groups, where people are sitting around with 12 strangers but are somehow expected to be 'open'. A skilled moderator can help some, but games will be played. An alpha male or female group member may, in effect, take over the discussion. Another big problem related to this limitation is that people will give answers that make them look smart. Rational, defensible answers are great – but not if they're unrelated to people's true feelings or motivations.

The answers aren't in real time

People's rational reactions aren't likely to be given in real time. In large part that's because of the pervasive influence of our subconscious, which we can't access but which is likely to drive our reactions more quickly than we can report verbally. There are other problems, too. In focus groups, people can sit back and wait for the consensus to form before safely joining in. In response dial testing, subjects may move a hand-held dial to indicate a positive or negative reaction before they really intend to, not move it often enough to reflect shifts in response, or go too slowly as they rationalize their responses. Finally, in fMRI brain scan testing that tracks blood flow, people's responses tend to peak around 8 seconds after exposure to the stimulus (Banich, 2004).

Darwin noted that there was no specific body language that denoted emotional response. To help prove his point, consider this graphic. Can you correctly identify the emotional state of each model? Neither can I. While body language undoubtedly helps us read the feelings of those around us, only facial expressions provide the precision necessary to truly uncover what's going on behind the mask.

Emotions aren't being adequately accessed

While brain scans can capture the physiology of specific emotional responses, they're likely to remain expensive and invasive. Verbal input suffers from all the limitations cited above. In contrast, ethnography is good because it can tell you what people are doing. But it can't access how they're internalizing their emotional response, so as to show how they feel about what they're doing. That leaves facial coding and its originator Charles Darwin (1998 edition), who notes that:

> Emotions are shown primarily in the face, not in the body. The body instead shows how people are coping with emotion. There is no specific body movement pattern that always signals anger or fear, but there are facial patterns specific to each emotion.

In summary, what researchers, analysts, consultants, strategic planners and anybody else in the business world trying to understand how consumers and employees are feeling needs to recognize – and address – is that quite often our responses are cast in a silent language. Most of us still aren't always comfortable honestly discussing them out loud, especially with strangers. And for those who are, it is sometimes impossible to accurately describe how we truly feel, which is where facial coding enters the picture as a viable solution.

And now – facial coding

Facial coding is incredibly versatile in terms of applications

For readers who know nothing of facial coding and may be inclined to consider it a fairly esoteric topic, please think again. Not only has the tool received some surprisingly mainstream press coverage in recent years, it also has a way of showing up in the most unexpected places.

Consider one of my own experiences. A few years ago I was in Beijing to give a speech at the American Chamber of Commerce. It was the Sunday beforehand, during a visit to the Great Wall, when a fellow tour group member asked me what I did for a living. When I said consumer research, his eyes glazed over. So I tried to peak his interest by adding, 'But we do it somewhat differently. Rather than just depend on what people say, my company also studies people's facial expressions to learn how much they're really buying-in emotionally.'

'Oh, micro-expressions,' he replied, referring to brief expressions that typically flit across the face in less than a fifth of a second.

Startled, I couldn't help but lean in toward him and ask with an inquisitive smile, 'Yes. How do you know about them?' After all, micro-expression isn't exactly a household term. It turned out he had just ended a 15-year stint in the Middle East, where he used facial coding for surveillance and general counter-intelligence purposes.

Alarmed? Don't be. The applications to be covered in this book are much more benign than interrogation. But beyond business uses for the tool, yes, it's true that the CIA, FBI and the Pentagon (including the defence contractor my fellow traveller had been working for) have turned to facial coding for the same reason any company might: to gain a competitive edge by learning more than people may be willing or able to communicate through words alone. As a result, everyone from national security to police forces relies on facial coding to be of assistance.

Just how versatile is facial coding? Listed below are various ways in which Sensory Logic uses it to gain emotional insight because traditional market research methods aren't able to do so.

Copy testing	Offer design and positioning
TV spots	Segmentation
Print ads	Price elasticity
Direct mail	Brand equity
Outdoor	Brand icons and characters
Radio	Personnel
Casting	Sales force training
Usability	Hiring
Products and packaging	Media coaching
Websites	Negotiation training
Customer experience	Morale and retention
Customer satisfaction	Change management
Strategy	

At the same time, however, facial coding also has a far softer side to it in terms of possible applications. For example, my first brush with facial coding was in an academic text devoted to psychology that I happened to read in 1998. So imagine my surprise when the tool first hit the mainstream in 2001. That's the year John Cleese, of *Monty Python* fame, produced and starred in *The Human Face*, a five-part series for the BBC. Part psychology, part biology, with lots of interjected humour, the series was ultimately about how central the face is to communication, mating and other types of social activities.

Coverage in *Esquire* (Torday, 2003) and Oprah Winfrey's *O* magazine (*Oprah*, 2002) soon followed, emphasizing the tool's benefit in daily interactions with a loved one. Then a year later Malcolm Gladwell (2002) wrote an essay on facial coding for the *New Yorker*. That publicity led, in turn, to a front-page article in the *Wall Street Journal* (Davis, Pereira and Bulkeley, 2002). Capping it all off was the eventual publication of Gladwell's international bestseller *Blink: The power of thinking without thinking* in 2005.

So facial coding has obviously received a fair amount of popular attention. But how accurate is it? In *Blink*, Gladwell cites the success of the 'Love Lab' at the University of Washington. There, psychologist John Gottman has spent well over a decade studying couples talking to each other. Using only an hour of video footage, his ability to predict whether a couple will be married 15 years later is 95 per cent accurate. By viewing only 15 minutes of videotape, his success rate is still around 90 per cent. Gottman's tool of choice: facial coding.

The marriage counselling Gottman practises is of course highly emotional in nature, a territory few companies have investigated and even fewer have staked out effectively. As stated earlier, business is already very knowledgeable about and comfortable with rationality. Criteria related to it can be measured using verbal input. But now through facial coding, it's also possible to tackle business issues involving emotions – as we're about to see. Daniel Goleman is right to note that 'Just as the mode of the rational mind is words, the mode of the emotions is non-verbal.' The bottom line? While at present, almost all companies rely on rationally oriented input such as comments and ratings to help them make decisions, facial coding provides a means to extract emotional data with insight about the feelings that drive behaviour.

Origins and scope: why and how facial coding works

Synopsis: This section details the origins and refinement of facial coding, including an explanation of its biological basis. But the heart of the section involves profiles of the seven core emotions that facial coding can universally gauge, as well as how deceit is most likely to reveal itself.

- The founders of facial coding worked from careful physiological observations.
- Facial coding is robust because of the face's unique properties.
- Every codeable emotion has its own meaning or 'script', but there is no specific muscle movement that betrays a liar.
- Computer-assisted coding will enable quicker, less expensive results.

Discovery and development of facial coding

The founders of facial coding worked from careful physiological observations

Facial expressions are uniform and universal. Indeed, even a person born blind, who could not possibly learn expressions through imitation, has the same facial expressions as everyone else. Moreover, a team of Israeli scientists has recently gone even further. Their conclusion? People born blind exhibit characteristic expressions nearly identical to those displayed by their families and close relatives.

Charles Darwin first discovered this amazing truth about the innate, hard-wired nature of facial expressions. As a father, he was eager to know what his young children were feeling before they could talk. So as a scientist, Darwin began to observe them carefully. What he found stunned

As DNA has shown, we are quite genetically similar to apes. Darwin made a discovery about emotions while observing an orangutan and comparing its facial expressions to his children's.

him. Their facial expressions were very similar to those of an orang-utan named Jenny also under his observation on a regular basis, albeit at the London Zoo.

After an extensive amount of research, Darwin published *The Expression of the Emotions in Man and Animals* in 1872. The *Blink* of its day, it quickly became a bestseller. In his book, Darwin provided evidence that the facial expressions of humans correlate with those of other primates. He went on to note that the face is the primary vehicle used to communicate emotions to others.

From an evolutionary perspective, the key to Darwin's pioneering research was that we have universal facial expressions because communicating emotions in this way is an adaptive advantage. Long before we could speak, humans communicated with each other primarily via what their faces 'said'. But from a business perspective, Darwin was laying the groundwork for a scientifically valid means of measuring emotions in order to manage outcomes more successfully.

Unfortunately, it took until the mid-1960s before modern science picked up where Darwin had left off. It was then that Dr Paul Ekman, a professor at the University of California San Francisco, received a grant to confirm or disprove Darwin's theory regarding the universality of facial expressions.

Eventually Ekman travelled to Papua New Guinea, to study a tribe that lacked a written language and had lived in virtual cultural isolation from the western world. There he told stories and asked tribal members to select among photographs of various facial expressions the one that best fitted each given story. Except for some problems distinguishing between fear and surprise, the native people clearly recognized the other core emotions, providing evidence that Darwin's theory was correct (Ekman, 2003).

A contemporary of Darwin with whom he corresponded, the French anatomist, Duchenne, used electric shocks to force patients to show the facial expressions he wanted to study because emotion can trigger muscle movement in the face without control. What facial coding terms a true smile is also known as a Duchenne smile.

Armed with these findings, Ekman and colleague Wally Friesen from the San Francisco School of Medicine proceeded to spend over seven years systematically studying a large pool of facial expressions. Their goal: to document precisely the movements of people's facial muscles. When they were done, Ekman and Friesen had created the Facial Action Coding System (FACS), which categorizes the activity of 43 facial muscles. These muscles moving in various combinations form 23 key action units (AUs), which serve as the basic building blocks of all facial expressions related to emotions. Finally, Ekman and Friesen documented the AUs in terms of which specific core emotions they express.

Darwin's discovery of the powerful universality of facial expressions had originated in comparing his children to a primate. Now his discovery had become a sophisticated system for deciphering human feelings. Thanks to FACS, it has become possible to quantify emotions by systematically reading other people's faces. As a result, a thorough, precise feel-your-feelings approach exists, enabling companies to know consumers' and employees' actual emotional responses to company initiatives and to plan accordingly.

When I learnt about the Darwin-to-Ekman connection, the business applications intrigued me. Nearly three decades after Ekman first travelled to New Guinea, I would arrive at his office in San Francisco eager to learn how best to bring this astounding capacity to the business world.

Paul Ekman and his colleague Wally Friesen spent over seven years scientifically decoding the muscle movements of every type of facial expression. Their end product: the Facial Action Coding System (FACS).

It was my belief that the old joke, 'Half of my advertising is wasted; I just don't know which half' reflected a crucial truth

The purpose was clear: FACS's scaleable, repeatable method of gauging emotional effectiveness could be used to find out what was working, what wasn't and how companies could improve on their best options.

The brain-to-face connection

Facial coding is robust because of the face's unique properties

When Ekman and Friesen created their facial coding system, they relied on two facts which make it a natural and highly effective tool. The first is that human beings have more facial muscles than any other species on the planet. This fact alone makes analysing the face a gold mine of data. Second, the face is the one and only place on the body where our muscles attach directly to the skin. As a result, the face is highly mobile, with skin that shapes itself quickly in response to impulses from the brain (McNeill, 1998). Thus the face provides a spontaneous window on to people's feelings.

The expressiveness of our facial muscles provides the basis and the rationale for facial coding. Whenever the brain generates emotionally encoded impulses, these impulses are delivered to the face via a single facial nerve that controls all our facial muscles and resulting facial expressions.

Much as an ocean wave forms, builds and dissolves, facial expressions have an onset, a peak and a fade. The duration of expressions will typically range from half a second to four seconds. Meanwhile, the length of time and the type and degree of movement all combine to serve as barometers by which to gauge the intensity of the underlying causal emotion.

The seven core emotions

Every codeable emotion has its own meaning or 'script,' but there is no specific muscle movement that betrays a liar

To help get a better grasp on facial coding as a method of determining the true emotional response of consumers and employees, let's look at its basic elements. What exactly emerges? Regardless of race, ethnicity, age or gender, people's faces reveal seven core emotions. One is essentially neutral: surprise. Five are negative: fear, anger, sadness, disgust and contempt. The other is positive: happiness. Moreover, happiness can be divided based on two different kinds of smiles, true smiles and social smiles. The latter involves only the mouth and may indicate deceit.

Seven core emotions
Positive: happiness
Neutral: surprise
Negative: fear, anger, sadness, disgust, contempt
As good as the dinner was, it never makes doing the dishes fun. The reason that
negative emotions predominate is because humans respond more quickly to bad news
than good news as a matter of survival.

As shown in Chapter 3, this core set of emotions can be expanded
through gradations and mixtures. But these are the essential emotions, of
which, yes, only one involves upbeat feelings.

In evolutionary terms, a ratio favouring the negative can be explained
by the fact that life is kind of like making dinner. We have to buy the
groceries and do the cooking. Eating the food is fabulous fun. But it only
takes a few minutes, after which the dishes sit waiting to be washed. In
other words, survival instincts dictate being more alert to hearing bad
news than good news – and our core emotions reflect that reality.

Now that readers have been forewarned about the negative tilt, let's
review the core emotions. In each case, an emotion's meaning or script
will be explained. (Script refers to what typically causes the emotion and
what kind of physical response and behaviour happen as a result of it.)

Please note that the following photographs of yours truly were staged
and may be a little exaggerated, like caricatures, to make studying them
easier. Furthermore, note that references to the early age at which these
emotions appear on the face is to reinforce the point that facial expressions are universal and innate (McNeill, 1998).

Surprise

Our ability to express surprise appears at birth. Uniquely, surprise is neither inherently positive nor negative. Its valence all depends on what we perceive after the surprise has passed. In the basic surprise script, we're confronting a 'mystery' we haven't faced before, one that's yet to be solved. We don't know whether pleasure or pain awaits us, and we tend to freeze until we know the outcome.

A surprised face expands upward and downward, north and south, and has much in common with one expressing fear. Here's how the face may show surprise:

- Eyes go big.
- Eyebrows fly high.
- Mouth falls open.

Fear

This is the single most important emotion. Prominent in politicians' campaign messages – from John F Kennedy's 'missile gap' to George W Bush's 'War on Terror' – its use is also a mainstay of business. Fear is constantly monitored by consumers in the marketplace. After all, an offer's safety is the first item on people's intuitive checklist, the equivalent of looking both ways before crossing the street. No wonder fear rips through companies when employees hear the latest reorganization rumour. In short, fear cuts through the clutter like nothing else and is used to sell everything from snow tyres to toothpaste.

In fear's basic script, we seek to escape some perceived danger in order to protect ourselves. The loss aversion concept, emphasized by behavioural economists, fits right in here.

The ability to express fear appears about five to nine months after birth. Fear opens the face, which will blanch and, in extreme cases, tremble. Here's how the face may show fear:

- Eyebrows lift up and in.
- Eyes widen.
- Chin pulls wider.
- Lips stretch back horizontally.
- Jaw drops open.

Anger

Talk to people who work in customer service and they'll probably suggest that anger, not fear, is the single most prominent emotion! What they witness is anger's reactionary nature. It involves a lashing out. It's the fight part of our fight-or-flight instinct, and arises whenever our expectations are violated. In anger's basic script, people seek to remove or otherwise attack a barrier they believe is unfairly blocking progress or undermining their personal identity and sense of self-worth. A secondary script related to desiring progress is that anger arises in response to experiencing a loss of control.

The ability to show anger appears three to seven months after birth. The angry face contracts – like a snake coiling to strike – and its appearance becomes more concentrated and intense. When a person becomes red-faced or 'boiling mad', blood floods the face's capillaries. Here's how the face may show anger:

- Eyebrows lower and knit together.
- Eyes narrow into 'snake-eyes'.
- Lips will tighten or form a funnel.

Sadness

In business, sadness as expressed in the marketplace is usually about buyer's regret. In the workplace, the despondency created by alienation, stress and fatigue robs a company of its most vital resource: an engaged employee. When we're sad, we slow way, way down. Withdrawal, listlessness and general avoidance behaviour become typical. 'Always sell hope' is a valid motivational mantra because sadness means feeling helpless. With respect to employees, companies can defuse feelings of rejection and irrevocable loss by offering the prospect of feasible rewards instead of threats of further reprimand.

Sadness appears between birth and three months. Generally speaking, sadness makes the face sag, giving a person a 'long face' frown. Here's how the face may show sadness:

- Wrinkles form a mid-forehead 'puddle'.
- Eyebrows drop, but inner corners rise slightly.
- Corners of eyes crease in a wince.
- The 'trench' running between the corners of nostrils and upper mouth corners will deepen.
- Lip corners sag or form an 'upside-down' smile.

Disgust

Disgust is an adverse reaction shown when we attempt to distance ourselves from an offensive source. It's our way of showing that an object, person, place or even an idea 'stinks'. Not surprisingly, disgust manifests itself in an upturned nose and curling lips, and can be seen as the equivalent of having a foul taste in one's mouth. Unfortunately for those offers lacking spice, a mild form of disgust – boredom – which signifies no taste for what is being offered is very prevalent.

Disgust appears between birth and three months. It involves a lifting up and away, like a gag reflex, as we try to protect ourselves from 'poison'. Here's how the face may show disgust:

- Nose turns up and wrinkles.
- Upper lip rises, sometimes as part of an 'upside down smile'.
- Lower lip pulls down and away.

Contempt

Less physical and more attitudinal – one might say moral – in orientation than disgust, customers may feel contempt in response to feeling deceived, for instance. Contempt can be fatal for companies. After all, Dr Gottman's 'Love Lab' research has shown that nothing predicts the collapse of a couple's relationship better than the settling in of contempt. And what's bad for marital bliss surely isn't going to be healthy for company/customer or manager/employee relationships, either.

This emotion reflects deep disdain: a belief that the other party in the deal is beneath you. It's an emotion hard to recover from. Watch out for contempt in others, because it means one's offer, promotional efforts or managerial style has become repugnant to that audience.

Contempt is expressed in subtler but more profound ways than is disgust. When feeling this emotion, people's lips will tighten and lift on one side of the face, forming a little pocket or cavity in the cheek like the eye of a hurricane. Here's how the face will show contempt:

- A unilateral expression (the left side of the face is generally more expressive than the right side), with one upper corner of the mouth curling into a sneer.
- Upper lip rises.
- Eyes may partly close and turn away.

And the winner is ...

As mentioned earlier, there is only one truly positive emotion in Ekman's set of core emotions: happiness. That's because in evolutionary terms survival is job number one, and we don't need happiness to survive. Once we move past meeting basic survival needs, we grant happiness more and more importance.

In therapeutic terms, and based on measures of finding authentic meaning in life, the Positive Psychology movement classifies happiness in levels ranging from fleeting pleasure to deep, sustained contentment. Meanwhile, recognize the reality that people are willing to pay more for their dream-like wants than needs. So making happiness possible can be handsomely rewarded. The happiness script is fairly stable: we've experienced a gain or success and are now making what we deem to be reasonable progress toward a goal.

> Happiness makes up in height what it lacks in length.
>
> Robert Frost

The true smile or Duchenne smile

Like surprise, our unique capacity for expressing true smiles is present from birth. Maybe that's why the front of breakfast cereal boxes are always full of cartoon characters like a smiling Tony the Tiger, who is meant to coax children into pulling at the heartstrings and wallets of parents worldwide.

a **TRUE** smile

A true smile's signature features are eyes that twinkle or gleam because the muscles surrounding them are animated. Ekman calls a true smile a Duchenne smile in honour of the French anatomist whose photographs of people's expressions aided Darwin's work. Here's how a true smile looks:

- Skin near the outer corner of the eye pinches together into 'crow's feet'.
- The upper eyelid slightly droops and skin under the eye may gather upward.
- The corners of the mouth move up and out, the cheeks lift upwards.

The social smile

If there are true smiles, there must also be false smiles, right? Correct. Human beings have more ability to manipulate the muscles around the mouth (we like to eat, after all) than we do those around the eyes. It's why we have sayings like 'the eyes never lie' and 'the eyes are the window to the soul'. Just think of the 'grip and grin' photos present in numerous print ads, television commercials and public relations events. What they have in common is that viewers can intuitively tell that the smiles on the people's faces are 'phoney', or at least less substantial.

Social smiles appear at one and a half to three months after birth. In other words, toddlers quickly pick up this skill (a revelation that caused a department store researcher I once met with to remark, 'I knew my kid was manipulating me!'). While there is only one true smile, Ekman has catalogued a score of slightly different social smiles. In essence:

- The face becomes rounder as the corners of the mouth move up and out and the cheeks lift upwards.
- Missing, however, is the activity around the eyes that would cause them to twinkle or gleam, thereby indicating the presence of a true smile.

a **SOCIAL** smile

Lying smiles and other signs of deception

The presence of a social smile may simply reveal a degree of enjoyment that falls short of spirited, joyful happiness. Consumers or employees who are pleased with what they've received may nevertheless not experience an exalted happiness. That's because, while their expectations were met, they were not exceeded. How they then respond to being satisfied, but not thrilled, could involve the exhibiting of a social smile. But if there's pressure to be happy about the raise a boss has just given you, for example, the employee may gamely put a happy face on the situation. Or a prospect put off by a salesperson's overly aggressive style may exhibit a social smile to hide the fact that the deal is headed south.

In those cases, a degree of deception is involved. And later on, the manager or salesperson may wish he or she had been able to tell from the other party's facial expressions that the end was near. But alas, there is no one muscle movement that categorically reveals deception.

What better example for deceit than the classic clown face?

Painted to look like it's always full of smiles, one glance beneath the make-up can dispel the myth of continuous merriment.

Facial coding does much the same thing by gleaning true, unfiltered, positive or negative emotional reactions.

Bear in mind that while Adolf Hitler practised his speeches in front of a mirror to test his accompanying expressions, most of us aren't that deliberate. All of us can adequately guard against 'two-faced' people whose smiles aren't the real thing by being alert to a few, basic situations or patterns.

In particular, be alert to a polite, masking smile in situations where:

- It doesn't involve the whole face. The cheeks will lie flat and still and the eyes don't narrow as they do during a genuine smile.
- It lingers too long. A true smile tends to fade around the four-second mark. A false smile may run from five to ten seconds.
- It has odd timing. A deceitful smile tends to start or end too abruptly or arrive too early or late. A smile may also be deceitful if what the person is saying and the expression are out of sync.

- It's asymmetrical and much more pronounced on just one side of the face. That happens because the smile is likely to have been consciously delivered.
- Finally, watch out for smiles given when the person's face hints of other, darker emotions at or near the same time. In a case of **mixed signals** like happiness and anger, be careful not to discount the anger on display.

That last description of a deceitful smile involves what Ekman (1992) calls 'leakage'. Basically, it amounts to unintended, fleeting glimpses of what the person is really feeling. Leakage involves the kind of brief, micro-expressions referred to by the fellow traveller I met at the Great Wall in China. On a related note, a micro-expression may happen because of 'squelches'. These occur when a person interrupts his or her natural expression, usually to cover up a negative feeling with a smile. The squelch is something skilled politicians the world over attempt to master.

Data capture and analysis

Computer-assisted coding will enable quicker, less expensive results

In practice, facial coding begins by capturing video. While it can be done by placing cameras in store environments, for instance, Sensory Logic most often tests by running individual interviews with webcams mounted on a laptop computer. Those tests can be administered in focus group facilities, mall facilities, and over the internet, among other settings. The tests are pre-programmed so that the intervals when the webcam will turn on to record video and audio of subjects looking at stimuli and/or answering questions are timed, and they include the option of rotating the order in which stimuli are shown.

A webcam on top of a laptop screen captures digital video of all responses to computer-programmed tests in which the individually tested subjects may look at stimuli as well as answer questions and provide ratings.

How can this help? Consider the prevalence of internet surveys. Cheap and relatively easy to do, they run the risk of being garbage in, garbage out. Look at the frames captured from webcam recordings. The woman on the left is letting out her dog while 'watching' the TV spot she went on to comment about. The woman to the right is talking to her boyfriend the whole way through the spot she also went on to critique. The value of a webcam starts, but doesn't end, with knowing whether the subjects are really paying attention or, in other cases, even fit the screening criteria.

As revealed by webcam footage, both of these subjects went on to critique a TV spot they didn't watch (in favour of letting out the dog and talking to a boyfriend instead).

Once the video is captured, it is then manually reviewed at intervals as precise as 1/30th of a second, looking for signs of the action units that serve as the building blocks of Ekman's facial coding system. But the ultimate business model involves automated facial coding. Sensory Logic has secured a technology partner in order to eventually automate the coding of the action units, creating the opportunity for greater scale, time efficiencies and reduced costs.

Deliverables: facial coding in practice

Synopsis: Until now emotions have been hard to quantify and, therefore, even harder to plan for. Facial coding changes all that, providing precise metrics that companies can use in plotting strategies and handling tactical executions. To that end, this section shows sample result formats and a couple of case studies. Then it concludes by summarizing Sensory Logic's findings about the extent of the gap between what people say versus what they feel in response to marketing efforts.

Key take-aways

- Each emotional data set provides its own unique insights.
- Being on-emotion is more important than being on-message.
- There is verbal 'grade' inflation in people's responses.

What the results look like

Each emotional data set provides its own unique insights

As is true when learning any new skill, one can learn some of the basics of facial coding within a short time. But it takes countless hours of practice to master all of the intricacies, let alone decide how best to tabulate the results. Serving as a consultant to Sensory Logic during its start-up phase, Ekman provided my company not only with training materials, but also with advice and feedback as we learned our way.

What Ekman did not have, however, was a scoring system that would enable facial coding to realize its potential as a scientific, cross-cultural tool for quantifying emotional responses. To bring it to scale globally and access a platform of applications, Ekman's FACS system would have to be given additional rigour. In utilizing facial coding on a daily basis in a business context, I and my company, Sensory Logic are uniquely qualified because we've added a scoring system, norms and deliverables suitable to business practice. As protected through US patents, granted and pending, our scoring and reporting methods had to be developed and refined over a decade of ongoing work in order to fulfil facial coding's ability to guide companies forward.

The following topline review of a few key charts shows how the data derived from facial coding can be presented. Seven charts will be shown:

- emotional response rate (Figure 2.1);
- percentage of positive/negative emotional response (Figure 2.2);
- specific emotional spectrum (Figure 2.3);
- quadrant chart (Figure 2.4);
- second-by-second chart (Figure 2.5);
- benefits of facial coding versus the dial score (Figure 2.6)
- eye tracking and concurrent emotions (Figure 2.7).

The first decisive measure is whether anybody notices or cares. A company can't win people over if it hasn't awakened them by causing an emotional reaction. At Sensory Logic, we track emotional response rate by discerning the exact percentage of subjects who show at least one action unit (AU), or 'hit', on their faces (Figure 2.1) in reaction to experiencing a stimulus and/or while answering a question.

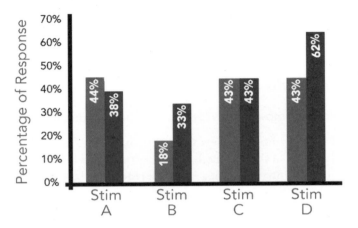

Figure 2.1 Emotional response rate levels.
This chart compares the emotional response rates of four components of two different campaigns. Note the variance in response rates for different components. Campaign 1 has an average response of 37 per cent and Campaign 2 has an average response of 44 per cent. Keep in mind that emotional response rate doesn't measure like or dislike, but rather whether or not subjects get emotionally engaged by what they're experiencing.

Once a company knows whether it's engaging people, the next step is to learn the general type of response. From facial coding, a company can also determine whether good or bad responses are more prevalent: the percentage of people whose overall emotional response can be categorized as positive, neutral or negative across the sample population (Figure 2.2). Remember, however, that negative emotions don't always correlate to bad outcomes. In a problem/solution TV spot, for example, it's vital to establish the problem as real and relevant in order to sell the branded solution.

Figure 2.2 Percentage of positive, neutral and negative response overall.

So negative emotions early in the commercial will be an indication that a credible connection is being made.

Then there is also the matter of identifying the specific emotions expressed by subjects (Figure 2.3). As we know by now, each emotion has its own 'script' or meaning. It can be helpful to understand the amount each specific emotion contributes to the overall response of a group.

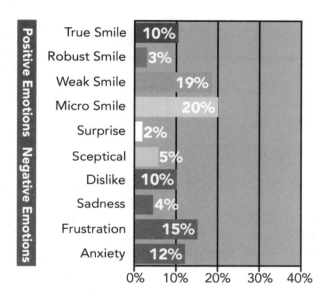

Figure 2.3   Specific emotional spectrum.

For our purposes Sensory Logic has divided social smiles into three categories (robust, weak and micro smiles shown briefly on only one side of the face). Surprise is categorized as a slight positive here because of the urgency of obtaining attention in a crowded marketplace. Meanwhile, among the negative emotions scepticism refers to a social smile used to mask or soften a negative comment. Dislike encompasses disgust and contempt. Frustration and anxiety correspond to anger and fear, respectively.

Next up is a quadrant chart (Figure 2.4), whose importance resides in the fact that each of the emotions shown on people's faces will vary in terms of the impact and appeal values of those emotions. To illustrate, there are about five primary ways in which people may exhibit anger on their faces. Those ways vary from outright, blood-curdling rage to far more mild annoyance. Based on the facial muscle activity or AUs, the emotional outcome must take into account the degree of impact or intensity of those AUs as well as the degree to which the appeal being exhibited

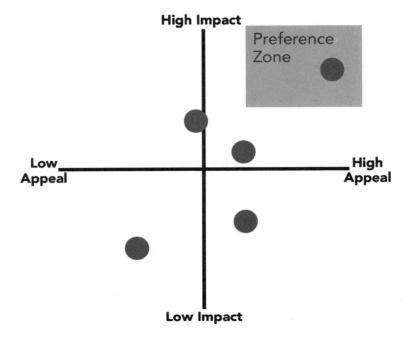

Figure 2.4   Quadrant chart.
Quadrant charts graphically represent the impact (intensity of emotional response) and appeal (degree of positive or negative response) of stimuli. Especially when it comes to purchase intent, the ideal result is in the top right quadrant – an indication that the target market is enthusiastically positive.

is positive or negative in orientation. As a result, a quadrant chart maps data reflecting the *emotional temperature* of those AUs we've detected.

Next, in regard to examples like TV commercials, offer usage or customer service experience, people's emotional response unfolds over time. In those cases, a second-by-second chart is in order (Figures 2.5 and 2.6).

Taken together, these six charts account for the primary ways in which Sensory Logic shows results, with each version providing a slightly different insight. Because people have such a hard time accurately articulating responses to stimuli (whether visual or word-based), there is also one more relevant measure that we use. To specifically link emotional responses to what is causing them, it's helpful to be able to determine *exactly* what people are looking at.

That's where eye tracking enters the picture. Eye tracking is the recording of where people look and what they focus on. When tied to facial coding, the results indicate the precise amount of gaze activity

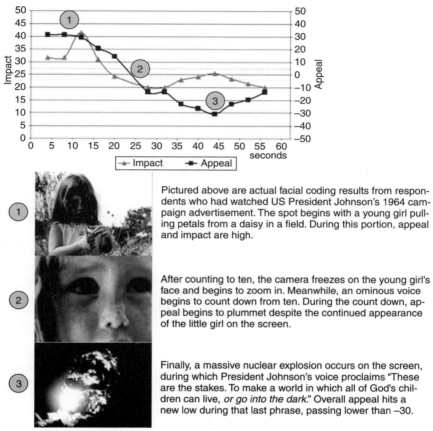

Pictured above are actual facial coding results from respondents who had watched US President Johnson's 1964 campaign advertisement. The spot begins with a young girl pulling petals from a daisy in a field. During this portion, appeal and impact are high.

After counting to ten, the camera freezes on the young girl's face and begins to zoom in. Meanwhile, an ominous voice begins to count down from ten. During the count down, appeal begins to plummet despite the continued appearance of the little girl on the screen.

Finally, a massive nuclear explosion occurs on the screen, during which President Johnson's voice proclaims "These are the stakes. To make a world in which all of God's children can live, *or go into the dark*." Overall appeal hits a new low during that last phrase, passing lower than −30.

This famous spot – shown only once, like the equally famous '1989' Apple spot – is notable because of the large number of connective data points. Moreover, it accomplishes a large emotional swing to drive home President Johnson's warning about his rival, Barry Goldwater.

Figure 2.5   Second-by-second chart.

(where people looked) and specific emotional response to elements of a stimulus (how people feel about what they see). This synchronization of emotional response and visual focus provides a reliable method for understanding what is driving subject reactions (Figure 2.7).

In effect, the combination of eye tracking and facial coding provides a one–two punch based on people's actual behaviour. The eye tracking correlates to awareness: does one get noticed? Meanwhile, the facial coding correlates to consideration. Yes, they noticed but is the company winning them over?

Figure 2.6   Benefits of facial coding versus the dial score.
This second-by-second chart details one minute of a network television series. The dial score appears in grey along with appeal (dark) and impact (light). The dial test does not present a natural indication of one's feelings because it is consciously filtered and not truly spontaneous. Instead, it requires respondents to think about their feelings and then to make a judgement. Facial coding on the other hand, represents natural gut reactions captured in real time. In this instance, the dial score misses a key emotional fluctuation when appeal and impact drop about 40 seconds in.

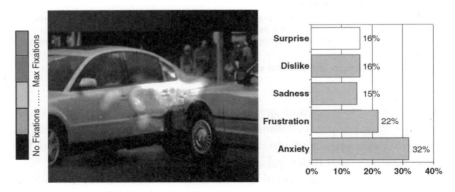

Figure 2.7   Eye tracking hot spots and concurrent emotions.
This photo and bar chart represent the ability of eye tracking and facial coding to provide specific insight into the emotional effect of stimuli. Based on the advanced eye trackers available from the Swedish company Tobii, the photo shows the results of eye tracking relative to a scene in a TV spot. As is evident, the main focus of people's gaze fixations is where the collision has occurred. The chart above shows the specific emotional responses present during the viewing of the scene.

The power of being on-emotion

Being on-emotion is more important than being on-message

The ultimate, big-picture story being conveyed here is that, yes, it's important to be rationally on-message. But it's even more imperative to be on-emotion. A company's message will only be successful if it attracts interest and emotionally appeals to the receiver enough to commit to the proposition being promoted.

As the examples of deliverable formats illustrate, facial coding is a repeatable, actionable methodology. Moreover, companies can also use it to gain a more complete picture of people's responses across a wide range of applications from offer design and advertising to personnel issues, as well as other opportunities.

> Rational motives are merely a cover-up of unconscious, archaic motive complexes.
>
> Ernest Dicher

So now that we've seen how significant emotions are, how they are measured and how to understand the information they can provide, let's look at a pair of real-world examples that will combine these elements and demonstrate the importance of being on-emotion.

Case 1: Direct mail pieces in the financial sector

We tested almost 30 direct mail pieces for a financial services company. (Note that unless permission was granted, the names of clients and examples of their work won't be shown in this book in order to protect their confidentiality.) Of those mailings, eight qualified as part of what might be called a 'hell' strategy. In general terms, that means the company attempted to use fear to motivate consumers into opening a mailing by creating enough concern over the mailing's contents that recipients would be afraid of throwing it into the bin without looking at it. In order to succeed, the 'hell' strategy needed to generate a strongly negative emotional reaction.

As shown in Figure 2.8, in four of the five instances where facial coding detected a very negative emotional reaction, the in-market response rate to the mailing was high. In other words, the mailers were on-emotion and elicited the negative response necessary to convince people that the mailers were important and that not opening them could have negative consequences. In contrast, when the facially coded emotional response result was positive – and therefore off-emotion – the response rates for the 'hell' mailings were abysmally low.

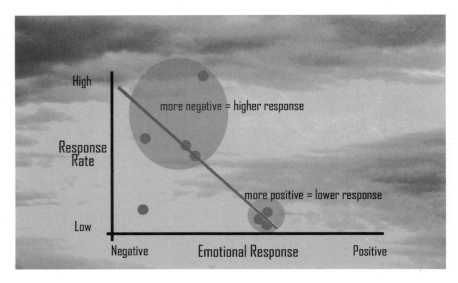

Figure 2.8   Hell strategy.
88 per cent of fear-based direct mail offers demonstrated strong correlation between
increasing negative emotional response and market response. The more negative the
emotional response, the higher the market response proved to be in accordance with
this strategy for breaking through the clutter.

The 'heaven' strategy reveals similar results (Figure 2.9) in regard to the
importance of being on-emotion. Seven of the 11 'heaven' mailers were
off-emotion. They failed to generate strong positive emotional responses
because they didn't emotionally convince the recipients that they would
find good news inside an envelope promising either an attractive interest
rate or other generous terms. In every case, those seven off-emotion
'heaven' mailers had low in-market response rates.

As for the other four 'heaven' mailers, they were 50 per cent accurate.
Half the time, a high response rate was the result of generating a very
positive appeal reaction. But the other half of the in-market wins came
from 'heaven' mailers that didn't generate favourable emotional reactions. As a result, the predictive power for a 'heaven' strategy proved to be
slightly less robust.

Overall, however, Sensory Logic correctly predicted the in-market effectiveness of 16 of the 19 mailers using either a 'heaven' or 'hell' strategy and
proved the power of being on-emotion. What does generating the desired
emotional reaction accomplish? It enables success in a fickle medium like
direct mail, where the average response rate per piece hovers around 2
per cent (according to the Direct Marketing Assocation – DMA).

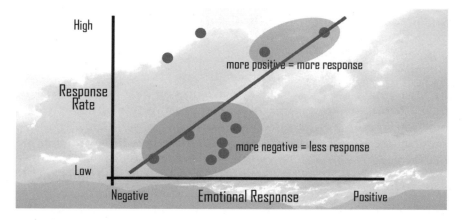

Figure 2.9   Heaven strategy.
82 per cent of hope-based direct mail offers demonstrated strong correlation between increasing positive emotional response and market response. The more negative and off-emotion the response was, the lower the odds that it generated a strong market response.

In this case, our ability to gauge which 'hell' and 'heaven' strategy executions would work reached:

- 88 per cent for 'hell' mailings – seven of eight right (Figure 2.8) – based on knowing that highly negative reactions were the key for this strategy to pay off.
- 82 per cent for 'heaven' mailings – nine of 11 correct (Figure 2.9) – based on knowing that the mailers meant to be positively received but unlikely to generate that kind of response were likely to fail.

In other words, plucking the correct emotional heartstrings was the key to determining which direct mail pieces were worth sending out the door.

Finally, it is important to note that the overall percentage of direct mail pieces leading to the preferred response rate was higher among 'hell' mailings, proving that 'going negative' does pay off. Half of the 'hell' executions – four of eight (Figure 2.8) – were successful, while approximately 35 per cent of the 'heaven' strategy – four of 11 (Fig. 2.9) – were successful. So it would appear that mailers meant to sell hope but failing to generate positive emotional responses – we might say, landing in purgatory – fall flatter in market than do mailers pushing people's fear buttons.

Case 2: Designing the next big pickup truck

For a major motor vehicle company, we looked at various design options for a forthcoming pickup truck model. In Case 1, the degree of positive or negative appeal was the key measure in detecting what would work. This time around, the key proved to be the impact or intensity level of the emotional responses we saw in the subjects. In short, weak positive support – lacking enthusiasm – proved insufficient to be a winner in the marketplace. Here's what happened.

As shown in Figure 2.10, there were six design options the company was considering for final production. Of the six, two designs were the only ones to receive positive rational verbal responses. And this duo also received positive appeal results based on the emotional facial coding, although the impact results were worrisome. They were dishearteningly low.

Our concern was that subjects said and showed that they liked both options; however, their smiles were tepid. They lacked the fire of conviction. Wouldn't this lack of enthusiasm prove fatal in a sector where price tags are high, competition fierce and innovation so constant that a company risks looking dated by the time its design hits the streets?

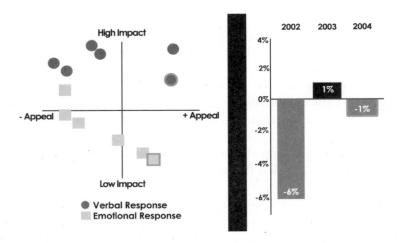

Figure 2.10   Responses to pickup truck designs and sales results for the selected model.
The chart on the left shows the emotional and verbal response of subjects to proposed pickup truck designs for a 2004 release. On the right are preceding sales figures and the outcome for the year of the model's release. Though emotional appeal was strong for the chosen design (outlined above), impact was low, reflecting a lack of enthusiasm. As is evident based on the 2004 sales results, the design's lack of emotional impact during testing proved to be an accurate prediction of eventual marketplace response.

We thought so. And as the eventual sales results show, the marketplace unfortunately proved us right. Our advice was to go back to the drawing board. Instead, the client opted for one of the rational 'winners' and put it on showroom floors. As the right side of Figure 2.10 shows, the 2004 sales (the year the design was put into production) fell by 1 per cent.

Exploring the say/feel gap

There is verbal 'grade' inflation in people's responses

With years of projects and thousands of examples behind us, Sensory Logic is in the unique position of being able to quantify the extent of the gap that can exist between what people say and how they actually feel. So in the closing section of this chapter, let's examine the gap, knowing that actions really do speak louder than words. Thus it makes sense that Ekman refers to the various types of facial muscle activity as action units (AUs). Though miniature in scale, what people show on their faces is still behaviour. As a result, facial expressions are reliable guides to how people are likely to respond as consumers or employees.

The key question is, 'To what extent do people's verbal and facial coding responses conflict with one another?' To answer it, Sensory Logic has engaged in extensive reviews of our database (see also Figure 2.11). Here are some general guidelines as to what we have found true over the years:

- **Grade inflation exists.** As a rule of thumb, the percentage of positive verbal results often exceeds the percentage of positive facial coding activity by at least 10 per cent. At times, the gap gets as large as 20 per cent to 30 per cent either way – more negative or positive – depending on whether people feel comfortable disclosing what they like. Overall, the track record suggests that people tend to say they like something more than their actual feelings merit.
- **There are racial differences.** We often get asked about differences between races and cultures, especially whether the Japanese reveal their emotions enough to do facial coding. The answer is, yes. Playing video-tape on a split-second basis and freeze-framing it for further review helps. The Japanese may be more subtle and reserved in their facial movements. But as fellow human beings, they show their emotions using the exact same facial muscles moving in identical patterns. The difference is something Ekman calls display rules: that is, the degree to which emotions are easily evident or else get 'squelched'. Suffice it to say, the ability to detect micro-expressions is crucial in doing work in Japan given that cultural differences favour the discreet. In contrast, we've

seen some fairly profound differences in America regarding the size of the say/feel gap. Caucasians and Hispanics are in one group. They typically have a fairly large gap, tilted toward positive exaggeration. In the other camp are African-Americans, who are much more forward about saying exactly what's on their minds (and in their hearts).

When survey ratings were...

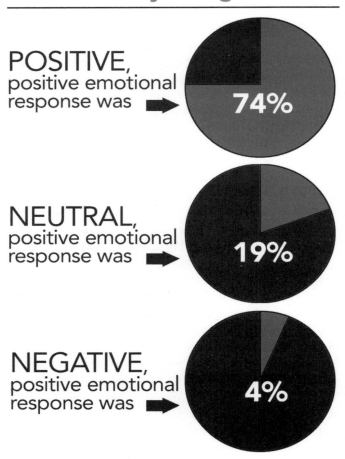

POSITIVE,
positive emotional
response was ➡ **74%**

NEUTRAL,
positive emotional
response was ➡ **19%**

NEGATIVE,
positive emotional
response was ➡ **4%**

Figure 2.11   A say/feel gap discrepancy.
Using statistics Sensory Logic has calculated from two major projects, this chart demonstrates the fact that people don't always know how they really feel, even if they think they do. The top pie chart shows that when our subjects said they had a positive reaction, it was emotionally positive only three-quarters of the time. When they stated a neutral reaction, they actually responded in an emotionally positive manner a fifth of the time. And when they voiced negative feelings, they had a positive reaction unbeknownst to them 1/20th of the time.

- **There are really two tribes: men and women.** Is there a gender gap related to the say/feel gap? Yes, we've found one. For men, the say/feel gap is smaller than it is for women for two reasons. First, men tend to have a lower percentage of positive verbal response than women. In other words, they're less inclined to 'make nice'. Second, men tend to have a higher percentage of positive facial coding activity than women. In other words, they're more emotionally promiscuous – less choosy than their more discriminating female colleagues.

Now that we've established how facial coding works, both in theory and practice, it's time to move on to Chapter 3 and build the rest of the analytical model that will form the basis for the application chapters to follow.

3 Emotions and motivations

Like meshed gears that transfer power to an engine, emotions and motivations are the source behind all human action. How can companies anticipate and leverage this essential knowledge? Read on.

Overview

To explore, not ignore, the role that emotions play in how people respond to circumstances is vital. Only then can companies secure insights that lead to success. Being better able to decide among options that aren't being viewed through only a rational perspective is the key. At the same time, however, the motivations that compel people to act are also important. Without taking motivations into account, it's as if those emotions supposedly arose without cause or reason for being. In this chapter we'll take a deeper look at emotions while linking them to motivations. More specifically, we will focus on:

- **Contextualizing emotions:** in Chapter 2, the seven core emotions were briefly profiled. Now in this section, we shall establish a deeper understanding of emotions. That requires, first, defining what emotions are. Next, the secondary emotions that arise from blends of the primary or core emotions will be identified. In turn, those secondary emotions will be subdivided into internally oriented versus externally oriented emotions. Finally, how the core emotions correspond to specific action tendencies will also be identified. The implication for business? When executives understand emotions and the context in which they are experienced, companies can plan for and better manage the behaviour linked to them.

- **Motivations:** numerous business models exist in which industry sector and offer-specific needs have been identified to aid a company in its strategic planning. But how about the basic, underlying needs that exist across cultures and relate to the basic human condition? Fortunately, a pair of Harvard professors has identified four core motivations or needs that drive human behaviour. They will be profiled here. The implication for business? To create and communicate initiatives that will engender long-term commitment from consumers and employees alike, companies must link those initiatives to motivations that are essential and eternally relevant.

- **The Emotionomics Matrix:** what is the Emotionomics Matrix? It's an actionable model that companies can use in broadening their strategic business planning. Improvement will come from including not only rational elements but also the often neglected human factors of emotions and motivations. Think of the matrix as an architect's blueprint. It tells us what the underlying structure is. The implication for business? Creating these matrices as, for instance, a platform for an advertising campaign or for introducing a new initiative to employees will enable companies to anticipate the feelings and needs most likely to create engagement and buy-in.

Now let's look more closely at how companies can initiate more incisive business planning, starting with a fuller understanding of emotions.

Contextualizing emotions: how feelings fuel behaviour

Synopsis: This section lays the groundwork for being able to gain a richer, working knowledge of what emotions are. It will also show how the core emotions often blend to create secondary emotions. Next, this section will describe the meaning of those secondary emotions before finally looking at correlations between feelings and the actions that typically result from them.

Key take-aways
- Unlike rational thoughts, emotions are action-oriented.
- It's possible to expand the set of core emotions to anticipate more situations.
- Some emotions we effect, while others reflect external forces dominating us.
- Specific emotions signal that specific behavioural outcomes are likely.

Defining what emotions actually are

Unlike rational thoughts, emotions are action-oriented

Not only are emotions messy, but so are the discussions involving them. Look closely at the business writings and research or strategic planning models that attempt to address emotions and what do we find? Confusion. People rarely know what they're talking about when they refer to emotions. Too often, the discourse gets cloudy with terms that aren't emotions at all but, rather, business objectives masking as feelings. For instance, relevant isn't an emotion. Nor is warm. Nor is familiar. And yet these words appear as emotions that companies are attempting to generate in target markets.

To begin, let's define what an emotion is and, therefore, what it isn't. Thankfully, real experts have already looked at this issue and provided us all (me included) with some answers.

In sifting through the various expert opinions available on this matter (Cornelius, 1996), a psycho-physiological (mind/body) consensus emerges. These are the three universal qualities that characterize emotions:

- a feeling component – physical sensations, including chemical changes in the brain;
- a thinking component – conscious or intuitive 'thought' appraisals;
- an action component – expressive reactions (like smiles or scowls), as well as coping behaviours (think fight or flight).

Sometimes an optional sensory component exists.

- a sensory component – sights, sounds, etcetera, which intrude and serve to trigger the emotional response.

When executives understand emotions and the context in which they are experienced, companies can plan for and better manage the behaviour linked to them

Emotionality is distinguished from rationality because the latter only involves one of these four components: *thinking*. Unlike an emotion, thinking may, but is less likely to, have a sensory component. That's because we frequently think in 'the abstract'. In contrast, there are often specific circumstances or events that bring an emotion into being and give it a time-sensitive urgency that thoughts rarely have.

More importantly, a rational thought remains fairly abstract. A thought will be likely to cause a sensory, bodily sensation only if it triggers an emotion. Meanwhile, surely the single most important distinction for business is that thoughts, unlike emotions, aren't action-oriented. They don't necessarily cause anything to happen.

In short, rational thought involves conscious, deliberate, evaluative assessments. A thought is about arriving at a judgement. Think of it as a dog riding in a car with its head out the window. In contrast, it's as if an emotion happens to us. They're more like spontaneous events that unfold inside us. So think of emotions as a dog finding itself in a fight with a cat. Everything's relative. Chaos reigns. The dog's just happy to survive.

Now we are halfway through establishing a comparative framework for emotions. On one side of emotions are rational thoughts. What's on the other side of emotions? The answer is moods, which in comparison are far less intense than emotions because they aren't associated with a triggering, sensory stimulus. The strength of emotions is that they help mobilize the body to get through an emergency. As revealed in our faces, emotions have an onset, a peak and typically fade in a matter of seconds. Moods tend to linger for hours or days, and again live more in the abstract – like thoughts. Unlike rational thoughts, however, with moods the feeling component is in play along with the thought itself.

Joy	Amazement	Rage	Loathing	Grief	Terror
HAPPINESS	SURPRISE	ANGER	DISGUST	SADNESS	FEAR
Satisfaction	Curiosity	Annoyance	Boredom	Pensiveness	Worry

Above = **high-intensity** / Below = **low-intensity**

Figure 3.1   Emotional intensity spectrum.
Once contempt is incorporated into its related emotion, disgust, a set of six basic emotions emerge. Those six can then, in turn, be expanded on by taking into account higher and lower intensity versions of them.

A wider range of emotions

It's possible to expand the set of core emotions to anticipate more situations

Now that emotions have been defined as highly prone to triggering stimuli that lead to action, we're alert to the need to tread carefully in interactions with others. How consumers and employees get treated on a daily basis will have consequences. But before we can factor emotions into strategic and tactical business planning, there is still one step left. We need to have as wide but accurate a range of emotions to talk about as possible. Only then can we address the variety of human behaviours likely to arise in different situations.

Aiming to leverage only the core emotions on Ekman's list could begin to seem limiting. It's a little bit like asking an agency to draft a creative brief on a par with da Vinci's *Mona Lisa* while using just a pair of colours to do so.

Fortunately, two simple steps help create a wider array of emotions to utilize in planning and analysis. First, realize that the emotions showcased in Chapter 2 exist on a spectrum. While emotions are much more intense than moods, they also vary in regard to their own degrees of intensity, as Figure 3.1 indicates.

Second, think of Ekman's core emotions as the primary colours, which, when mixed in different combinations, create all the other colours. Emotions rarely occur alone; they are usually felt in combination with another emotion. In fact, the number of action units in Ekman's system that reference only one emotion are the exception, not the rule.

By plotting the primary emotions on both a horizontal and diagonal axis, Sensory Logic created a chart, illustrated in Figure 3.2, which shows how secondary emotions are formed. Every secondary emotion is a combination of two primary emotions. (Here, Ekman's core emotion

	Surprise	Anger	Disgust	Sadness	Fear
Happiness	Delight Relief	Pride Vengeance	Morbidity	Yearning Nostalgia	Hope Guilt
	Surprise	Outrage		Embarassment Disappointment	Awe Alarm
positive emotions / neutral emotions / negative emotions		**Anger**	Contempt Resentment	Sullenness Envy	Jealousy
			Disgust	Regret	Shame Prudishness
Primary Emotions and Secondary Combinations				**Sadness**	Despair Distress

Figure 3.2   How the primary emotions combine to create the secondary emotions.
When the primary emotions get combined (as they usually are in real life), a much richer palette of emotional response emerges. Quite obviously, the bulk of the secondary emotions are negative in orientation, reflecting people's innate desire to survive by choosing either fight or flight. (Chart based on Zeitlin and Westwood, 1986.)

of contempt appears as a combination of disgust and anger.) For example, to understand how outrage is formed, locate outrage in one of the white boxes that denotes the secondary emotions. Next, find the corresponding primary emotion in a grey box above outrage on the horizontal axis, in this case anger. After that, locate the other primary emotion directly to the left of outrage, also in a grey box, in this case surprise. Now it is easier to understand that outrage is a combination of anger and surprise.

When we take all combinations into account, the initial list of emotions grows from Ekman's seven to 30. This chart provides a much richer palette of emotions to work with. Whether used as an inspiration for innovative marketing or for motivating employees, these primary and secondary emotions offer universally measurable benchmarks against which specific goals can be scientifically quantified. They will be referenced in subsequent chapters as we discuss how they may apply to various issues.

Figure 3.3   Internally and externally focused secondary emotions.

While there are only seven core emotions, in interpreting human responses it's possible to blend the core emotions to create a broader array of feelings that provide specific insights

Of the 30 emotions listed here, notice that even given the most generous of interpretations, only seven of them are positive in orientation. Two others – surprise and nostalgia – are neutral. The remainder are negative to some degree, again reflecting the drive to survive that keeps us particularly alert to bad news.

Internally versus externally focused emotions

Some emotions we effect, while others reflect external forces dominating us

In Chapter 2 we defined each of Ekman's core emotions, the ones that are labelled here as the primary emotions. Now it's time to briefly define the other, secondary emotions so that they can also serve as a reference point (Figure 3.3).

With 24 of them to cover, some sort of categorization will no doubt prove helpful. Let's break them into two sets: the 13 internally focused versus the 11 externally focused emotions (Roseman, Antoniou and Jose, 1996; Ortony, Clore and Collins, 1988). By internally focused, what's meant are emotions that are either caused by the person experiencing them or are inwardly directed. These emotions typically relate to either self-esteem issues or how we internalize our responses to changing conditions based on the expectations we held going into a situation.

An example of an internally focused emotion is pride, which involves how we feel about our own accomplishments. In contrast, vengeance is an externally focused emotion because the person feeling it wants to harm somebody else.

That leaves the 11 externally focused emotions. These are the emotions caused by external circumstances or where the emotion's energy or resulting actions get directed at somebody else. Concerns about status and the fortunes of other people – especially when linked to how well our own goals are being realized – tend to cause these emotions.

How emotions influence and reveal behaviour

Specific emotions signal that specific behavioural outcomes are likely

With a working definition of emotion in place and specific definitions for the primary and secondary emotions established, it's now possible to start modelling how specific emotions lead to specific outcomes. Thanks to facial coding, it's also now possible to know what exactly consumers and employees are feeling. But in order for this amazing new knowledge to make an actionable difference on behalf of business practitioners, it's necessary to close the loop by linking emotions to behaviour.

In short, we need to know: what does each of these emotions mean in terms of understanding and influencing people's behaviour?

For simplicity's sake, we shall focus on five behavioural results. As a reader's guide to Figure 3.4, here's a summary of what the academic research indicates about how emotions influence a handful of key, recurring business-oriented behaviours.

Related to attention is what kind of outcome orientation people have based on the emotion they're feeling. The choice is basically carrot or the stick, reward or punishment. Here *happiness, anger* and *sadness* are related because all three of these emotions involve being strongly focused on getting the reward (*happiness* is the best because the reward we seek is either in sight or already in hand). The polar opposite is *disgust*, where avoiding the punishment of a negative condition is everything.

In regard to level of attention, advertisers and executives, for instance, are right to emphasize the positive in order to get the audience's attention. Research indicates that only *happiness* or *surprise* ensures a high attention level. Losing hope and interest as reflected by *sadness* or *disgust* brings about the lowest attention level.

When it comes to getting something done, each emotion also involves a different action bias. Four of the six emotions under study here drive people

Behavioural Result	Primary Emotional States					
	Happiness	Surprise	Anger	Fear	Sadness	Disgust
Outcome Orientation	High focus on receiving reward	Split focus between reward & punishment	High focus on receiving reward	Split focus between reward & punishment	High focus on receiving reward	High focus on avoiding punishment
Level of Attention	High	High	Medium	Medium	High	Low
Action Bias	High: strive for results	High: strive for results	High: prompts retaliation	Low: delay/ freeze	Low: delay/ freeze	High: engage in avoidance
Risk Tolerance	High risk, low reward	NA	High risk, high reward	Low risk, low reward	High risk, high reward	NA
Decision Making	Quick (not concerned)	Cautious (uncertain)	Quick (impulsive)	Cautious (wary of outcome)	Cautious (delays)	Quick (not concerned)

Figure 3.4   A profile of feeling/action interdynamics.
(Chart from Roseman, Antoniou and Jose, 1996; Smith and Ellsworth, 1985; Frijda, Kuipers and ter Schure, 1989; Raghunathan and Pham, 1999; Loewenstein and Lerner, 2003; Tiedens and Linton, 2001; Mackie and Worth, 1989; Bodenhausen, Sheppard and Kramer, 1994.)

to action, but the type of action varies. Feeling *happy* or *surprised*? We'll strive for results. *Angry*? We're seeking revenge. *Disgusted*? We can't get away fast enough. *Fear* and *sadness* are, in contrast, the emotions that slow us down.

For consumers and employees alike, risk tolerance is a major consideration. The mantra 'No pain, no gain' only makes sense to an audience that feels as if the mantra is right for them. We'll take the risk of trying to secure a gain more often if we're *happy, angry* or *sad*. The difference between these three emotions, however, is that when we're happy we tend to take a risk even if the reward is low. With *fear*, the risk is considered low because danger already exists. With *sadness* we feel like we've got nothing to lose.

Finally, decision-making styles also vary by emotion. Feelings provide information. They also influence how we process information. If we're feeling *happy, angry* or *disgusted*, we go quickly – because we're unconcerned (*happy*), impatient (*angry*) or discouraged (*disgusted*). In contrast, feeling *surprise, fear* or *sadness* leaves us more paralyzed.

Overall, these findings indicate why the business world needs to take emotions seriously. They shouldn't be ignored because they influence and, at times, even dictate outcomes. Moreover, simply describing a person as feeling positive or negative isn't good enough either. As we've seen from these five behavioural results, two negative emotions like anger and sadness, for instance, can lead to very different outcomes.

Simple categorizations like positive or negative simply aren't insightful enough to help strategize. As Figure 3.4 makes evident, the various negative emotions can lead to sharply contrasting behaviours.

Motivations: what spurs us on

Synopsis: Emotions don't exist in a vacuum. Some sort of stimulus is forever tempting our emotions to turn on, provided it's powerful enough. But while the stimuli will vary, the argument has now been made that the key motivations underlying why and how those stimuli strike us don't vary and haven't varied across the course of human history. The four core motivations that have been identified from research will be emphasized here.

> **Key take-aways**
>
> • Four core motivations cover the reasons why people take the actions they do.

Understanding needs that drive human behaviour

Four core motivations cover the reasons why people take the actions they do

On learning how the core emotions can influence our behaviour, it would also be helpful to know about the core motivations that cause our emotions to turn on. In *Driven: How human nature shapes our choices* (2002), Lawrence and Nohria, two Harvard University organizational psychology professors, have analysed human motivation. While their focus is on the workplace (that is, company employees), their conclusions apply to consumers as well.

Much like Ayers Rock in Australia, the core motivations that drive human decisions and emotional responses are speculated to have been around since the beginning of time.

After an extensive review, the authors propose that there are four basic human motivations: to defend, acquire, bond and learn. While these motivations will be explained in greater depth shortly, in essence they can be defined as follows:

- Defend: the oldest, most primitive need is pure instinct: survive.
- Acquire: while not a matter of survival, feathering the nest adds to comfort.
- Bond: having allies provides both pleasure and security.
- Learn: akin to the spiritual/self-growth at the top of Maslow's hierarchy of needs.

Depicting the order or interrelationship of these four core motivations is open to interpretation. In Figures 3.5 and 3.6, as well as in all of the application chapters to follow, I've decided to diagram the four motivations a little differently than in *Driven*. Lawrence and Nohria depict each core motivation as occupying a corner of a four-sided diamond. This format could suggest that the diametrically opposed motivations of defend/acquire and bond/learn cancel each other out. Yet nothing in their book makes that claim.

Figure 3.5   Four core motivations.

In contrast, I've sought to avoid such a misunderstanding by showing the oldest, in effect, most negative motivation – defend – in the centre of the diagram. It is obviously protective in nature and likely to be closely related to fear. As a result, placing *defend* in the middle makes sense because nothing is more basic, more central, to humanity than the urge to ensure our survival.

The other three motivations are, as Lawrence and Nohria observe, more proactive in nature. So they've been arrayed around the more constrictive *defend* motivation. Meanwhile, all of the motivations have been linked to make the point that – like the primary or core emotions, and the way they can blend to create secondary emotions – the four core motivations may likewise either interact or work independently of one another. So they will be depicted accordingly in the examples to follow.

As complex as that may seem, the bottom line is simple. Lawrence and Nohria propose that, taken together, these four core motivations form a complete, universal set. Let's follow their reasoning.

Motivation 1: Defend

The most fundamental motivation is to ensure our survival. Protecting ourselves from danger and creating security is as basic as it gets. In addition to preventing physical harm, this motivation also encompasses defence against psychological harms like lower self-esteem or stress: a combination of mental and bodily harm. While essentially negative and reactive, the defend motivation can be viewed positively to the extent that it preserves useful achievements and guards against making rash changes.

The reactionary defend motivation can likewise be understood in relation to the other motivations. For example, when attacked we seek to protect: *resources* (belongings that we have acquired), *relationships* (loved ones with whom we have bonded) and *belief systems* (values we've learned during life). See Figure 3.6 for details.

In the end, however, the defend motivation stands alone in the centre of the diagram because it's markedly different from the other three motivations, which are more expansive in nature, inspiring us to extend our horizons. The motivation to defend risks a fight to the death in a classic evolutionary win/lose scenario. In contrast, the other three motivations provide an opportunity for win/win situations in which everyone enriches his or her physical, social and mental well-being (Figure 3.7).

Figure 3.6   The defend motivation.
The single most primal motivation is to defend our existence. Reactive in nature, this motivation can nevertheless interact with the other, more expansive motivations to arrive at goals broader than individual survival.

Here then is what the more evolved motivations are about

Figure 3.7   The proactive motivations.
The diagram shows the special goals or points of focus related to each of the other three, more proactive core motivations.

Motivation 2: Acquire

When not harnessed on behalf of benefiting one's immediate family and other loved ones, acquire becomes the selfish 'me, myself and I' motivation. At its most basic level, this motivation ensures our survival by prompting us to gather essentials such as food and shelter. At a more advanced level, however, the goal is to gain control of objects and symbols of power that improve our status relative to others. Often, this motivation also entails accruing money and allies to bolster our identity and make life more secure and pleasant. People seem to have a natural desire to establish dominance within hierarchies, which is why the fear of disgrace is this motivation's dark underbelly.

Motivation 3: Bond

The collective of me is we. Bonding is based on the reality that a life shared with others can be more fulfilling as well as more comfortable. Moreover, from a strategic vantage point, opportunities to be part of a community and engage in reciprocity can result in mutually supportive, long-term relationships. Everyone seeks acceptance.

Motivation 4: Learn

While the motivation to acquire is materially expansive and the motivation to bond is emotionally expansive, the motivation to learn is intellectually and spiritually expansive. It's based on our innate curiosity about the world around us. It can be thought of as non-material foraging. At a rational level, learning is about collecting information to plan and predict likely outcomes. But at heart, this motivation explains our quest for spiritual, ideological and aesthetic ways to appreciate and make sense of the world around us.

In summary, those are the four core motivations companies should always bear in mind. Why? Because to create and communicate initiatives that will engender long-term commitment from consumers and employees alike, companies must link their initiatives to motivations that are essential and eternally relevant.

The Emotionomics Matrix: introducing a strategic model

Synopsis: With both of the human factors of emotions and motivations explained, it's now time to introduce the deliverable referred to at the start of this chapter: the Emotionomics Matrix. In literal terms, it refers to the integration of emotions into economics. But in richer, operational terms, the Emotionomics Matrix is meant to give the business world a way to take into account two factors: what motivations cause people to act, and how people's feelings will, in turn, further influence their actions. In this section let's first define the Emotionomics Matrix and then show it in practice, using as a case study the marketplace battle involving premium beer.

Key take-aways

- The Matrix reflects the reality that behaviour can arise from a mixture of factors.
- Underlying the growth of premium beer is a drive for authentic uniqueness.

Defining the Emotionomics Matrix

The Matrix reflects the reality that behaviour can arise from a mixture of factors

The purpose of the Emotionomics Matrix is to use it to strategically frame business issues in a way that gets beyond pure rationality. To achieve that goal, the matrix must be at once both simple enough to understand and use. But it must also be flexible enough to reflect the reality that behaviour arises from – and is guided by – a mixture of the motivations and emotions already introduced in this book.

In the application chapters to follow, the matrix will be employed repeatedly to help frame the discussion of the three key business issues each chapter is organized around.

But first let's explain what exactly the Emotionomics Matrix is. While the four core motivations are central to it, the matrix would be woefully incomplete if it didn't take into account emotions. So Figure 3.8 shows how it might be possible to assign a place within the matrix for each of Ekman's core emotions, based on which motivations are the most likely to invoke them. While these are not rigid assignments, the objective is to give readers some sense of how the core motivations and the core emotions may be related.

In subsequent examples, each business issue will be framed in terms of which motivation or pair of motivations is most relevant. The issue's placement relative to the motivations will then be shown by an arrow labelled with the emotion that is also most relevant to the issue. Most

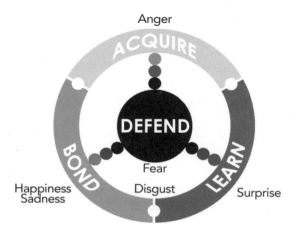

Figure 3.8   The Emotionomics Matrix.
How do emotions and motivations pair up most naturally?
● Defend and fear form a likely combination, given concerns about survival.
● Acquire and anger fit together because anger often involves seeking control.
● Learn and surprise make sense together because of the discovery process.
● Bond fits together with both happiness and sadness as we either celebrate being with those we care about or are sad about missing them.
● Disgust can involve rejecting an idea (learn), person (bond) or object (acquire).

times, the emotion deemed most relevant or revealing of the business issue being discussed will be the one business people should strive to *create* in their targeted audience, whether it be consumers or employees. But at other times, it will be the negative emotion they should seek to *diffuse* so as not to imperil their goals.

But we're getting ahead of ourselves. First, let's look at how the Emotionomics Matrix operates by taking it through a practice run.

The emotionomics of premium beer

Underlying the growth of premium beer is a drive for authentic uniqueness

The US beer companies Anheuser-Busch, Miller and Coors were worried. The increased popularity of wine, martinis and micro-brews was cutting into the opportunity for growth. Wine consumption had increased by 63 per cent since 1991. Beer sales were relatively flat and beer's share of the total alcohol market had dropped from 56 per cent in 1999 to around 53 per cent in recent years. Even more worrisome was that in 2005, for example, mass-market beer sales were down 0.3 per cent overall while the country's craft brewers recorded a 9 per cent increase in sales volume for the year (Daykin, 2006; Quaid, 2006).

The solution? If you can't beat them, join them. Mass brewers have done so in numerous ways. They've been buying micro-breweries, signing distribution deals for both foreign and craft beers, revamping their own current offers and creating new ones. Their underlying strategy is to have an offer whose status enables it to compete with cosmopolitans and merlots by providing more authenticity and sophistication than mass-market beer.

But knowing how best to enter the growing premium beer market depends on understanding why the shift from beer to wine is taking place in terms of the motivations and emotions in play. So let's use the Emotionomics Matrix (Figure 3.9) to look at three key opportunities mass-market beer companies are seeking to address.

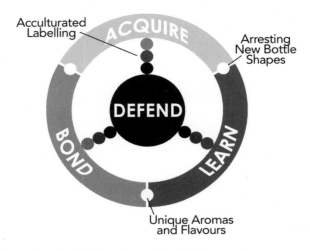

Figure 3.9   Emotional solutions for craft-style beers.

Opportunity 1: unique aromas and flavours

To offset the lack of enticement some consumers might usually associate with non-craft beer offerings, the big three beer companies have begun to provide new, premium beers with rich aromas for the nose and more tantalizing flavours for the taste buds. Anheuser-Busch has introduced B-to-the-E and Tilt, which feature sweet flavours, caffeine, ginseng and guarana, a Brazilian stimulant. That edge helps to battle a rival like SAB-Miller's entry, Leinenkugel's Sunset Wheat, which uses coriander to create a unique taste. Another notable contender is Sam Adams' Utopias, described as having a cognac-like aroma and a taste that's slightly fruity with maple syrup 'notes'. With a current asking price of $100 for a 750ml bottle, Utopias promises the drinker something that can't be found in a bottle of malt liquor.

Emotion and motivations

From a human factors point of view, let's start with the underlying emotion most relevant here: how the yearning for fulfilling sensory sensations can be met. A blend of sadness and happiness, yearning transformed into unalloyed happiness must be the emotional goal of beer companies seeking to overcome a legacy of less than exciting offers. The pertinent motivations are learn and bond. Why? Because companies seizing the opportunity will, first, get consumers to learn about their enticing aromas and taste bud treats; second, they will then get consumers to form a sensory bond with their offer through experiencing it.

Opportunity 2: arresting new bottle shapes

The wineries have moved to easy-open screw-tops, cans and party-friendly boxes to remain upmarket but soften their image. What can the beer companies do? Well, since we see the beer's packaging before we experience its smell or taste, the shape of the beer bottle is a good means of signalling that a new, non-advertising form of differentiation has arrived. Anheuser-Busch's Celebrate packs a double punch. It appears under its Michelob brand as an oak-aged, dark vanilla beer and its bottle looks more like a bottle of champagne than beer. But for an even more extreme positioning, again look to Sam Adams' Utopias, which come in a bottle styled like a copper decanter and resembling a trophy.

For the past 15 years, major beer producers were growing nervous, with flat sales, a rise in wine consumption and a drop in total market share.

Wine, on the other hand, enjoyed a surge in popularity to the tune of a 63 per cent rise in consumption since 1991. It was different, classy and aesthetically pleasing. Vintners toasted each other all the way to the bank.

Emotion and motivations

In this case, the emotional goal is clearly surprise. Beer companies want to differentiate their offer by having consumers feel surprise on encountering the new packaging, followed by yearning transformed into happiness upon sampling the beer it holds. The advantage isn't just limited to pleasing consumers. Motivationally, the goal is that they will discuss these new unexpected shapes with fellow beer connoisseurs, also eager to learn about and then acquire the new 'finds' on the market.

Opportunity 3: acculturated labelling

One big advantage that wine and martinis enjoy is that they often carry more social cachet than beer does. To counteract that perception, the big breweries have learned from the micro-breweries and the wineries by adopting more exotic labels and names. Sometimes those names are classy: Coors sells Blue Moon Belgian White Ale. Sometimes they're healthy-sounding, even organic: Anheuser-Busch has Wild Hop Lager. A cool label can help, too. Dogfish Head Brewery has commissioned the award-winning artist Tara McPherson to create labels for its Fort and Chateau Jiahu beers.

Who says drinking beer isn't an art?
Dogfish Head Brewery is a craft brewer that
cares about more than the taste of its beers.
Dogfish Head adds to the consumer's
experience through its labels, some of which
(like the two above by Tara McPherson) are
created by award-winning artists.

Emotion and motivations

Sometimes the emotional goal isn't about proactively achieving so
much as it is about avoiding a negative. This time around the
emotion to diffuse is contempt. That may not be how beer drinkers
feel about themselves, but it could be what they suspect other, more
seemingly sophisticated drinkers could be feeling about them as they
sit together in public places like bars. Therefore, the motivations
involve wanting to defend oneself by being able to acquire more self-
esteem through the 'good taste' status other forms of alcohol enjoy.

We've come to the end of Part One. Now readers should have all the foun-
dational knowledge required for the application chapters to follow.
Chapter 1 covered insights from brain science about people's decision-
making process. Chapter 2 established facial coding as a tool to measure,
and therefore manage, people's emotional responses. Finally, Chapter 3
built the Emotionomics Matrix that will provide a psychological context
for the various business issues awaiting discussion. So let's move on, first
to the marketplace and then to the workplace, looking at opportunities
for emotional buy-in.

Part Two

Marketplace applications

4 Branding

Branding is 200 per cent proof emotionality. And what's better evidence than the sale of vodka – an odourless, colourless, tasteless liquor – where brand equity, aided by a great name, great packaging and great advertising, is essential to creating loyal customers.

Overview

Branding is primarily emotional in nature and, without the benefit of a tool like facial coding, also almost hopelessly abstract. After all, the essence of brand equity is that a company has managed to create a sense of loyalty among its customers. What is loyalty if not a *feeling*? Devoid of a tool like facial coding that measures loyalty in emotional as opposed to rationalized, verbal input survey terms, companies are hard pressed to know whether they really enjoy brand equity or not. To help them achieve true emotional buy-in, this chapter will focus on:

- **Reflected beliefs:** the first key to building brand equity is for companies to pursue a customer-centric brand strategy that protects the emotional health of their relationship with consumers. To do so requires them to, in turn, ensure that consumers see their deeply held, personal beliefs mirrored in the brands they purchase. As a result, companies should reflect the target market's beliefs, linking their beliefs about themselves to an enduring belief in the brand. The best strategy is always to sell people on themselves. That's because building on what's already been internalized works best.

- **Belonging:** a second brand equity key is to provide status so consumers enhance their self-identities in relation to potential membership in groups to which they aspire. To that end, build a bridge facilitating people's adoption into those very groups. That is, people should feel not only that the brand fits them, but that it fits the social group to which they hope to belong. With both 'me' (beliefs) and 'us' (belonging) covered, a brand is in a more strongly fortified position to guard against status-induced defections.

- **Telling a story:** while the first two keys to brand equity are strategic in nature, the third one is tactical. It's about creating a brand story rich enough to engage consumers. To do so, tell a story that builds a brand/customer relationship by offering a vivid personality people can relate to, and by creating hot-button associations. Over time a combination of personality and associations will help intuitively guide consumers to a brand. Just make sure they don't become concerned that they've invested their time and money on a company whose story lacks enough power.

Now let's look more closely at how to build brand equity, starting with the values to be found lodged in consumers' hearts.

Reflected beliefs: keep consumers' values in view

Synopsis: This section is about encouraging companies to make a practice of reflecting beliefs. That's because everything consumers see in the world gets 'bent' through the prism of the values they espouse. Companies should figure out what values emotionally matter most to their target markets and be sure to deliver on them. To bring that point alive, the rest of the section looks first at why customer relationship management (CRM) is a half-hearted approach to knowing consumers. Then it moves on to beliefs on the global scale as well as closer to home.

Key take-aways

- A beliefs strategy means consumers no longer think about which brand to buy.
- CRM provides data without any intuitive feeling as to what it all conveys.
- Given the strength of both religious and secular beliefs, never defame them.
- Figure out which values are for real and which are less imperative.

Staying power

A beliefs strategy means consumers no longer think about which brand to buy

Customers are the 'who' of brand strategy. A solid, self-sustaining strategy mirrors customers' preferences. Having such a strategy entails speaking to them on their level: who they are and associate with, what they do and value. An adept 'mirror' brand drives an emotional connection so deep that consumers no longer think about what to buy.

Emotion and motivations.
Pride is the key emotion here because consumers want brands that reinforce and enhance, not disrespect or ignore, their self-identities. In other words, consumers have belief systems they inevitably want to protect, having invested themselves in making sense of the world. To seize on this opportunity, companies must tap into consumers' motivations to **defend** their worldviews, which of course arose from what they have been able to **learn** from life's circumstances.

Unfortunately, all too often, companies choose the *what* (their products, services, etcetera) over the *who* (their customers). Too often the goal of getting ahead of rivals ends up having only a tangential relationship with getting closer to customers. The solution is to remember that customers buy the brand that makes them feel comfortable, happy, proud and successful. Competitive differentiation means nothing to consumers unless it's focused on what's in it for them.

Stages of Company Growth and Customer Focus

Entrepreneurial	Growth	Maturity	Decline

Figure 4.1   The centre of focus shift.
As a company grows in scale, it tends to become increasingly distracted by internal dynamics, losing sight of customers in the process (Slywotzky and Morrison, 2002).

Done correctly, branding becomes internalized and accepted as an extension of the beliefs and values of its loyal, hard-won constituency. Trust and faith add intensity to the quality of branded offers, making them less subject to erosion. Consumers buy brands that provide emotional reinforcement, notably pride, in who they are and the decisions they make.

Thus consumer beliefs and brand equity go hand-in-hand because both are concerned with the long haul. They are about staying power. Core beliefs are built on core emotions, the templates that drive business outcomes. Forget about changing beliefs. A brand makes headway to the extent that it ties into beliefs and avoids what isn't credible or relevant. How can a company know that its approach is on track? By gauging consumers' core emotional responses.

In the following example, Sensory Logic tested a resort and adventure travel company's vision of *what* it offers by scrolling its mission statement across a computer screen for a group of subjects, one by one. We wanted to learn how the *who* – the target market – would actually respond. In short, we looked for when, how much and what type of emotional response occurred (Figure 4.2).

Positive	Bold
Neutral/No Response	Underline
Negative	Italic

We will guide you through a **world of active travel,** providing access to places in nature and cultural experiences around the world where extraordinary things **happen to individuals** from sun-up to **sun-down.** We are committed to assisting you to realize your dreams for memorable, unique and ultimately **body-and-soul** satisfying *experiences ... again* and again.

Figure 4.2   Facial coding response to positioning statement.

The words in bold type are the parts of the positioning statement to which test subjects responded positively. What worked? The company was on-message and on-emotion when it could credibly promise an offer of individualistic adventure that would carry to day's end and please body and soul alike. In other words, the offer appealed to its target market when it reflected that audience's values and affirmed the importance of their being dynamic, independent and rejuvenated.

In contrast, the text in italic indicates times the positioning statement left people feeling negative because they might be encountering empty rhetoric, thus undermining the company's positioning strategy. Meanwhile, fully half of the statement invoked no response or a neutral response, as indicated by underlined text. In short, this draft of the statement was going to need some more work if the company was going to gain real buy-in.

CRM and its future

CRM provides data without any intuitive feeling as to what it all conveys

Because customer relationship management (CRM) emphasizes *what* over *who,* it's too bad that the most common approach to the brand/customer relationship nowadays relies on the various CRM software packages. That's a good first step toward customers. But the current CRM toolkit never makes the whole journey (Rigby, Reichheld and Dawson, 2003). It starts by recording and organizing individual transactions. Then it determines how much the customers spend, how often they buy, and where and how they make purchases.

Customers, however, have much bigger stories to tell. Executives who understand that an emotional connection is central to the creation of a viable relationship will want to get a bigger perspective. Without a way to get a feel for what the data really means, isn't CRM software merely a glass half full? The missing void could be filled with vital emotional insight. That step would inform management, designers, marketing staff, salespeople and others at a more comprehensive and pertinent level. Such insight in tandem with transactional history would provide the knowledge required to build a more powerful connection between a company's brand and its customers.

Without a way to understand what CRM data means emotionally, it's a glass half-full solution. It needs to be topped off with an emotional kick.

Beliefs, religious and secular

Given the strength of both religious and secular beliefs, never defame them

A good way to start determining any target market's beliefs is to examine how different societies mould people's worldview. Companies engaged in global marketing, take note: in *The Clash of Civilizations and the Remaking of the World Order* (1997), Harvard University professor Samuel Huntington argues that since the fall of the Berlin Wall, the world has divided itself into eight different power blocks. They're organized around language and religious value systems, requiring companies looking to achieve optimal emotional buy-in to customize their approach.

Just how prominent is religion in defining these power blocks? It's extremely pervasive. Even in the west, where religion is less prominent, 85 per cent of Americans believe God exists. Moreover, the percentage of 'born-again' Christians in the United States has risen 12 per cent in the past two decades to 45 per cent (Phillips, 2006).

Therefore, branding directors and advertising agencies should be deeply attuned to religion's influence and its role in consumers' value systems. Otherwise, they risk giving offence. Pride isn't a trivial emotion. As a mixture of happiness and anger, pride has an edge to it. It contains an element of defiance, a don't-tread-on-me spirit. Given the emotion's quality of certainty and triumph, a brand wants to be a facilitator of this emotion rather than an obstacle. No company wants to be seen as an enemy of its target market's belief system.

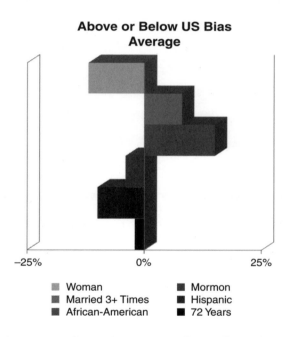

Figure 4.3   Sensory Logic results versus Gallup poll.
In 2007, both the Gallup organization and Sensory Logic ran studies asking potential voters in the United States, 'Would you be reluctant to vote for a ___ candidate?' The results were staggeringly different. Sensory Logic's facial coding results found more than twice as much bias amongst voters regarding the 2008 presidential race as had been reported in the Gallup poll. The verbal input vastly under-reported the amount of bias, particularly on socially sensitive dimensions such as racism (5 per cent versus 43 per cent) and sexism (11 per cent versus 40 per cent). Worse off, however, was thrice-married ex-New York City Mayor Rudolph Giuliani, whose messy personal life violated many voters' moral compass. Giuliani was followed by a strong sign of hostility toward Mitt Romney's Mormon faith.

In short, reflecting beliefs needs to be a front-and-centre strategy. That's true because beliefs result from a lifetime of learning. They constitute the essence of selfhood, which a person will adamantly defend, sometimes even to the death.

For his part, Huntington emphasizes three global mega-trends. The first two involve the relative decline of western countries' economic strength, especially America's, given the rise of Asian countries and China in particular. American and East Asian cultures share few values in common, except hard work, as illustrated by the percentages of the populations endorsing the importance of the eight values in Figure 4.4.

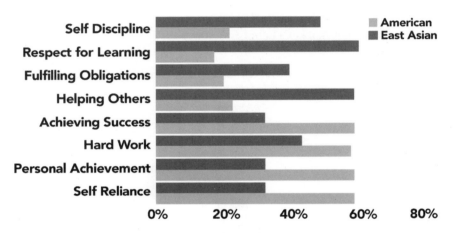

Figure 4.4   Value orientation differences between the United States and East Asia.
With regard to the percentage of citizens endorsing these eight values, American and East Asian cultures have little in common except for honouring hard work. Brand strategists must therefore be careful to customize their approaches (Hitchcock, 1994).

Likely to boast seven of the top ten world economies by 2020, Asian countries are quick to emphasize how the virtues of Confucian culture have bolstered their successes. Their leaders herald order, collectivism and restraint over the self-indulgent individualism they see rampant in western society.

Huntington's third trend? The Muslim share of global population is expected to surge to 30 per cent by 2025, making the differences in values between the predominantly Christian west and the Muslim world even more prominent. To disregard the differences between the two is to disregard a potentially huge market.

Closer to home, let's now look at two examples of how consumers' belief systems affect the outcome of brand marketing efforts. But in doing so, bear in mind that great brands evolve organically and have few, if any, tangible levers companies can pull to effect quick, deep-seated changes. A brand is hard to manipulate because a brand message involves no call to action, no need for audience participation. In practice, branding becomes the accumulation of a series of tactical steps. Remember that emotional testing is essential to avert long-term drift brought about by otherwise potentially undetectable short-term missteps.

American beliefs involving cars and sex

Figure out which values are for real and which are less imperative

The first case involves a major US auto manufacturer that ran ads with themes emphasizing family safety and environmental awareness. While people claimed that the environmentally conscious ad had greater impact, emotional data captured through facial coding came to a different conclusion. It revealed a large enough drop-off in interest that safety was actually slightly ahead in both appeal and impact (Figure 4.5).

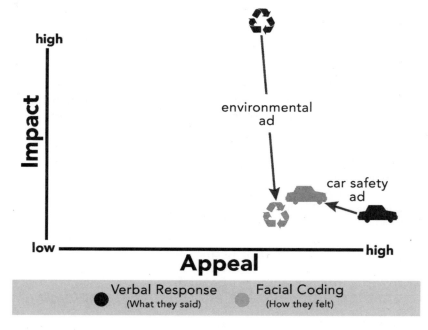

Figure 4.5 The planet versus the family unit.
Although people claimed to be more affected by the environmentally conscious advertisement, facial coding revealed that the family-oriented ad was stronger in both appeal and impact. In other words, people liked it more and responded more intensely to its message.

It seems that being 'green' sounds good. But when push comes to shove, people want to protect themselves and their families more than the species at large. As a result, the green advertising may be more suitable as a subtle, incremental building block of help to the company long-term.

The second case involves another company in the automotive sector. This company planned on running some 'sexy' TV spots, joining a growing trend. But it wanted to be sure it wasn't going to offend women by doing so.

The good news? That would be the company realizing it would be smart to test the spots before launching them in order not to risk alienating a 'segment'. What a good idea, since women represent over half the planet's population and therefore aren't exactly a niche market.

The bad news? The 'cheesecake/beefcake' spots elicited a lower degree of positive response from the study's female subjects. Clearly, women didn't find the content as compatible with their value system as men did.

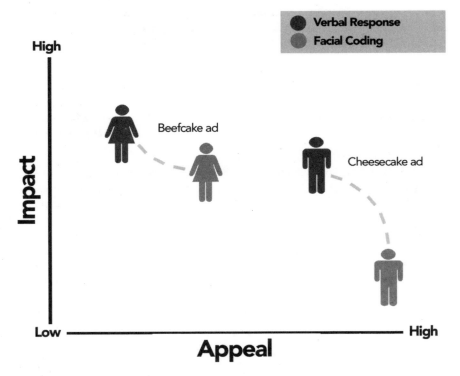

Figure 4.6   Gender differences in 'sexy' spot response.
No surprise: men found the 'cheesecake' commercial much more appealing than they were willing to acknowledge. But perhaps given the dulling surplus of titillation on TV, they were actually less impacted by it than they stated. In contrast, the women liked the 'sexy' commercial less than men did. But they were also a little more impacted than the men as well as more pleased by the 'beefcake' commercial than they admitted.

Why in commercial terms would it be important to know that women were likely to find the commercials distasteful? Consider these statistics (Barletta, 2003; Sharpe, 2000):

- Women are estimated to be responsible for 83 per cent of all consumer purchases, including 80 per cent of healthcare decisions, 91 per cent of general household purchases, 94 per cent of furnishing purchases, 92 per cent of vacation expenditures, and 62 per cent of car purchases.
- Today, over 30 per cent of women earn more than their husbands.
- Women also control over 50 per cent of the private wealth in America (a number certain to rise given their longer life expectancy).

Two decades ago, a study found that only 1 per cent of magazine ads contained implicit sexual activity. A decade later thinly veiled depictions of intercourse had risen to 17 per cent. Meanwhile, the percentage of sexily dressed women went from 28 per cent to 40 per cent, while men in varying states of nudity rose from 11 per cent to 18 per cent. No known current study has addressed the topic, but surely the trend continues to grow, whether in accordance with people's value systems or not (Davenport and Beck, 2001).

Belonging: where status and security meet

Synopsis: Because brands are social in nature, we rely on them to reinforce our sense of membership in a tribe. Companies whose brand position is so broad that there's no 'us' and no 'them' become, in effect, all things for all people, which is impossible, and therefore meaningless. This section opens by affirming the need for the brand to serve as a bridge to a consumer's desired community. Then it looks at two segmentation factors that companies have a hard time navigating well: age and race.

Key take-aways

- In branding, the desire to achieve 'in-group' status is paramount.
- For seniors, emotions become ever more the currency of persuasion.
- People's subconscious bias is to rely on their own tribe.

Across the great divides

In branding, the desire to achieve 'in-group' status is paramount

In *The Culting of Brands* (2004), Douglas Atkin defines a cult brand as:

> a brand for which a group of customers exhibits a great devotion or dedication. Its ideology is distinctive and it has a well defined and committed community. It enjoys exclusive devotion (that is, not shared with another brand in the same category), and its members often become voluntary advocates.

Emotion and motivations.
Hope is the key emotion for those who see a brand as a tribal destination. A brand that nurtures and reinforces our identity by helping us to affiliate with others is invaluable. On the Emotionomics Matrix, this opportunity lies between the motivations of to **acquire** and **defend**. The former is related to status and power, and the latter to protecting ourselves against getting hurt because of rejection by a group to which we aspire to belong.

In other words, great brands leverage our innate impulse to belong to an inner circle. That circle affirms who we want to be, with three factors being especially significant here.

The first factor is that, in response to the evolutionary desire to impress others, great brands make it possible for us to feel unique, special and worthy of affinity in the eyes of whatever our preferred group happens to be. To that end, the key step is to take a position a little bolder than that of rivals. Being average just won't get a brand noticed any more. If a brand's positioning isn't both readily perceivable and important to people, the brand is at risk.

The second factor is to remember that a brand's edginess and the reflective glory it theoretically casts on loyalists are not ultimately as important as whether the social fit is both right and authentic. After all, our social aspirations have to be plausible for them to be sustainable, rather than mere pipe dreams.

The previous two factors involved groups that we as individuals decide to join. They are distinctions that we pursue on our own. But sometimes the brand community we belong to gets decided for us, at least to some extent. Thus, the third factor involves non-electable signifiers like age and race, which we'll look at next.

Great brands play to our inner desire to break through barriers and become part of a group that represents who we are as well as who we want to be

Age and age-ism

For seniors, emotions become ever more the currency of persuasion

The new consumer majority consists of people beyond the midpoint of life. Brand strategists, take note: the level of spending by those over 45 years of age will soon exceed that of people between the ages of 18 and 39 by US$1 trillion. Meanwhile, in the United States those over 50 years of age represent 44 per cent of adults and control 70 per cent of the country's wealth. Despite those statistics, only 10 per cent of all branded advertising expenditures target older consumers (Wolfe and Snyder, 2003).

As we age, the word-oriented left hemisphere of the brain overloads more easily. But the right hemisphere's ability to process visual images holds steady. So companies will find the senior market less attuned to rational, persuasive arguments. What's the better approach? The answer is emotional, visual, subjective appeals that play to older people's rich networks of long-term memories and associations.

Once again, emotional measuring is the key. How much of a difference can one's age make in calculating likely buy-in? Quite a bit, is what Sensory Logic found in a study involving equally wealthy investors segmented by age. The underlying brand strategy issue? Would a company's famous name provide enough equity to put people at ease with an online offer requiring them to share financial information?

Younger Segment   Older Segment

■ Postive Emotions
■ Negative Emotions

Figure 4.7   Age differences in online buy-in.
When it came to determining true willingness to participate in banking activities online,
Sensory Logic found some interesting responses. While both groups professed great
willingness to provide the personal, even intimate information required, the emotional
response of the younger segment was over 20 per cent ahead of the older segment.
But neither segment was as comfortable with the concept as they said they were.

For younger people this proposition proved to be less worrisome than it
was for older people. The latter group worried far more about matters like
ease-of-use, program quality and, especially, online security. In the verbal
responses, there was essentially no difference between the younger and
older segments in regard to the question, 'Are you willing to provide
personal information?' But the facial coding revealed that the older group
were actually far less willing to do so than they claimed (Figure 4.7).

Race and racism

People's subconscious bias is to rely on their own tribe

Nowhere does the idea of 'tribes' surface more strongly than with regard
to issues involving race and racism. For instance, an academic study investigating racial stereotypes concluded that people are hardwired to prefer
their own race. That's because bias unconsciously permeates people's attitudes (Wartik, 2004). Intriguingly enough, however, as we saw in regard
to research shared in Chapters 1 and 3, different emotions can lead to
different outcomes.

Specifically, students in this study who were coaxed into *anger*, for
instance, were more likely to have negative reactions to members of
other racial groups than they were to people of their own racial groups.
In contrast, *sadness* actually eased the degree of bias (perhaps because
being 'down' inspired greater sensitivity). Not surprisingly then, its

opposite – *happiness* – proved to be like anger because it increased the students' rapid-response rejections of 'outsiders'.

At times, clients have directly asked Sensory Logic to check for issues related to racial bias.

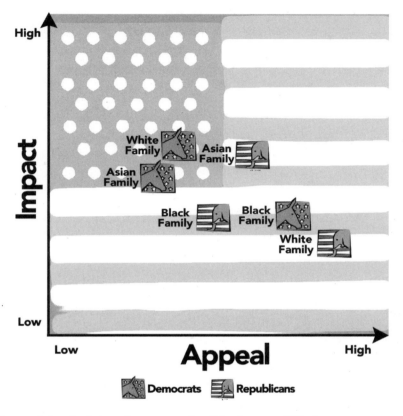

Figure 4.8   Racial preference and political party affiliation.
A financial services company had us test in the United States three print ads which were textually identical but had families of different races in them. Party affiliation was the key demographic variable. Although more than half of the Democrats analysed were Caucasian, they were most positive about the African-American family shown to benefit from a financial services offer meant to assist families buying a first home. In contrast, the mostly Caucasian Republicans felt more supportive of their own race.

In one case (Figure 4.8), the stakes involved determining how best to appeal to US Congress members and their staffs in order to protect the company's government charter. The specific focus was testing three print ads to see how well they promoted a programme to assist first-time home buyers. In another case (Figure 4.9), the company feared it might offend

Asian-American sensibilities. Why? The risk was that a TV spot showing a dishevelled Caucasian executive meeting his Japanese counterparts might signal disrespect.

Figure 4.9 Asian persuasion.
A TV spot in which an American is revealed to have food in his teeth didn't offend Caucasian Americans. Nor, according to the sizeable Asian-American segment included in the study, did it seem like a blow against the dignity of the Japanese delegation with whom he was meeting. Instead, both groups contributed to a consistent rise in appeal as opposed to the turn-off the company wanted to guard against.

What's the overall verdict based on these two cases alone? It's that bias can give way to harmony. Still, in a contest between the hopeful motivation of acquiring status and power and the protective motivation of defending oneself against getting hurt, beware; it's hard to imagine that the more primitive, fear-oriented part of the brain doesn't hold sway.

Telling a story: selling familiarity and comfort

Synopsis: Stories engage us, so companies should tell stories lively enough to build a protective layer of value around their offerings. Here, we go through the steps required to build a robust story. After establishing the importance of storytelling, this section will examine the key story components: personality and associations. Finally, three quick case studies will make the point that associations and beliefs collude in ensuring that brand equity works.

> **Key take-aways**
> - To avoid being a blank slate, a brand must exude a personality.
> - Since a warm, attractive personality is vital, gauging awareness isn't enough.
> - Brand equity resides in neural networks forged through associations.
> - Confronted with new, disruptive information, we favour the familiar.
> - Pride gets in the way of accepting apologies or re-examining our beliefs.

The brand as storyteller

To avoid being a blank slate, a brand must exude a personality

A great brand is a myth perched on top of functional attributes that deliver on the brand's promise and make the story feel like reality. In other words, if a brand delivers emotionally, its myth is transformed into reality for its tribe. So an offer must comply with the brand's promise, or both risk being destroyed. Like a myth, a brand is hard to start, hard to establish and difficult to dislodge.

Emotion and motivations.
The inverse of pride is shame. A brand story is always vulnerable to a scandal. But shame is often too strong an emotion to describe the reaction of previously loyal customers who end up feeling like a brand story they adopted as their own has failed them. More accurate is an emotion like **disappointment**. It is felt when consumers conclude that a brand story they listened to and accepted in their hearts isn't worthy of support. In terms of the Emotionomics Matrix, companies can guard against that outcome by crafting a story that enables consumers to **defend** their self-esteem while retaining the desire to **bond** with the brand.

If consumers' faith in the brand's story gets broken, they'll see the brand's message as an epic lie. Then the fall from success will be horrendously fast. To avoid taking this plunge, a company must ensure that there's substance behind its brand's promise.

That being said, brands – especially great brands – are ultimately more about their implied, emotionally oriented promises. The functionally based benefits that initially created a need for a company will fade over time. This progression happens for two reasons.

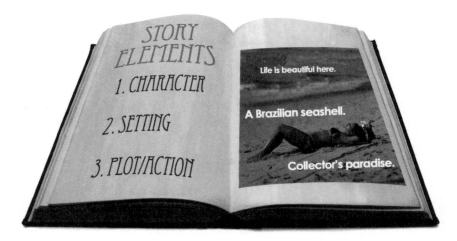

Figure 4.10   Brand story elements.
In order to successfully tell its brand's story, a company must make sure that all elements of the tale relate to the target market and appeal to their desires. This example shows a common ploy used to incite foreign travel. The goal is to show a scene that intended customers can not only project themselves into but also desire to take part in.

The first is that whatever technical or operational innovations originally provided the company with an advantage will eventually suffer. This change happens as competitors adopt a 'me too' stance.

The second and far more positive reason is that over time robust brands move from framing their offer's appeal in terms of facts, to framing the appeal in terms of fiction. By that I don't mean telling lies. Instead, what's meant by fiction is that over time the branded story supersedes the literal offer and becomes the value proposition. A brand is no longer a platform for the rationally oriented offer. Rather, the brand has acquired emotional power that doesn't reside in facts; it resides in faith, enjoyment and ease of connection.

As a result of this shift from nonfiction to fiction, brand equity accrues to the extent that a company's brand story provides the two main components of a successful story. The first is an attractive personality. The second is positive signature associations by which the company becomes familiar and comfortable to members of its target market.

Let's leave aside associations until a little later. For now let's concentrate on what it means for a company to develop a distinct brand personality for the products and services it offers.

First up, remember the formula: recurring emotions form the basis for traits, which in turn create personality. So in addition to belief systems and seeking to belong to a tribe, another primary reason that branding is deeply emotional is that it involves developing a distinct brand personality. The ability to make that happen helps a company because:

- It enables consumers to express symbolically themselves, their ideal selves or selective dimensions of themselves in relation to the brand.
- It ensures a relatively stable and distinct context for a company's offers, strongly differentiating them from those of other companies and cementing consumer preferences and usage.
- It provides a common denominator to aid in marketing a brand globally, across cultures.

Given these crucial benefits, companies should – but often don't – seize on the opportunity to develop robust personalities. Instead, they only go half-way toward that goal. In *Emotional Branding* (2001), Marc Gobé characterizes how branding falls by the wayside by observing that, 'American Airlines has a strong identity but Virgin Airlines has personality.'

Recognition and awareness are enough to give an identity. But to project an engaging, attractive brand personality, a company must become not only a familiar face, but the face of a friend. Only then can a brand be on its way to creating an emotional shortcut in the brain. Trust enables consumers to relax and more intuitively select an offer. With more goods and branded advertisements to look at than time in the day, this subconscious, emotionally based differentiation is a gold mine in persuading the consumers of today's global economy.

Talk about personality in action. What's more comforting than Mrs Butterworth? Undoubtedly, the mental image of the kind, grandmother figure makes the syrup taste that much sweeter. (Picture from Pinnacle Foods.)

Personality in action

Since a warm, attractive personality is vital, gauging awareness isn't enough

Branding isn't a feature or even a benefit. It's a relationship based on an emotional connection. Therefore, pure economic models miss the mark. So do brand descriptions, which attempt to quantify brand value based on formulas involving awareness, saliency and so forth. Why are they inadequate? The reason is that they don't – and can't – quantify in emotional terms how it feels to be in that brand relationship from the consumer's perspective.

Depending on whether there's a good personality match, we do or don't fall in love. To prove this point, Sensory Logic decided to look at brands to see how much of a spark exists in a company's projected personality.

Our decision was to test *Advertising Age*'s top ten icons of the 20th century to learn which ones retain emotional brand equity among consumers of the 21st century. Do these famous American brand icons still provide the comfort and reassurance people desire? And since we're talking about relationships, are there gender differences in how men and women relate to these icons?

Here's a summary (Figures 4.11 and 4.12) of what Sensory Logic found. It addresses both the emotional response rate (how interested people are in the icons either positively or negatively) and how much appeal the icons have (amount of preference or likeability).

Overall Emotional Response Rate

82%	Marlboro Man
80%	Elsie the Cow
73%	Betty Crocker
73%	Aunt Jemima
73%	McDonald
66%	Doughboy
66%	Energizer Bunny
61%	Michelin Man
55%	Green Giant
54%	Tony the Tiger

Gender Differences (% Response)

Marlboro Man	37%
Green Giant	33%
McDonald	33%
Betty Crocker	31%
Aunt Jemima	31%
Michelin Man	21%
Doughboy	18%
Energizer Bunny	18%
Elsie the Cow	17%
Tony the Tiger	7%

Figure 4.11   Brand icon emotional response rates overall and by gender.
These charts show the response rates that each brand icon created overall and by gender. The gender differences reflect which gender had more of a response, and to what degree (dark = male, light = female).

Figure 4.12   Brand icon preference overall and by gender.

These charts show the level of preference (positive emotional response) that each icon created overall and by gender. The gender differences reflect which gender had more of a positive response and to what degree.

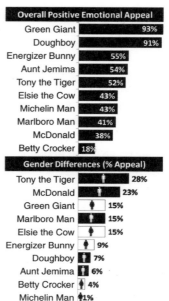

Response rate: overall

● Even after being pulled from the national spotlight, the Marlboro Man is still the most emotionally captivating, thanks to 100 per cent male response. Every man tested felt some reaction to the Man as a symbol of what it means to be a man.

● Otherwise, however, the masculine icons fared badly. The female icons did no worse than tie for third, while Tony the Tiger, for instance, had a response rate almost 30 per cent lower than Marlboro's cowboy.

Response rate: by gender

● The Marlboro Man, Green Giant and Michelin Man are manly men, with more stopping power for guys. In contrast, Ronald McDonald and the Pillsbury Doughboy generated cross-over interest by getting more of a rise from women than men. Not surprisingly, both Betty Crocker and Aunt Jemima did likewise among women.

Preference: overall

● Best liked was the Jolly Green Giant, followed by the Pillsbury Doughboy. No other icon came close. Way at the bottom was Betty Crocker, thereby validating General Mills's decision to change its packaging by replacing the rather grim-looking Betty with a spoon!

Preference: by gender

● Emotional response rates split by gender: men had more of a reaction to male brand icons and women to female brand icons. But no such split occurred in regard to preference. Best at creating equal degrees of appeal from men and women alike was the Michelin Man.

Why associations matter

Brand equity resides in neural networks forged through associations

A recognizable personality gets the brand story rolling. But ultimately the story unfolds based on the clues we consciously or unconsciously pick up when interacting with a brand. As for where the brand story unfolds, well, it's mostly hidden. Ultimately, as Al and Laura Reis note in *The Origin of Brands* (2004), 'Branding occurs only in the mind and has no physical reality.' This fact makes branding hard to manage because branding effectiveness is primarily subconscious, emotional and dependent (at least in part) on neurology.

As noted in Chapter 1, neurons that fire together wire together. In practical terms, this scientific insight means that experiences rewire the brain by fusing neural networks. As a result, what we've seen predisposes us to what we can and likely will see next time around. Memory builds around hot-button connections that grow more dense and weighty if they are repeatedly lit up and reinforced (Figure 4.13).

So in addition to featuring strong, impression-generating personalities, companies should also strive to reinforce their brand stories by creating mental landscapes rich in associations. A case in point is McDonald's. Despite some problems in recent years, founder Ray Kroc built it to last by drawing on what he learned about storytelling from fellow Second World War Red Cross member, Walt Disney.

Figure 4.13   Branding via neurons.
Constantly used neural pathways create stronger, quicker connections (Banich, 2004).

Is it pure luck that McDonald's is the place children want to go? Hardly. Carefully crafted associations have been skilfully embedded in the minds of America's youths for decades (Figure 4.14).

What Disney and Kroc knew is something that every brand director needs to know: brands are for tribes. But brands must nevertheless be executed at the individual level because that's how strong, internalized emotional responses get born.

Once upon a time in business, grand, large-scale strokes like national TV commercials worked just fine. Nowadays, however, they aren't enough unless reinforced by paying attention to all the little details. The new branding involves a consumer's real-time, less scripted interactions with the brand across multiple touch points and on multiple occasions.

Figure 4.14   McDonald's associations.
McDonald's has worked hard over the years to make sure its brand name is associated with certain elements. That we think of these same words when we think of McDonald's is no accident.

How associations work

Confronted with new, disruptive information, we favour the familiar

In practice, branding becomes a matter of trying to leverage the power of a psychological phenomenon known as top-down versus bottom-up processing (Schermerhorn, Hunt and Osborn, 1999; Compton, 2003). In essence, the top-down wins most often. That's because the power of emotions means that existing beliefs influence and even dominate how we react to any new sensory input, such as advertising for example.

Why does that happen? The explanation is that fired and wired neurons don't just build a network, they build the entire context in which we mentally see our lives. As a result, we're mentally and emotionally invested in what has come before (Figure 4.15). Our brains favour suppressing any new sensory input – or bottom-up content – that conflicts with what we have already accepted and internalized. Who has perhaps most memorably noted this tendency? One candidate would have to be the famous author and social critic Upton Sinclair, who remarked, 'It's hard for a man to understand something when his salary depends on his not understanding it.'

Everybody has biases and vested interests that limit their perceptual powers. Therefore, unless a new perception is really disruptive, top-down contextual processing dominates bottom-up content processing. That

Figure 4.15   Top-down processing typically wins.

Remember the games you played as a child? How about the one with the little wooden shapes you had to fit through a corresponding hole? The first few times you had to try out different holes to see which one fit the shape. But soon you knew which block went with which opening. That's the difference between bottom-up and top-down processing. In bottom-up, the brain is learning and forming associations with stimuli. In top-down, the associations built previously are instantly accessed, then used as filters and to guide subsequent action.

happens because the top-down version quickly, subconsciously and emotionally frames a stimulus in three ways:

- First, it emphasizes what has been important in the past.
- Second, it often downplays what doesn't fit with established values in order to avoid cognitive dissonance.
- Third, the emotions and motivations invoked help define the meaning found in new perceptions.

Associative, top-down processing in action

Pride gets in the way of accepting apologies or re-examining our beliefs

To show how mental modelling really works, let's look at three examples. In each case, the context of brand equity stands in conflict with sensory content, causing emotions to be the decisive factor in how a company fares.

Case 1: Wal-Mart

The first example concerns Wal-Mart, which has used the power of positive, associative, top-down processing to its advantage. For starters, Wal-Mart is famous in the United States for its omnipresent slogan, 'Always low prices. Always.' The choice of that slogan is already in itself a triumph of top-down processing. It affirms the widespread and widely accepted notion that low prices is a valid – if not the single most important – criterion in choosing where to shop and what to buy. In other words, the slogan affirms the context, framing the way in which we look at and evaluate our shopping options.

Moreover, the slogan invites the mind to equate Wal-Mart not just with low prices, but with the lowest prices as a means of telling people, 'You will be smart to shop here. You will get low prices, even the lowest prices. And you can do so without having to take the time and make the effort to shop elsewhere. Here you can not only practise price comparisons, but also secure the lowest actual prices for your purchases.'

As a result, not having the lowest prices could threaten Wal-Mart's brand equity and its bottom-line profitability. Well, guess what? That threat is real because, as a study has documented, Wal-Mart doesn't always have the lowest prices (Wellman, 2002). Instead of offering the lowest price generally, the company relies on top-down processing and, on a daily basis, a key tactic. It selectively undercuts some big-brand items (by 15 per cent to 25 per cent) when the items have high household penetration and high purchase frequency.

Those items are known as *signpost items*, and they are a decisive factor in how Wal-Mart plays the pricing game. Signpost items matter because consumers often really don't know whether a price is a low price for an item. So first they rely on the retailer's reputation. Next, they look to prominent and popular items to form an overall impression of a store's prices, thereby pre-empting bottom-up processing.

As a result, Wal-Mart can get away with content – not always having the lowest prices – that stands in conflict with the assumption that Wal-Mart is the place for lowest prices. Why does the strategy work? Brand equity delivers. The contextual equation that Wal-Mart is the place for lowest prices overrules content, aided by two factors:

- The first is that signpost items reassure shoppers that the store is, indeed, the one and only place required to get items at the low prices their top-down processing has come to accept as the key criterion. Signpost items help suppress the chance that shoppers will begin to notice a disconnect between the promise of low prices and the reality, thereby switching to bottom-up processing instead.
- The second is that shoppers are eager to accept the signpost evidence in support of an equation they have already bought into. That's because acceptance saves them time and energy (versus shopping in many stores). Besides, emotional equity gets tied to brand equity. In other words, by now Wal-Mart is so well established that countless shoppers have come to accept the idea that Wal-Mart is the place for lowest prices. Over the years they've spent their money at Wal-Mart in the belief that Wal-Mart has the lowest prices. So, they are now emotionally loath to disrupt that belief because it would mean they have been wrong, and people hate to admit mistakes. Consumers have in that sense become partners in the strategy and are complicit in its success.

Case 2: the automotive sector

In this defensively oriented case, a US automotive manufacturer came to Sensory Logic after paying for an extensive national print ad campaign that included an apology for previous lapses in quality. We tested the reception of this particular ad by three segments. They consisted of recent purchasers (Owners), people who were indifferent to the brand (Apathetics), and those who would not consider it (Rejectors).

How was the apology received? Badly. The average percentage of positive emotional response was a measly 22 per cent. Even worse, the Owners' collective facial coding results were barely ahead of the other two segments despite the fact that fully one-third of them considered the company the leading quality provider in the category. What went wrong? Let's look at the strategy and outcome in contrast to Wal-Mart. Both the retailer and the auto company start with a contextual belief that consumers buy into. In Wal-Mart's case, it's primacy of price. For the auto maker, it's primacy of quality as consumers' key criterion in making such a major purchase (Figure 4.16).

Wal-Mart makes its customers feel like winners by giving them enough signpost items to support their belief that they have made the right choice in shopping at Wal-Mart. In contrast, by making the overt apology the auto maker was providing content evidence that the primacy of quality belief wasn't being honoured. Therefore, the loyalists who had bought in the past were, in effect, being told that they were losers. Their mistake? Having made the wrong choice by deciding to buy the company's cars.

Figure 4.16   The wrong road.
Always know what one's apologizing for. This example shows the emotional responses of three segments to an ad by an auto maker. The ad was an apology for the sub-par quality of its previous vehicles. That's great – **unless you already own one of those cars!** Then it feels like not only were you lied to when you bought the car, you were an ignorant sucker as well. Furthermore, those who weren't owners simply had their initial belief that the car was inferior reinforced. All around, it was an advertising failure.

Case 3: the healthcare sector

The third example had a more positive outcome. In this case, the company came to Sensory Logic after a wave of publicity cast doubts on a pharmaceutical offer's safety. The company and its ad agency were considering two versions of a TV spot, one more defensive than the other. The percentage of positive self-report rating results hardly varied across segments. But the facial coding results were clear: the company should not run the defensive spot. On our advice, the company wisely shelved it.

Given the data from facial coding, we determined that this spot would decimate support from its key audience and not gain ground with the other segments. Ironically, this defensive measure was intended to be so widely disseminated that the likelihood of this new sensory stimulus being hard to ignore was high. The net result would likely have been to disrupt the advantageous, top-down processing associations that had previously brought the company success with its supporters. In this case the context was the primacy of safety. The risk was that the company would be providing evidence strong enough to potentially disrupt the implicit equation by which the company's offer was viewed as safe.

Market Segment	Occasional Users	Supporters	Wavering Supporters
Upbeat TV Spot	52% (80%)	69% (83%)	44% (60%)
Defensive TV Spot	47% (75%)	31% (77%)	42% (65%)

Figure 4.17   Pharmaceutical product scandal results.
Bold numbers indicate the percentage of positive facial coding response and the numbers in parentheses reference positive verbal response. Based on our study, the defensive commercial – had it actually been aired – would have decimated the ranks of supporters without bolstering the ranks of the other two segments. Interestingly enough, verbal input alone barely hinted at the shame and embarrassment supporters would have felt because of using and trusting in a product that was shown to be subpar. Their level of emotional affirmation – 31 per cent – was less than half what it was for the upbeat TV spot.

The bottom line, emotionally speaking? As these three examples show in regard to telling a brand story, people want tales in which they get to be a hero rather than a fool. Wal-Mart aside, the other two cases highlight the danger of causing disappointment in consumers who had purchased and believed in the brand. When that happens, the loyalists' relationship with the company gets put into jeopardy, threatening a hasty, nasty unravelling of the hope and pride so fundamental to success.

> It's more intuitive than analytical. We have gone from something easily measurable – how many people are aware of your brand to something far more difficult to measure – how do people really feel about your brand.
>
> Scott Bedbury (1999)

Conclusion

Nothing in business is less tangible, and therefore more purely emotional, than branding. All the levers for changing brand equity exist. But where? While the literal answer points to consumers' minds, the underlying answer is in their hearts. To be effective, a strong brand strategy must accomplish the following:

- Reward customers for their loyalty by mirroring the beliefs that frame their top-down processing. Figure out what values emotionally matter most to the target market and make sure your brand can truly deliver on representing them.
- Remember that a brand is social in nature because we rely on it to reinforce our status as members of the tribe with which we identify. The community we join serves as a bridge to adoption by giving us the extra confidence to declare the brand our choice. In contrast, amorphous brands lacking symbolic power don't help consumers impress other people or help orient them to the group that feels right.
- Tell a story that involves a vibrant brand personality whose enduring traits resonate in harmony with the key associations by which consumers know and accept the brand with enthusiasm. A company whose name doesn't invoke mental imagery is in trouble.

An action plan

To make sure that the company's brand is emotionally healthy, here are some important points to remember when assessing effectiveness:

- Create a story so that customers and employees want to say 'we' or 'us' when talking about the brand. Strive for a sense of membership.
- Brands should project a destination that is greater than reality. At the same time, don't forget that a brand should over-deliver emotionally, not over-promise rationally. If a company has excelled at accomplishing this goal, rivals will use its brand as a benchmark.
- The brand/customer relationship should feel like a friendship. A great brand creates a group of friends who share an emotional bond.
- Use research to determine whether the company's brand delivers a strong story so that consumers intuitively respond: this is where I want to be. Given the mind's preference for images, find key visuals that work effectively on an emotional basis. Provide an intellectual alibi to support the emotional brand story.

5 Offer design, packaging and usability

Ooh! Aah! The exclamations heard when people see fireworks are what a company wants consumers to experience emotionally when they encounter or use its products.

Overview

As Tom Peters (2000) writes, 'Design is about emotion.' That's because well-designed offers work if they hook people emotionally with an enticing promise that proves to be rewarding in the end. How to accomplish that feat? Vividly establish the offer's superiority by pleasing the senses and creating a compelling emotional benefit. The original, intuitive connection must be so strong that it motivates consumers to try something new and is remembered fondly enough to induce repeat purchase decisions. To help companies accomplish those goals, this chapter will focus on:

- **Winning superiority:** at the concept stage, the goal should be to make consumers feel like they've won when they purchase something. To truly be considered by consumers, an offer must ignite fantasy as they envision an emotionally enriching outcome. There's too much abundance and lack of true differentiation in the marketplace to approach design any other way. Therefore, the key is to protect the offer's conceptual 'wow' element from compromises that would rob it of the ability to awaken a latent desire or create a new one.
- **Sensory payoff:** at the sensory stage, the goal should be to get consumers to investigate a new offer through perceptions that trigger subconscious emotional responses. More specifically, utilize the sensory bandwidth of sight, hearing, touch, taste and smell as an opportunity to ignite interest. The packaging must accomplish this first because it is the final touch point before purchase. Then it's up to the offer itself to seduce the buyer by continuing the sensory excitement begun at the store. In a crowded marketplace, an offer's failure to be stimulating in sensory terms will also make it emotionally invisible.
- **Functional fulfilment:** at the usability stage, the goal should be to ensure that consumers don't experience design flaws that test their patience and prevent or limit repeat sales or usage. If rationally oriented, utilitarian ease of use is neglected, an emotional backlash is inevitable. Usability properly anticipated reduces frustration with trying to use the offer. That step also enables the offer's use to be emotionally gratifying based on easy, enjoyable functionality that doesn't reduce the offer's uniqueness.

Now let's look more closely at how to design an offer with an interruptive call to action that actually gets acted on, starting with the concept stage.

Winning superiority: nurturing a 'wow'

Synopsis: Conceptually, consumers will be more readily enticed if the offer isn't merely utilitarian, but rather strikingly unique. It should be the result of inspiration, instead of the dutiful necessity of getting the job done and the deal made. As this section will discuss, what often gets in the way are compromises that take precedence over creating true excitement. In contrast, success stories will likewise be shared that range from designing a specific product to an entire hours-long experience of an offer.

Key take-aways

- Too often, let's-make-a-deal compromises obstruct bold, enriching designs.
- The basis of great design is to be both awe-inspiring and emotionally relevant.
- The highest level of offer design is to create a story-like experience.

Emotion and motivations.
Creating **awe** is the emotional objective. The substantial lift consumers gain by acquiring an offer that inspires awe is a huge payoff that they will seek time and time again. To achieve the wow that comes with superiority, great designers will tap into the consumer's motivation to **learn** while also whetting the urge to **acquire**. What consumers find out about the offer must motivate them to want to own it and enjoy its power.

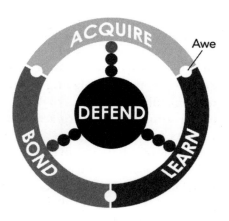

Overcoming design obstacles

Too often, let's-make-a-deal compromises obstruct bold, enriching designs

More than any other facet of a company's operations or output, the design of a product, service or experience possesses the potential for delight. Why is that the case? First, direct, intimately personal exposure gives companies the opportunity to invoke any or all of our five senses so that consumers will notice, comprehend and ideally enjoy the offer. In other words, unlike advertising, where only sight and possibly sound can be leveraged, an offer that uses the entire sensory bandwidth allows for greater engagement. Second, actually laying our hands on a new offer makes tangible the hope that comes with anticipating new experiences. Third, many offers and especially the successful ones will be encountered repeatedly, thereby expanding their influence on our lives.

As a result, offer design has power. It can touch a consumer's inner self to a greater degree than any other part of the company/consumer relationship, save customer service.

Creating an emotionally engaging offer should be a high priority for every company. Maybe it is for many, but the statistics seem to suggest otherwise (Berkowitz et al, 1994; Cooper and Kleinschmidt, 1990; Kotler, 1994):

- Yes, over 30 per cent of a typical company's profits are projected to come from new offer launches.
- But new offers fail 90 per cent of the time.
- Moreover, in trying to improve the odds of success, companies often rely on extensions or other forms of knockoffs that mean only 10 per cent of their 'new' offers are actually new.

In other words, these dismal figures mean consumers aren't biting – despite companies playing it safe with knock-offs instead of introducing truly new offers. No doubt a large part of the problem is today's highly saturated marketplace. But isn't it possible that there are other reasons, too?

Specifically, there are five likely mistakes responsible for design failing to live up to its emotional potential. Constant among them is that designs may fail to create an emotional high for consumers. Here are the five reasons why designs fail and, more importantly, how that can be prevented from happening.

Feature-itis (too many features)

A consumer's mind prefers to take short cuts. It does so by quickly categorizing stimuli based on pattern matching aided by repetition. As a result, the high percentage of offer extensions and other forms of knock-offs are somewhat justified from not only a financial (cost savings) point of view but also a psychological perspective. After all, something entirely new or overly complex creates extra mental work.

Music. Games. PDA. Computer. Espresso maker? Pocket knife? (Just kidding.) Talk about feature-itis! Does anyone remember when mobile phones were used *to make calls?*

At the same time, however, most extensions and knock-offs aren't succeeding. Clearly a fresh approach is required. Companies need to track the emotional response rate and the degree of appeal to ensure that people won't emotionally jump ship. Why might that happen? Either because the work of assimilating the offers is too taxing – consumers rarely reward a company that makes them work harder – or because the offers simply aren't of much interest.

Let's concentrate here on the first problem: hard to assimilate. What's the likely culprit behind this problem? It's *feature-itis*: a company's tendency to over-think and over-execute the design of a product, service or experience. Doing so weakens the opportunity for consumers to respond with happiness or joy.

Because ignoring consumers' emotions is never a wise business move, the solution is to radically simplify the design. Don't get caught up in explaining the offer's rational benefits. Instead, lavish most of the design energy on targeting the sweet spot that will provide the single most attractive benefit. Understand the problems faced by consumers. These are problems consumers want offers to solve. Then think of scenarios in which the company can provide solutions to those problems. The scenarios should involve actions that elicit positive emotions (such as awe or hope) or promise to meet emotional needs. Use these emotional access points as the basis for inventing the advantage the company's offer can best deliver.

Cost-cutting (too few features)

While every company considers design, it's usually cost-cutting analytics that dictate final production. But no matter what offer a consumer considers, that offer will be incomplete unless it has a pleasing emotional payoff: a what's-in-it-for-me (WIIFM).

Why a paper bag? Because it's a great example of what can happen if all the features are taken out of a design – in this case a fancy woman's handbag. In losing the fine-grain, pebbled Italian leather, the 18-carat gold accented hardware, myriad internal pockets and matching clutch just to keep costs down, a company ends up with nothing more than a paper bag. And when's the last time consumers got excited about one of those?

The solution that gets consumers attracted, buying and satisfied? Provide a solution to a problem or shortcoming. Figure out the rational benefit – the intellectual alibi – that best provides justification for purchasing the offer. But in doing so remember that people feel before they think. The emotional benefit should come first in developing the design. It may be that what consumers desire most in emotional terms is exactly what rationally oriented or cost-cutting analytics recommend a company skimps on. Given competing agendas, the smart choice that will ultimately drive sales is the one that's emotionally based.

Myopia (selfish features)

A quest for artistic glory may be the reason the end-user's emotional needs are being ignored. An ingenuous design consumers can't readily comprehend will rob it of emotional punch, and the desire for functional superiority may mean the onset of feature-itis. In these and other ways, a company's natural bias can prove harmful. By starting from its own inwardly oriented and potentially myopic perspective, a company can keep consumers from getting the features they want and the emotional connection they desire.

What's required for love of an offer to flourish? The answer is reciprocity and an emotional hook. While the engineer is the 'Can it be done?' person and the marketer is the 'Will it be done?' person, the designer should ideally be the 'Should it be done?' person who looks out for the end-user by knowing which concessions don't matter and which will kill the design.

But eliciting, and gauging, consumers' emotional response is vital. Aim at knowing how potential buyers feel in order to determine what they will do. In conducting research, find the early adopters whose emotional model matches that of the company's largest target market. A non-verbal emotional connection with consumers will indicate success in fulfilling unexpressed preferences for an offer.

Ikea's spoof on hoity-toity designers.

Tunnel vision (irrelevant features)

Many offers fail because they were designed in response to a competing offer, to utilize factory capacity or to reposition existing offers. In short, the design is driven by the economic criteria of the business instead of the goal of fulfilling the consumers' emotional preferences. For example, while healthcare providers tend to emphasize technology and medicines, patients are concerned with service and information.

Talk about an irrelevant feature. Although this packaging example is slightly over-the-top, features that have nothing to do (or no direct connection) to the offer are simply clutter to the consumer. And what's hard to understand doesn't get purchased.

A company's best bet is to exaggerate the emotional benefit for the target market. Make sure the offer connects with people by determining the one thing the target market remembers two weeks after exposure to the offer. Then adjust the design to eliminate irrelevant features.

No vision (only safe, rationally driven features)

A great design, we love. A bad design, we hate. And a safe design, we don't even see. Sadly, it's easy to hate something and way too easy to build something invisible. Often a company will put effort into developing an offer that ends up being invisible because a focus group has said, 'Well, I would consider that.' Consumers fall back on giving utilitarian-oriented descriptions of what they would buy. However, most communication isn't verbal and great design isn't rational. A prospect's report that something is 'acceptable' isn't acceptable. The effort a company puts into developing an offer that's been verbally identified as 'acceptable' will produce apple sauce instead of apple pie.

> In a world of largely saturated markets and many alternatives, astonishing the customer (through superior design) is the path to exceptional growth and profits.
>
> Robert Heller (in Peters, 2000)

Proven winners: concepts that work

The basis of great design is to be both awe-inspiring and emotionally relevant

Given all the competition, form-follows-function is no longer an adequate mantra for gaining market share. Great design needs to go deeper than rationalization. Over time, it has to please our senses and win us over emotionally. But first it has to capture the imagination. What are the essential ingredients to success at the offer's concept stage? Two independent studies provide us with answers.

The first (Cooper and Kleinschmidt, 1990) found that the number one success factor is having a unique, superior offer. Providing greatness results in a 90 per cent success rate. Is there a caveat? Yes, the superiority must involve something consumers care about. What's the proof? A second study (Madique and Zirger, 1998) showed that success is also based on as deep and rich an understanding of consumer needs as can be ascertained.

Let's look at three successes as well as at one partial success.

Success 1: the new Love Bug

One example of imaginative power is the Mini Cooper. Like any really great offer, it captures the imagination by establishing a fantastical sense of superiority. No, that doesn't mean the offer is false or doesn't work. Rather, the offer inspires awe.

After all, it is a ridiculously small car – which makes its wide-eyed, pronounced headlights all the more noticeable.

Figure 5.1
The ridiculously small Mini.
Sometimes the small dog wins the fight. The Mini Cooper has managed to sell 40,000 units a year because people simply love the charm of it.

And speaking of exuding a sense of differentiated superiority, how was it launched? By being mounted on top of SUVs and driven around 21 cities with signs on top that read, 'The SUV backlash officially starts now.' There's an offer certain to annoy some people, but enthral others. The approach says, in effect: express your uniqueness and values by buying this car. You could be here, too – above the humdrum SUV fray, living a superior life of fun and fantasy.

Success 2: babes in toyland

A second example of imaginative power in action is from the toy industry. The sector has always leveraged the way children focus on the faces of others – something they do from the moment of birth. Nothing illustrates the emotional way kids relate to toys better than a girl's connection with her dolls. And for years no doll was more loved than Barbie.

Figure 5.2   Barbie is under attack from the Bratz gang.
Its parent company reported sales of over $2 billion in 2005. It's estimated that Bratz now has over 30 per cent market share.

Then in 2001, MGA Entertainment introduced its Bratz line of dolls as a hip alternative to Mattel's offer. Barbie smiles. The Bratz pout. The differences, especially the Bratz's air of superiority, go on from there. In short, the Bratz capitalized on the emotional needs of young girls in search of fun and attitude better than Barbie did, and financial rewards followed from taking a more extreme position.

Success 3: the $2,000 washing machine

Premium goods have surpassed $400 billion in annual US domestic sales, with expected growth of about 15 per cent a year (Silverstein and Fiske, 2005). The explanation for the rise has to be emotions, at least in part. Clearly, paying lots of money for an offer isn't 'rational'. Driven by consumers' willingness to pay more for goods in the categories that are most emotionally meaningful to them, new luxury goods have upended the traditional price/volume demand curve.

A case in point is Whirlpool's upscale Duet product line. The line retails for three times the average washer/dryer set. Surely nobody wants to pay $2,000 for a washing machine. Talk about a purchase that's purely functional and not emotional, right? But in actuality Whirlpool's innovative, European-style machines have sold very well to enthusiastic owners and the premium washing machine category has grown by 9 per cent (Silverstein and Fiske, 2005).

Incorporating sleeker designs and more aesthetically pleasing materials, Whirlpool's Duet® retails for three times the price of the average washer/dryer combo. The premium washing machine category has grown by 9 per cent overall. (Picture courtesy of Whirlpool.)

In testing that Sensory Logic did on the Duet line, we found that despite some verbal expressions of doubt, the emotional responses of subjects were strong and positive, with high emotional response rates. Consumers were extremely interested in learning about additional innovations and the wider array of colour options being considered.

Charles Jones, Whirlpool's vice president of global consumer design, was quoted about our research in the *Wall Street Journal* (Zaslow, 2006). About consumers he observed, 'They'd say, "I don't know if I'm comfortable with this," but their facial expressions were saying, "This is pretty cool!" It saved us from going down a number of blind alleys.' This focus on design has helped Whirlpool's stock price rise 31 per cent since introducing the new upscale Duet washer and dryer set in 1999.

Partial success: ergonomic handles

Finally, here's an example of an offer design that can work well, depending on which target market is being addressed. In another study involving the household, Sensory Logic moved from the laundry room to the kitchen. There we pitted an ergonomic, upscale OXO Good Grips® spatula against a basic, utilitarian 'Fred Flintstone' model (Figure 5.3). Unlike the Whirlpool study, which involved only women, in this case the sample was split between men and women – as were the results.

Verbally, women didn't indicate a preference either way. Indeed, their strong 'wow' preference for the softer and more flexible OXO spatula only

Figure 5.3   Getting a handle on gender.
OXO's Good Grips® are great. They're ergonomic, stylish and comfortable. But that doesn't mean they are for everyone. Testing we did on the product showed that, emotionally, men actually preferred a regular old steel spatula to the fancier (and more feminine) Good Grips® model.

became clear after analysing the emotionally based facial coding data. Interestingly, men somewhat similarly to women were verbally unenthusiastic about the crude model. But unlike the women's results, the men's facial coding data showed a win for the no-frills flipper over what they apparently took to be the frou-frou OXO Good Grips® model.

> It is only shallow people who do not judge the world by appearances.
>
> Oscar Wilde

Designing the experience

The highest level of offer design is to create a story-like experience

The previous examples were about products. But in addressing imaginative power in action we need to acknowledge the design of services and experiences as well. After all, America has moved away from being the producer of things: only 12 per cent of its economy is manufacturing-based. About 80 per cent of both the country's economy and its workforce belong to the services realm (Pine, 2004). Therefore, the topic of service deserves a more in-depth discussion, which comes in Chapter 8.

That being said, almost everything discussed so far in this chapter also applies to services and to what Joseph Pine II and James Gilmore (1998) and Bernd Schmitt (1999), among others, have been calling the next, more evolved stage of business: the providing of experiences.

As first Walt Disney, and now Starbucks, have shown, there are financial rewards in creating a sensory and emotionally immersive experience that involves a setting, characters (the employees) and a plot (experiencing the offer). Amusement park rides and coffee are merely the offer platforms. On to them, these companies add specially designed opportunities for consumers to feel emotionally satisfied in ways that they can't attain anywhere else.

The way for a company to move out of the commodity trap – which is to say, go beyond having its offers regarded by consumers as undistinguished, interchangeable entities, vulnerable to price pressure – is to differentiate emotionally. When engaged customers find meaning in an experience, there's a collaborative outcome. Linking what the offer presents and what it represents to consumers emotionally provides the ultimate degree of customization.

In short, while service is a transaction, an experience should be more encompassing. Consider American Girl Place. We could label its two sites in Chicago and New York City as 'stores'. But while consumers can buy the popular dolls, books, furniture and clothing on-site, there's also a doll hospital admissions centre, a hair salon, a restaurant and places set aside for

Figure 5.4   The progression of economic value.
Pine and Gilmore (1998) see four stages of growth: the agrarian extraction of natural
resources, the industrial manufacturing of standardized goods, the service and delivery
of customized care, and now akin to Disney, the staging of memorable, personal
experiences that are creatively designed to provide more emotional payoff.

souvenir photo shoots linked to *American Girl* magazine. The 'store' even
contains a 150-seat theatre, which helps explain why the average customer
spends two and a half hours in the building. To call it integrated marketing is
only half-correct. It is really more like offer design integrating the consumer.

A coffee shop. So what? There's plenty of those.
Except this isn't just a coffee shop. It's an ING DIRECT Café. Though it does serve java,
ING has created major oases in the middle of cities and staffed them with certified
financial planners. The goal is to provide customers with a peaceful environment where
they can check their stocks, get financial advice and enjoy a nice cup-of-Joe.

The intent is to make the enrichment of the customer's life the end 'product'. At American Girl Place, there are many features but no likelihood of feature-itis because the optional activities are clear and emotionally relevant.

Sensory payoff: the way to the heart

Synopsis: The key here is to create enough sensory excitement that consumers get emotionally intrigued. Only then can they overcome any previous disappointments in the category. As reflected in the content of this section, sensory engagement typically starts with the packaging as experienced in-store, but then it moves on to the offer itself, which is usually experienced at home.

Key take-aways

- Great packaging is about eyeballs and fingertips, leveraging sight and touch.
- A great offer design has a payoff for each part of our three-part brain.

Wrappers that work: enticing packaging

Great packaging is about eyeballs and fingertips, leveraging sight and touch

The goal of establishing an offer's superiority is conceptual in nature. It happens consciously in consumers' *minds*, inspiring fantasies about how the offer will be emotionally satisfying. But the next opportunity, overcoming marketplace invisibility through sensory sensations, happens more subconsciously. It unfolds in consumers' *bodies*. After all, the whole proposition of getting consumers to discover and investigate a new offer starts with engaging them. We're talking eyeballs and fingertips – the basics. The sensory bandwidth must be leveraged to ignite and sustain emotional interest in the target market.

This sensory intrigue must occur twice: once through packaging and again in actual usage. Let's concentrate on packaging for now.

While ultimately functional, product packaging must be as full of sensory enticement as possible to induce sales opportunities. Packaging's dual personality – emotionally stimulating in store, rationally satisfactory

Emotion and motivations.
Yearning is the relevant emotion here, as consumers, burned by disappointments, dare to hope again. This rekindled desire is less about trying to **bond** in the social sense than it is about a me/new toy relationship. The other motivation is to **learn**, as consumers gain a better experiential understanding of the offer.

after purchase – is necessitated by the difficulty of grabbing people's attention. In any retail setting, shoppers are now bombarded by so much sensory input that their minds immediately and subconsciously filter out what's not important to them.

'With its thousands of images and messages, the supermarket is as visually dense, if not as beautiful, as a Gothic cathedral. It is as complex and as predatory as a tropical rain forest' (Thomas Hine, 1995).

That brings us to our next issue: just how small the window of opportunity really is. The estimate is that designers have .06 seconds, on average, to make an impression on a shopper in the grocery aisle (Hine, 1995). Nor are volume, competition and limited time the only hurdles. For packaging to function effectively in such a short amount of time, it must do so while typically appealing to only two of the senses: sight and touch.

In other words, packaging needs to catch the eye and welcome the hand. At the sensory level, an offer's visual obscurity is the kiss of death. As people are primarily visual beings, we look at things to establish most of our impressions. So if a packaged offer doesn't visually engage

For inspiration, consider Red Bull. Not only did Red Bull create the energy drink category, it owns it, with worldwide sales of $1.5 billion annually (Reis and Reis, 2004). What makes Red Bull so effective? Let's start with the offer: it's not just a drink but a highly relevant way to improve performance during times of stress. Positioning? Red Bull says it all connotatively by packaging in smaller, 8.3 fluid ounce cans that suggest potency and fit nicely in consumers' hands.

consumers at first glance, it's either too complicated or has settled for look-alike invisibility. In creating an effective package design, quick comprehensibility and a firework-like pop are everything.

Then after pleasing the eye, it's time to invite touch. Make the offer tangible in such a way as to invite consumers to hold it in their hands. But remember that once a package is held, people's emotional brains – the second part of the brain in evolutionary terms – will assign value. So be sure to make the perceived value an emotionally positive one.

It's believed that 70 per cent of what we look at in stores is packaging (Nelson and Ellison, 2005). But what exactly are we looking at? At Procter and Gamble they call it the 'first moment of truth'. Soon, an offer is either in someone's hand or passed over. This output visually summarizes eye tracking data we captured from subjects looking at a store's toothpaste shelf. The dark centres of the blotches indicate the most attention.

Packaging must build trust and reassurance both visually and physically. That's because even though consumers might not be able to see the packaged offer directly prior to purchase, they must nevertheless decide the offer is worthwhile to buy. Successful packaging can fulfil this last requirement in multiple ways. Packages can influence through the use of clever colour schemes, size, material quality, unique shapes or weight.

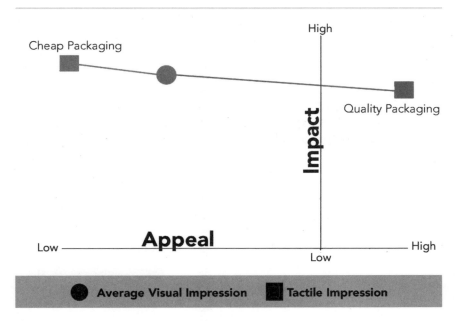

Figure 5.5   The effect of package quality on emotional response.
The difference between great and cheap packaging? A sale. As seen in this study on healthcare product packaging, there is a distinct difference in perception. The cheap packaging says, 'You don't think my health is important.' The heavier, more substantial packaging says, 'You're concerned about quality and will look out for me.' The bottom line is that flimsy packaging may save money on the factory floor but will definitely cost money on the sales floor.

A pleasing offer experience

A great offer design has a payoff for each part of our three-part brain

When it comes to getting the offer home from the store, out of its packaging and on to actual usage, all previous sensory experiences are mute. Enticing quick-moving shoppers to stop and, within just a few nanoseconds, 'consider' the purchase is over. The goal now becomes deepening and enriching the sensory-emotional experience. To learn how to do so, let's return to our model of the three-part brain and its implications for offer design.

How does the target market respond emotionally to the shapes, proportions and spatial relationships in the company's offer? Leverage the 27 universal and hard-wired sensory archetypes in Figure 5.6. They will help a company design offers more effectively by enabling it to invoke the patterns people already intuitively know and can relate to readily.

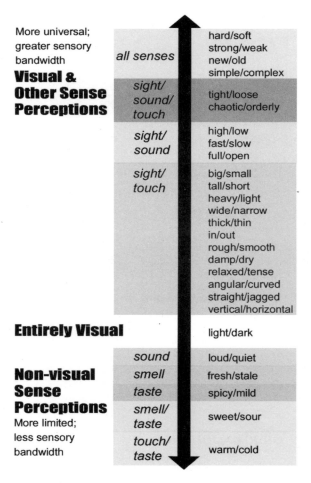

Figure 5.6 Sensory archetypes.
The chart shows dichotomous pairs of sensory attributes and where they fall in terms of engaging all or some of the sensory bandwidth. At the top are pairs that engage our sight and other senses. At the bottom are non-visual pairs that engage less of the sensory bandwidth and are thus less likely to be effective in a shopping environment (Lakoff and Johnson, 2003).

At the sensory level, appearances matter. But the key here isn't just aesthetics in a pure visual sense; it's essence and satisfaction. Strategic advantage doesn't lie in the form-follows-function mode, but rather in form-follows-soul. In other words, don't ignore functional utility, but concentrate on what the offer is really about in terms of its key emotional benefit and then choose which of the sensory archetypes can best help deliver on that benefit.

In general, at the emotional level strive for attachment. The secret of lasting love and enduring relationships is pleasure. Without it, no sparks will fly. And without sparks, nothing will endure over time.

Finally, at the rational level ask: are the functional qualities substantially addressed? Are consumers able to justify the purchase to themselves and others, using an intellectual alibi? Does the offer as designed readily provide such an alibi?

For a real-life example of just how much in conflict the sensory, emotional and rational levels can be, let's look at a study Sensory Logic did comparing two car interiors. One belonged to an upscale American car, and the other an upscale German car. As these results show (Figure 5.7),

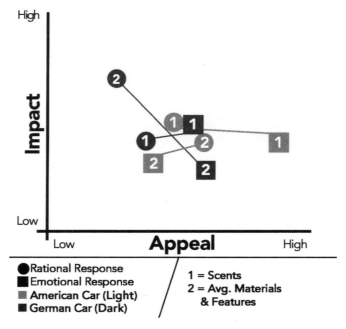

Figure 5.7   Emotional results: a German versus an American car.
Scent of a woman? Try scent of a car. On an olfactory level, the American car won easily. But when the eye and hand were involved in evaluation, experience belied adverse verbal responses toward the German car and revealed high appeal in favour of it. On average across a half dozen categories involving materials and features, the German car was consistently felt to be better, despite comments and ratings indicating the opposite.

subconscious, sensory-emotional responses can be at odds with consciously stated preferences. In this case, the people we tested in Detroit probably knew on a rational, reflective level that American pride and jobs could be at stake in their expressing preferences for a foreign-made car.

So they rationally sought to ally themselves with the American car. Thus, they consistently rated its design attributes as better, even though their own emotional responses indicated that, new car smells aside, they liked the German car more.

Functional fulfilment: joy, not frustration

Synopsis: A well-designed offer takes into account not only the sensory and emotional levels, but also the utilitarian needs that occupy the rational level. Otherwise, the potential for emotional enjoyment will get sabotaged by rationally-oriented frustration related to inadequate functionality. Protection against that fate lies in usability testing. That testing should, however, gauge efficiency and accuracy alongside the emotional aspects of the usage experience.

> **Key take-aways**
>
> - An offer that taxes our emotional resources isn't going to be viable for long.
> - True customer satisfaction is sensory-emotive and must be tested accordingly.

Emotion and motivations.
An offer that makes consumers feel less capable creates displeasure in general and **anger** in particular as they lose a sense of being in control. This emotional outcome is the exact opposite of what they want. An offer consumers sought to **acquire** because it would enhance their power, status or capability now, instead, becomes something they must **defend** themselves against.

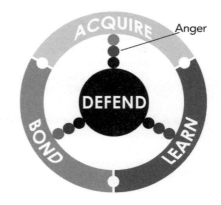

Effectiveness of use

An offer that taxes our emotional resources isn't going to be viable for long

At a very rational level, consumers want the offers they purchase to work easily, correctly and with as little effort as possible. For example, who isn't happier knowing that Microsoft Office now requires only four clicks to insert a text box, whereas the 2003 edition required 26 clicks?

Sounds like companies just need to address fairly utilitarian and rational issues, right? Let's not fool ourselves. Emotions are at play here, front and centre. The moment we're confused – poof! In a cluttered world, nothing spells an offer's doom more quickly than its being hard to assimilate. Every offer needs to sell itself without the aid of complicated, detailed advertising and instructions for use. So in development, consider this question: can a person encountering this offer without previous knowledge figure it out and be captivated by the outcome?

Designing for maximum ease and pleasure of use requires minimizing the potential for anger. How could it arise? If usability proves to be a hassle, it robs consumers of a sense of self-control during the usage experience.

Thus it's essential that consumers grasp how an offer works quickly and intuitively. Non-visual instructions won't be of much help, especially when written by a non-native speaker who lacks grammatical fluency. Even when instructions are well written, the truth is that words alone often aren't enough to avoid an emotional disconnect should the going get tough. The key to success is ensuring that consumers are able to form their own mental image of how the offer works.

In the end, the real reason an intuitive sensory approach to functionality is so vital is emotional in nature. That's because, first, frustration floods people and causes them to short-circuit and shut down when they feel unable to comprehend something new. Second, emotions control our muscles, hence our behaviour, robbing us of adeptness when rage takes over.

Imaginative power. Superiority. The symbolic role of the offer in people's lives. None of those qualities will be sustainable or matter if a consumer is frustrated with the offer and comes away feeling as if the original, conceptual promise wasn't fulfilled.

After all, if an offer looks great, feels great and performs terribly, then a company's marketing and branding dollars have been wasted and amount to nothing more than a very expensive opportunity to frustrate the customer. Making sure the offer lives up to expectation, in terms of both design and post-purchase usage, is the best way to ensure customer loyalty.

In the 1980s, in writing *The Design of Everyday Things*, I didn't take emotions into account. I addressed utility and usability, function and form, all in a logical, dispassionate way – even though I am infuriated by poorly designed objects. But now I've changed. Why? In part because of new scientific advances in our understanding of the brain and how emotion and cognition are thoroughly intertwined. We scientists now understand how important emotion is to everyday life, how valuable.

Donald Norman (2004)

Usability testing to the rescue

True customer satisfaction is sensory-emotive and must be tested accordingly

Fortunately, in recent years the usability movement has become stronger as companies realize that part of championing design is making sure the outcomes please consumers. 3 November 2005 was the first World Usability Day, with 35 countries participating in the Usability Professionals Association's inaugural event meant to promote user-friendly design. It couldn't have come a moment too soon.

Over the last 40 years the average American has grown in size so much that the trend has implications for all sorts of offers, not the least of which are new motor vehicles. As *Chicago Tribune* columnist Jim Mateja notes (2006), 'Hard to believe, but the last time attention was paid to how the size of people affects the size of the passenger cabin was when John, Paul, Ringo and George were an opening act in the '60s.' Mateja was writing about how Ford is updating its models using mannequins to help designers account for the increased size of the average buyer.

What explains the new commercial focus on user-friendly design? According to Randolph Bias, author of *Cost-Justifying Usability*, the return on investment for companies who do

Figure 5.8   Americans are getting bigger.
The sizes stated here account for the upper limits of all but the largest of Americans. Companies that create consumer comfort by acknowledging expanding waistlines set themselves up for bulging bank accounts (Mateja, 2006).

so is estimated at 100 to 1 (Baig, 2005). In other words, ease of use is good both for consumers and for the company's bottom line.

As the Apple iPod's clean, easy-to-use design proves through market domination, intuitive and easy-to-use offers simply sell better. Ikea is another example of simplicity in action. The instructions that accompany its assemble-yourself offers don't even bother with words. Instead, they rely on pictures and the fact that the designs are well thought-out and easy to assemble.

Ensuring that consumers don't suffer sensory confusion leading to an emotional disconnect should be obvious. Perhaps companies will take this information one step further and realize that design discussions involving designers, engineers and marketers are incomplete unless they include those who will service the offers. That's because an offer that can't be feasibly supported at the customer service stage post-launch needs to be re-evaluated pre-launch.

The good news is that usability testing is being performed increasingly, and for good reason. That's because the quality of offers impacts the quality of consumers' lives.

But now for the bad news: the challenge facing standard usability testing is that best practices means moving beyond evaluating only a consumer's rational responses. After all, at the point that really counts – the experience of the offer – satisfaction lives in the sensory impressions and the customer's heart. After all, value is determined based on a person's intuitive, emotional response to that experience.

On its own, consciously constructed, verbal input can't help you assess the quality of your offer. Nor can it tell how easily and enjoyably consumers are using it. Donald Norman is on track in *Emotional Design* (2004) when he notes that questionnaires are 'poor tools for learning about behaviour' because 'most behaviour is subconscious and what people actually do can be quite different from what they think they do.'

Actions do speak louder than words.

This cliché phrase is why observations, especially those done utilizing facial coding, can be of decisive help. Gauging emotional buy-in in this way and then using verbal input to identify the intellectual alibi can serve as an effective one–two combination. Then designs and revisions can be undertaken by drawing on a more complete picture of the situation.

Otherwise, usability testing too often gets reduced to capturing just speed and accuracy, proxies for gauging efficiency. The problem is that neither variable tells how consumers have internalized the usage experience, nor how they truly feel about the offer.

To fully grasp the implications of this frequent shortcoming, consider a pair of examples. The first one involves testing Sensory Logic performed at the conceptual level for a new feature that could seriously impact a machine's usability. The innovation seemed good, rationally speaking. Asked to rate potential advantages versus drawbacks, subjects saw more of an upside than a downside by nearly a two-to-one ratio. Furthermore, only 5 per cent of the subjects voiced concerns that the additional feature might be 'just another thing to go wrong' (Figure 5.9). Emotionally, however, the subjects responded with lots of doubt and no strong positives.

Figure 5.9   Offer attribute response.
Asked to evaluate a potential feature on a major home appliance, respondents provided verbal responses that saw the feature as a benefit by a ratio of two-to-one. But emotionally, that same feature was greeted by an almost 80 per cent negative emotional response.

The second study was conducted in Japan for a healthcare offer. In this case, Sensory Logic videotaped subjects interacting with the offer. Their facially coded expressions were caught on video and the visible reactions were segmented into five stages: 1) viewing the packaging; 2) reading the instructions; 3) opening the package; 4) applying the offer; and 5) smelling the offer's fragrance.

Figure 5.10 shows a screen shot of a participant at every step of the process. It also shows the breakdown of the overall emotional responses for all the people Sensory Logic tested in the project.

The results show that the best-received steps of the offer/use cycle were the initial contact (89 per cent positive) and smelling the offer (72 per cent positive). As one might expect, reading the instructions didn't prove

Figure 5.10 **Step-by-step emotional responses to product testing**

enjoyable (93 per cent negative). But our biggest concern was that opening the packaging proved to be a 100 per cent negative experience for the study's participants. Clearly, the possibility of joyful anticipation had been overtaken by responses mostly driven by frustration and dislike. Moreover, this strongly negative reaction threatened to create adverse momentum heading into steps 4 and 5.

Fortunately, the results revealed both current strengths and the largest opportunities for improvement. Armed with those insights, the company was then in a position to take the steps it deemed necessary to generate the best possible emotional buy-in to their offer.

Conclusion

We've all experienced both the highs and lows of offer design, packaging and usability. The ideal is for companies to create offers that intuitively grab and please us and that we can readily understand. Unfortunately, all too often consumers experience the opposite – and fear disappointment again. To be effective in the design phase, the following must be accomplished:

- At the concept stage, aim to create awe. This mixture of fear, curiosity and, most of all, delighted respect for what the offer can do is vital. Without an emotional breakthrough, there's no staying power or connection – only another 'deal'.
- At the sensory encounter stage, make hope spring eternal. Do so by engaging the senses, sparking a belief first in the packaging and then the offer in order to bypass the intellect and induce consideration. By inviting intimacy, commitment will follow.
- At the usability stage, protect consumers' fragile faith in the offer. Do so knowing that we love an offer only if it loves us in return. Bad design violates the love pact by creating a sense of betrayal when the offer doesn't fulfil its promise.

An action plan

To make sure that the company's offer design, packaging and usability efforts are emotionally healthy, here are a few check-ups to do when assessing effectiveness:

- Convene consumers to talk about the company's products, services and designed experiences. By listening carefully or, better yet, by quantifying the emotions underlying their words through facial coding, the company can learn valuable information about both its offers and those of its competitors. Then look for gaps that reveal opportunities for differentiation.
- Discern the emotional needs of the company's largest buyer segment, and then discern whether those needs are being met. In essence, learn consumers' values, aesthetic sense and the nature of their relationships to the company. Specifically, learn how they respond emotionally to shapes, proportions and spatial relationships. Learning those patterns will help the company design more adroitly.
- A company's offer is emotionally healthy if its life cycle is different from the offers of the rest of the industry. To maintain an edge, identify consumers who didn't repurchase to learn why they didn't feel rewarded.
- With regard to packaging, let the emotional connection and positive sensory experiences continue to guide changes that might be necessary to fit a distribution system or other company-centric utilitarian requirement. Do so to stay loyal to pleasing the external consumer audience – the one that pays the bills because their feelings should never be ignored.
- With regard to usability, resolve any problems that reduce the emotional connection consumers make with the offer. Utilitarian usage issues are a hurdle to be overcome. But never do so at the expense of ignoring the potential for originality or at the cost of undermining consumers' allegiance to the offer.

6 Advertising

Advertising's goal is to shed a brilliant spotlight on to a previously unseen or ignored offer. The mantra is for consumers to see it, want it, need it.

Overview

The best advertising addresses the enduring human desire for something big, new and positive. Plain and simple, advertising relies on enduring consumer hope. Fail to deliver on the promise of new, enhanced possibilities and the heart can't fight through the scepticism the mind will have about getting pitched to, yet again, in an advertising-soaked world. Done right, however, advertising generates images that consumers deeply feel, as well as see. As a result, the choice tilts in a company's favour the next time they are shopping for what it sells. To help companies present emotionally resonant advertising, this chapter will focus on:

- **Being absorbing:** in traditional terms, the first step to success is to generate awareness. But awareness by itself isn't enough because recognition isn't of economic value. So agencies are right in pushing the envelope in order to create stopping power that leads to emotional potency. The bottom line is that awareness doesn't indicate the potential – and necessity – for emotional buy-in. Everything starts with the ability to slip past people's filters by eliciting a strong emotional response.
- **The invisible line:** the second step, consideration, also needs to be recast. What's the underlying issue? Keeping the creative output on the right side of an invisible line so that the offer's appeal doesn't suffer emotional damage and limit consideration. In other words, to support economic gain, creativity needs to be defined as the creation of emotions in consumers that promote consideration rather than rejection of the advertised offer. That positive outcome can only happen if the agency has a grasp of where the invisible line exists. It's the divide between pressing 'hot buttons' effectively enough to be engaging and pressing them so hard that the target market ends up feeling offended instead.
- **Reassurance:** the third step, persuasion, is of all the traditional terms the one most fraught with baggage. Too often, it really serves as a code word for guaranteeing sales, which in reality is asking too much of advertising. Providing reassurance is a more credible and achievable goal. Removing barriers to acceptance is vital. The key is gaining and keeping the target market's faith through images and concepts tied to those it already emotionally endorses.

Now let's look more closely at how to creating advertising that breaks through the clutter and makes a connection, starting with the link between securing attention and generating emotional involvement.

Being absorbing: what stopping power entails

Synopsis: Advertising needs to be emotionally absorbing. Otherwise, it's irrelevant and stale. In this section, we'll look at how big the challenge to connecting with consumers has become, and introduce the five decision-making stages advertising must impact to be effective. But only the first two stages will be emphasized for now, with a focus on contrasting rationally oriented awareness with emotionally oriented stopping power as the first step to success.

Key take-aways

- The mind is geared to filter out stimuli, requiring emotion to break through.
- Current methods for gauging awareness really only capture recognition level.
- The goal of measuring stopping power leads inevitably to emotional potency.

Emotion and motivations.
Awe is the key emotion as advertising must be absorbing enough to interrupt and interest consumers as well as be able to enter their long-term memories. A lesser emotional response may not be substantial enough for the days, weeks or even months until the purchase decision is at hand. The dominant motivation is consumers' desire to **learn**. Even at this initial step, the drive to **acquire** the advertised offer is also an emerging factor.

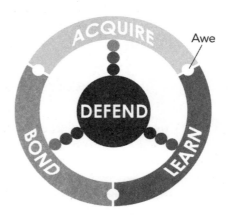

Overcoming indifference

The mind is geared to filter out stimuli, requiring emotion to break through

How big is the challenge of trying to secure the awareness – let alone the enduring emotional engagement – of consumers? Huge, of course. People are awash in information and glad to tune out what they don't need, which is why it is increasingly difficult to create a successful ad.

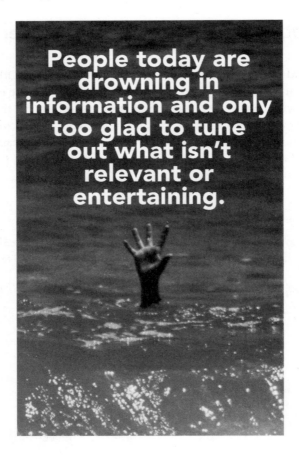

People today are drowning in information and only too glad to tune out what isn't relevant or entertaining.

Over a five-year period during the late 1980s, for instance, separate market research firms tracked the percentage of US and West German viewers who remembered the last commercial they had seen on television. The decline was over 40 per cent in America and nearly 20 per cent among the Germans. More recently, a third research firm found that in cluttered markets like the United States and Japan, TV commercials are only half as capable of increasing awareness as they are in countries with fewer commercials being aired per week (du Plessis, 2005). And that's just looking at the marketplace.

How about the mind? In that case, even under the best circumstances establishing awareness is difficult. As discussed in Chapter 1, the human brain takes in 400 billion bytes of information per second through our senses. But it only consciously processes 2,000 bytes. That ratio should make it evident that when it comes to awareness, keeping the door shut – not open – is far and away our basic impulse. In other words, filtering or screening out takes precedence over input.

As 400 billion bytes makes clear, the mind has remarkable elasticity when it comes to absorbing data. The problem lies in processing it all. Perhaps the authors of *The Attention Economy* (Davenport and Beck, 2001) put it best when they described sensory input as being processed in a large funnel. The narrow spout is what behaviour actually results from the influence of so much input (Figure 6.1). Let's add a little more detail to the five key stages of their metaphorical funnel to get a grasp on how emotions and advertising interact.

Figure 6.1   The awareness-to-action funnel and how attention works: traditionally and motivationally.
This diagram shows how stimuli are funnelled through the attention process. On the left side are the traditional ways to think about the process. On the right is listed, first, the role that emotions play in each step. Then it shows how Sensory Logic measures the emotional significance of each step in the attention process.

Stage 1: Awareness

This stage is about noticing something, becoming aware of it. Advertising proliferates in the hope that consumers will recall some of it. If properly diagnosed, recall is the first place in the funnel where emotion matters. That's because we remember something for only one of two reasons: it either sparks an emotional response or easily corresponds to something we have already retained. At this earliest stage, emotions serve as mobilizers. They're like an early-warning system, alerting us as to whether we might want to approach or avoid the advertising in question for innate, subconscious reasons we might not be able to articulate.

Some of the best 'advertising' in the world is conducted through street signs. They consistently create awareness, elicit relevant memories and responses and help us make instantaneous decisions that are acted on.

Stage 2: Narrowing

Survival instincts help explain the next, narrower part of the funnel. To function most effectively and ward off threats, people have to focus first and foremost on what they feel will matter most. Thus at this stage, emotions serve as relevance signallers. They turn on – and stay on – when a goal is at stake. To avoid being winnowed out at this stage, advertising must enhance or protect our lives.

Stage 3: Attention

This is the consideration stage. Here emotions serve as motivators, fuelling our response as we contemplate the advertising. As will be discussed in the middle part of the chapter, this is where creating sustainable interest is vital. Advertising that isn't ultimately very likeable or appealing will drop from consideration. That's typically for reasons related to the execution. The effort required to comprehend the advertising may be too taxing or else, more strategically, the advertising fails to square with people's emotionally-based belief systems.

Stage 4: Decision

This is as far as research can go in validating, prior to launch, whether advertising is likely to drive marketplace response. As will be discussed in the last part of the chapter, companies are looking for purchase intent or other forms of persuasion. In emotional terms, what they want to know, based on emotions serving as evaluators, is what's the gain versus harm equation? Emotions are judges of value. In judging the advertising, consumers are also judging whether the branded offer is worth pursuing.

Stage 5: Action

Only the post-launch tracking of sales results is truly relevant here. By this point, emotions have reached the critical point of serving as enactors. We take action either to change or regain the status quo. As a means to an end, the advertising will have caused people to resolve, evade or mitigate a situation that the advertising promised the offer could help us handle. Remember from Chapter 1 that only the sensory and emotional parts of the brain attach to muscle activity. The rational brain serves as a lobbyist, which is why functional benefits don't matter much unless they acquire emotional significance (often thanks to the advertising).

Finally, after all is said and done and the consumers' monies are spent, emotions and advertising have one final rendezvous. That happens because emotions also serve as monitors. As part of being evaluators, they monitor the degree or quality of the progress we've made as a result of the action we took. Here informal word-of-mouth advertising becomes an important alternative source of information. That's because as noted by many business people, there's nothing worse than great advertising on behalf of a terrible offer. Spurred to buy only to be disappointed, we then emotionally and financially withdraw – in favour of investing our time and money elsewhere.

Gauging awareness through rational means

Current methods for gauging awareness really only capture recognition level

Now that we have a sense of how – driven by emotion – people notice, focus and expend their mental energy and money in response to the presence of advertising, let's move on. Next up for review are the practices most commonly used to gauge advertising's effectiveness during the awareness stage. Inevitably, the advertising agency's client fears that all its costs for creative development and media placement will accrue without a discernible rise in sales. To address the very real and valid concern that advertising seemingly evaporates into thin air, agency planners and traditional researchers have arrived at three primary methods to assess awareness:

As part of being evaluators, emotions monitor the degree or quality of the progress we've made as a result of the action we took.

In other words, emotions provide our gut-level responses to decisions we've made and allow us to keep an eye out for offers that don't live up to their promises.

That way, we won't be duped again.

- **Assessing exposure.** One method of forecasting awareness penetration is for agency planners to proactively gauge the likely exposure level. By trying to choose the right media outlets and time slots as well as the optimal frequency of exposure, they seek to gain the most awareness for the least amount of money. What are the problems here? First, there's the fact that buying placement doesn't guarantee exposure. Next, no one can agree on what number of potential exposures best facilitates breaking through the clutter. Moreover, there are also disputes over what rate of exposure will best slow down the rate at which people may forget the advertising they've seen.
- **Assessing viewership.** AC Nielsen monitors the raw number of people taking in a particular TV programme and, advertisers hope,

also the programme's advertising spots. But future challenges to tracking viewership will involve ascertaining exposure to the new, less easily tracked media that are filling today's stimulus funnel. There's also the unresolved issue of whether a TV set on in the house guarantees actual viewership, especially in an age of zipping and zapping, let alone TiVo and the mute button.

- **Assessing recall.** The goal here is to answer the question, 'Does anyone remember your advertisement?' It's an attempt to learn whether consumers noticed and remembered a company's advertising. In practice, the question is typically handled one of two ways. The first is by describing an ad to a group of people to see if they can confirm their awareness or knowledge of the ad (aided recall). The second is by mentioning the brand and asking people to provide any recent examples of advertising for it (spontaneous recall). The possible limitations here consist of: a) the interviewed subject's ability to describe the advertisement, b) the interviewer's judgement that the subject's description is a satisfactory fit, and c) the fact that the subjects' descriptions reflect only limited, conscious, rationalized feedback unrelated to a deeper, emotional real-time response.

In short, these three methods may provide adequate means of gauging Stage 1 awareness as they are suitable for quantifying recognition. They give a company some idea of whether its advertising will be or has been noticed. But these more rationally oriented measures aren't in synch with what breakthroughs brain science has taught us about the importance of emotion in driving response. In addition, they are inadequate for Stage 2 narrowing because they don't get at what feels most important or most relevant to consumers among all the advertising they experience. To address that need, the terms and tools involved in the debate over awareness must shift in ways we're ready to discuss next.

It's better to be looked over than overlooked.

Mae West

From recognition to emotional potency

The goal of measuring stopping power leads inevitably to emotional potency

In acknowledging how the awareness-to-action funnel actually works, companies can't afford to settle for merely generating recognition. And here's why. What is recognition? It's awareness. It's merely having noticed the advertisement. Now, emotions may be turned on enough at this first stage so that they're mobilizers, prompting people to at least recognize and retain the advertising to some degree. But achieving measurable recognition won't prepare a company's advertising to survive the next stage on the way to being truly effective. There, being emotionally absorbing means being meaningful.

That stage is where the funnel starts narrowing and where emotions serve as relevance signallers. As a result, more than awareness must be gauged, because importance is signalled by the depth or extent to which consumers' emotions get invoked.

Therefore, more reflective of what is happening in Stage 2 narrowing – with its requirement to be emotionally absorbing – is terminology that goes beyond the meaning of recognition, recall, etcetera. The term the advertising agencies have always (rightly) favoured is an ad's 'stopping power'. That term describes whether or not an advertisement grabs people's attention by stopping them in their tracks. Stopping power beats surface-level awareness in value because it speaks to changing behaviour.

Stopping power beats awareness in value because it speaks to changing behaviour.

How to know that the company's advertising has that potential, however, requires a new tool like facial coding, geared as it is to tracking behavioural response (as shown on a person's face). More specifically, given what we discussed in Chapter 2, Sensory Logic proposes that deeper-level awareness (narrowing) can be determined, in large part, by quantifying the extent of an ad's emotional potency.

There are two different measures that help to do so:

- **Emotional response rate.** As previously stated, this is the percentage of the subjects who respond emotionally to the advertisement. In other words, it's a matter of learning how many people get absorbed or caught up by the stimulus to which they've been exposed.
- **Impact.** This measure reflects the strength of the emotional response felt by the subjects who had a response. It's a matter of learning how intensely people are affected by the stimulus to which they've been exposed.

Let's illustrate the difference, first in theory and then in practice. Imagine that 40 per cent of the sample population in a given study reveals at least one emotional expression on their faces while watching a 30-second video clip shown on the company's website. That percentage is the emotional response rate: the percentage of subjects whose emotions have been brought into play. Equally important, however, is knowing the strength of the emotional response in that 40 per cent share of the subjects. Lots of true smiles, lots of delight, will result in an impact score higher than if those smiles are wan, micro-smiles. That's in theory. Now it's time for a real-world example, but with the real company names changed.

Outdoor advertising is the perfect example of where emotional response rate and impact matter. Unlike its cousin the print ad, people probably experience a billboard at 70 mph in a car, with the radio on and without a chance to linger. The results shown in Figure 6.2 are for an actual award-winning Zen Cola billboard that shows a rival, 'Other Cola' delivery man eating lunch in a diner, pouring a Zen Cola into the can of Other Cola that he knows he should be drinking.

The eye tracking results are pretty provocative in their own right. They show people's eyes concentrating first on the action – the two cans and soft drink being poured – then on the Other Cola logo on the delivery man's uniform, then to the Zen Cola logo in the lower right corner, then back to the two cans and the offer again.

In short, the gaze of consumers is going where Zen Cola would want it to go, and perhaps even in the ideal sequence. Alone that knowledge is more a matter of awareness than of emotional potency, however. There the outcome is even better. Over two-thirds of the subjects we sampled had an emotional response to the billboard, and among those people the smiling, happy reaction was robust enough to secure a high impact score. In other words, the execution tested as being highly likely to break through to consumers emotionally so as to set up nicely the next proposition: driving consideration.

Figure 6.2   A great gaze fixation pattern and on-target emotional response.
Look back to our discussion of eye-tracking hot spots in Chapter 2. This illustration is a depiction of a real billboard Sensory Logic tested. The order in which test subjects viewed the visual elements (represented by the arrows starting at the face), contributes to the impact of the ad and creates great branding. Subjects saw the man, the cola switch, and realized – via the logo on his shirt – that he is an employee from the 'Other Cola' company who would rather drink Zen. Then they fixated on the Zen brand logo at bottom right before going back to the humorous cola switch, which brought a smile to their faces as a compliment to the surprise they felt on first noticing the logo on the disloyal delivery man's uniform.

The invisible line: why knowing the target market matters

Synopsis: The basis for choosing an advertising agency should be that it helps the client by knowing the target market best. More specifically, its creativity should help bridge the gap between company and audience. When is an execution interruptive or merely offensive? Where should the line be drawn? This section looks at the balancing act between the agency's innate desire for interruptive edginess and the client's need within that edginess for the offer to be liked. The interplay between the measures of Impact and Appeal will be examined, including how belief systems and likeability influence consideration.

Key take-aways

- Creating a relationship with the target market requires a mix of impact and appeal.
- The key to success is to stay focused on the target market and its belief systems.
- Consideration always trumps stopping power in deciding where to draw the line.
- With messaging, believability not comprehension drives consideration.

Emotion and motivations.
Alarm is the key emotion, which must be avoided here. Why? Because a target market tensing with worry in response to the approach used in the ad won't be inclined to internalize its content. Since consumers' belief systems are in play here, the challenge of being edgy but not too edgy falls between **learn** and **defend**. Seeking to protect their worldview, consumers will be open to new stimulation only if it doesn't endanger what they have come to accept over time.

Balancing act

Creating a relationship with the target market requires a mix of impact and appeal

To reiterate: traditional means of assessing target market awareness of advertising don't tell a company whether that audience has experienced any real, in-depth emotional response to it. Moreover, awareness alone certainly doesn't explain how it's been received. As such, a company can't bank on awareness. For instance, it's hard to ignore Carrot Top's flaming red hair in a telephone commercial. But taking note of his presence is hardly the same as responding positively to an ad that uses him as a spokesperson.

Therefore, determining how to break through is crucial. The ideal approach will both break through and captivate – in order to facilitate consideration. That's important because in the move from Stages 1 and 2 to Stage 3, attention, the focus is now on sustaining consumer interest. Only by establishing a relationship with target market members can the advertised brand offer eventually gets on their shopping lists. As a result, appeal, the ability to create liking and preference, ultimately becomes more important to success than generating impact alone.

In short, advertising involves a careful balancing act. Just as too little impact means it won't be interruptive enough to attract interest, too little appeal means it won't be able to sustain that interest.

Someone who profoundly understood the dynamics between impact and appeal was Sigmund Freud's fellow psychology pioneer, William Wundt (1897/1998). His research led him to conclude that, when aiming to connect with people, one needs to target a sweet spot that is either the right degree of complexity or novelty, but not a combination of both. The reason is clear-cut: people won't look favourably upon a company for making them work too hard to follow along. Instead, they'll just give up. The equivalent of arsenic in the marketplace is advertising that involves a high degree of both complexity and novelty, leading to lots of impact but also to appeal that runs into negative territory.

Meanwhile, the other part of achieving maximum appeal is either to pair simplicity with novelty or to pair complexity with familiarity so

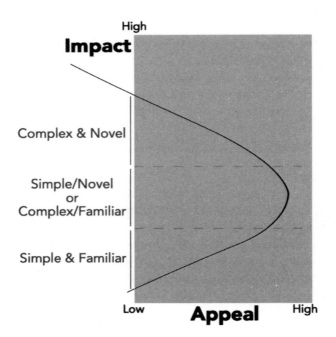

Figure 6.3   Wundt's curve: the sweet spot.
Psychologist William Wundt's research led him to discover that people respond differently to certain combinations of information. Achieving maximum appeal happens when a simple idea is presented using a novel approach, or a complex idea is introduced in a familiar manner.

people can be enticed but not overwhelmed. Once again, the underlying reason should be clear-cut: simplicity makes something new easier to digest, just as familiarity gives people a handle on a more complex approach. So include either simplicity or familiarity, but not both at once because the dull result will be a low level of impact.

Now that's in theory. In practice, getting the balance right is admittedly more difficult, for reasons we'll explore next.

Belief systems at stake

The key to success is to stay focused on the target market and its belief systems

The business reality of advertising is always inherently messy, with egos, budgets and turf battles all pieces of the puzzle. But the point here is to emphasize balancing impact and appeal to induce the optimal level of Stage 3 attention. That goal leads us to three different, often competing belief systems. Of the trio, only one, the target market's, should really matter in the end. Realistically, however, let's first look at the other two players in the drama. That's because they typically weigh in long before consumer preferences become a real factor in the outcome.

Who are those two players? The agency and the client, of course, with the former as creative instigator and the latter as paymaster and thus the final judge of what consumers will witness. It's an inevitably uneven relationship, about which Luke Sullivan (1998), a long-time copywriter at Fallon Worldwide, wistfully jokes:

> About 20 per cent of your time in the advertising business will be spent thinking up ads; 80 per cent will be spent protecting them; and 30 per cent doing them over. The elevator cables in your client's building will fairly groan hauling up all the people intent on killing your best stuff.

To illustrate how frayed and counterproductive the client/agency relationship can become, consider some recent results from an annual survey that studies the situation. As Figure 6.4 shows, perceptions of teamwork are skewed, with clients seeing it as improving far more than agencies do. Hassles and tension are seemingly forever increasing. Meanwhile, neither side believes that the best possible work is emerging from the process.

The underlying problem is that the two parties come from very different perspectives, complete with different belief systems. As Figure 6.5 seeks to explain with intentional exaggeration, advertising agency personnel and their clients are usually locked in an art versus commerce clash.

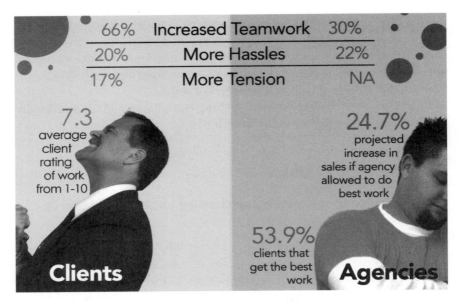

66%	Increased Teamwork	30%
20%	More Hassles	22%
17%	More Tension	NA

7.3 average client rating of work from 1-10

24.7% projected increase in sales if agency allowed to do best work

53.9% clients that get the best work

Clients

Agencies

Figure 6.4   Differences in client and agency perspectives.
These are the recent results from the Salz survey of advertiser-agency relations. The situation is improving compared with a few years ago, but clients and creatives are still out of synch (Elliott, 2006).

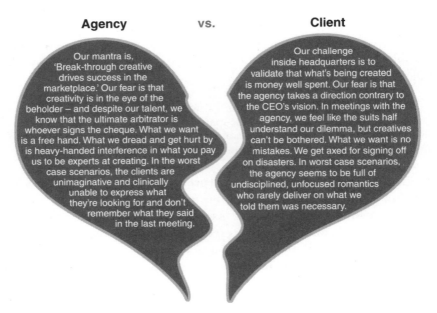

Agency   vs.   **Client**

Our mantra is, 'Break-through creative drives success in the marketplace.' Our fear is that creativity is in the eye of the beholder – and despite our talent, we know that the ultimate arbitrator is whoever signs the cheque. What we want is a free hand. What we dread and get hurt by is heavy-handed interference in what you pay us to be experts at creating. In the worst case scenarios, the clients are unimaginative and clinically unable to express what they're looking for and don't remember what they said in the last meeting.

Our challenge inside headquarters is to validate that what's being created is money well spent. Our fear is that the agency takes a direction contrary to the CEO's vision. In meetings with the agency, we feel like the suits half understand our dilemma, but creatives can't be bothered. What we want is no mistakes. We get axed for signing off on disasters. In worst case scenarios, the agency seems to be full of undisciplined, unfocused romantics who rarely deliver on what we told them was necessary.

Figure 6.5   The view from across the conference table.
These are the stereotypical perspectives that agencies and their clients can too easily fall back into amid the stress of dealing with each other.

What's the solution? It's remarkably simple: focus on the target market's belief system and the emotions related to that belief system. Good orientation requires being on-emotion for the audience in question. Fortunately, the measuring of emotions through facial coding helps facilitate this goal.

How is the business world doing with regard to understanding and reflecting consumers' belief systems? The answer is not very well. Consider these statistics:

- 91 per cent of women believe that advertisers don't understand them and 58 per cent are seriously annoyed by portrayals of their gender (Barletta, 2003).
- 79 per cent of men are alienated, barely able to recognize themselves in the advertisements portraying their gender (*Business Week*, 2006).

For *Advertising Age* critic Bob Garfield (2003), responsibility for this predicament lies squarely with advertising agencies. He sees creatives as all too often primarily interested in proving their 'pointless originality' by winning awards and becoming mini-movie directors. Given this focus, they fail to make emotional connections with target markets and waste clients' money.

Now, maybe Garfield's satirical portrait of creative directors is on target (although maybe it isn't). No matter what, it's hard to put all the blame on one party when somebody at the client's company signed off on the concepts.

Here's a case in point. Figure 6.6 shows responses to a potential TV spot for a company whose offer supports the consumer electronics sector. The storyboard in question involved a jogger using the company's offer when she was suddenly mugged. Apparently, the idea behind the spot was to emphasize the offer's desirability by implying that it was so desirable that a man would resort to mugging a woman who had it in order to obtain it himself. Amazingly enough, test subjects said they liked the storyboard fairly well. So this spot remained in the mix of those being considered. Based on positive verbal responses alone, it even seemed that producing and running the spot could lead to success.

The facial coding results, however, told a very different story. For only the third time in Sensory Logic's decade of research, a stimulus recorded no positive facial expressions. None. Zero. Zip. Even though the storyboard rated high in impact, it was strongly negative. Translation: underneath all their rational filtering, the subjects really hated the concept of a woman being mugged.

Wisely, the company didn't take it to full production. But imagine if the company had made its decision based only on verbal, self-reported input. In this case, facial coding was essential. It provided an objective, scientific

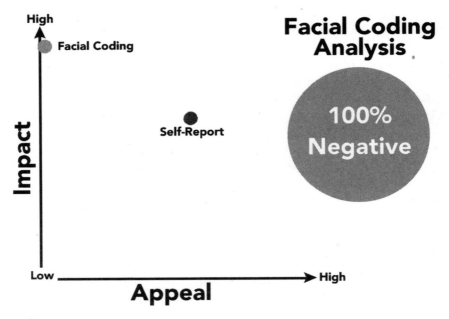

Figure 6.6   Breaking through – but broken.
These results demonstrate the importance of being on-emotion. Even though the TV spot received favourable verbal feedback, the facial coding showed a whopping zero per cent positive response. It turns out that although subjects rationally accepted the concept of a woman being mugged to obtain a desirable offer, in their hearts they were strongly against seeing that kind of execution.

tool able to unite the agency and client's mutual interest. That would be staying focused on ensuring emotional compatibility between the company's advertising and the target market's values.

> David Ogilvy is famous for observing, 'The consumer isn't a moron. She is your wife.' Well, David, God rest your soul, that's just not so. The consumer – the average consumer – isn't some ad guy's wife.
>
> Bob Garfield

The way forward

Consideration always trumps stopping power in deciding where to draw the line

Despite Garfield's jabs, the reality is that agencies and companies both share the credit and the blame for outcomes that either emotionally connect with consumers or else offend them. Indeed, in many ways the balancing act between impact and appeal runs parallel to a careful balancing act between the two parties' respective strengths. Only then will neither creativity nor nurturing the company/customer relationship gets unduly sacrificed. On the one hand, the need for stopping power justifies giving the agency's creative artistry something of a free rein. On the other hand, that strength must be balanced against the company's inevitably greater sensitivity to the buying public which enables it to stay in business.

Here then are a few guidelines and related observations to make this emotionally based balancing act easier to manage. The first is that in any potential conflict between Stage 1 awareness and Stage 3 attention, opt for the latter. Yes, the stopping power that leads to emotional potency is important. A consumer's perspective is always defined by the qualification, 'If I don't see it, I sure can't like it.' But a company should never sacrifice the long-term value of getting consumers to affiliate with the offer – that is, a chance for sales – in exchange for the short-term gain of generating the kind of stopping power that enshrines the advertising. In other words, the creative shouldn't take precedence over keeping the target market emotionally on-board enough to spur consideration.

Second, establish an 'us' versus 'them' dichotomy for the target market, otherwise there's no reason to belong and no membership status with which to entice consumers. A company will often be tempted to cast the net so benignly wide that no one could be offended and imagine *not* being part of the target market. The wisdom is that everyone's a potential sale. But don't give in to that thinking because creativity will suffer accordingly.

An us versus them position is necessary to create a feeling of exclusivity on behalf of the target market. If the tent is too large, there's no cachet to being invited inside.

Third, there's always a temptation to give into gimmicks. But speaking directly to the essence of how the offer emotionally benefits consumers will not only be more appropriate, it will also be more effective.

Fourth, in pursuit of stopping power, be careful of going for too much too quickly. Steve Jobs' motto is that elegant simplicity works. What Warren Beatty said about words, 'Take any script and cut it in half,' can be applied to advertising imagery and special effects, too. Remember the example of Wundt's curve. The combination of complexity and novelty blunts appeal.

Fifth, as is about to be explored in greater depth, negative emotions can be invoked to generate Stage 1 awareness and survive Stage 2 narrowing. But over time, the emotional net outcome must be positive to avoid generating the kind of negative emotion that will scuttle consideration.

Why being heard but not felt isn't enough

With messaging, believability not comprehension drives consideration

The coalition of the Advertising Research Federation (ARF), the American Association of Advertising Agencies (AAAA) and the Association of National Advertisers (ANA) is involved in an unprecedented collaboration to define and decide how to measure 'engagement'. Why has engagement become the hot new term (Spillman, 2006; Manning, 2006; Howard, 2005)? The business reason starts with the limitations of assessing awareness, as discussed earlier. But it also involves the pressure of how to gauge consumer response to exposure and thus the effectiveness of all advertising platforms, including emerging forms and the internet.

To that end, a measure is needed that encompasses the traditional benchmarks such as message comprehension, believability and the likeability or acceptance of feature, attribute or benefit claims. As a means of gauging effectiveness particularly at the attention stage, that measure could be emotional engagement, as practised by Sensory Logic.

Let's examine why. The coalition's current working definition of engagement is 'turning on a prospect to a brand idea enhanced by surrounding context'. But as of now, there is no emerging consensus about how to measure engagement. To do it properly will require directly addressing the role of emotions in advertising. After all, turning people on to a brand idea is more than just making sure they turn on their TV set. Awareness isn't the key here, because turning them on really means that emotions have been turned on.

Generating momentum in favour of a brand idea means that feelings of acceptance become central to the engagement proposition. Conscious, cognitive, verbalized input can only tell whether consumers find that brand idea plausible from an intellectual alibi perspective. A tool like facial coding is required to learn whether or not that brand idea will be emotionally embraced by consumers, thus setting up the opportunity for persuasion.

That distinction is decisive because whether consumers heard and understood a brand idea isn't nearly as important as whether they find it both believable and likeable. So a second facial coding metric is required. Yes, measuring emotional potency, based on emotional response rate and impact, gets at an ad's stopping power. But adding emotional engagement, based on emotional response rate and appeal, also helps by measuring the degree to which a branded offer, as advertised, is engaging and the proposed solution worth considering.

For example, consider a test Sensory Logic conducted in which there were four main messages the company hoped to convey through a series of three different print ads. The format or style of the ads was largely identical. Each showcased a person offering a testimonial about a benefit being provided. But as Figure 6.7 shows, the emotional engagement results couldn't have been more varied for the trustworthiness message considered central to the campaign.

Figure 6.7   Results for conveying trustworthiness.
Here we have the emotional engagement results for three print ads in a campaign. Given very similar layouts and content, it was the spokespeople who primarily caused the responses to vary. Emotional engagement is the product of emotional response rate (ERR) and appeal. The larger the bubble, the more salient the emotional engagement – whether positive or negative.

The bottom line? Without the emotional barometer of faith in the offer, the persuasion goal about to be addressed loses its viability.

Reassurance: defusing scepticism

Synopsis: Given the doubt and disinterest sown by today's advertising saturation, defusing scepticism becomes the key to achieving persuasiveness. As this section will explore, appeal is again crucial. Only with an ad that emotionally sums to a positive result can progress really be made. Finally, this section also looks at two other qualities a persuasive ad exhibits: enough emotional 'white space' for the offer's value to register and a corresponding opportunity for the offer to be branded clearly.

Key take-aways

- As to emotional net outcome, likeability and persuasion go hand in hand.
- An over-reliance on rational messaging won't achieve persuasion.
- Introducing the branded offer should create a positive emotional response.

Emotion and motivations.
Hope is the perfect emotional end-state for advertising to create as consumers contemplate the happiness an offer will bring. The goal is to build positive momentum in the face of doubts that may linger. Two motivations that pull in opposite directions are operating here: an instinct to **defend** or hold on to one's money versus the urge to **acquire** the advertised offer.

Plausible preference

As to emotional net outcome, likeability and persuasion go hand in hand

It's now time to talk about the third and final goal of advertising: spurring a favourable verdict at Stage 4, decision. As with emotional engagement, again the appropriate facial coding metric involves the emotional response rate and appeal. But this time the metric is emotional buy-in because Stage 4 is where persuasion and the goal of achieving a sales lift become the focus.

Since consideration and persuasion are a function of appeal, it follows that positive appeal (or likeability) is serious business that can drive sales. Marketers ignore this relationship at their own peril.

> Advertising that creates a positive emotional response performs better than that which does not – a fact repeatedly borne out by tracking studies the world over.
>
> Nigel Harris, Millward Brown (in du Plessis, 2005)

Indeed, no less a source than market research giant Millward Brown now believes that likeability is decisive. In *The Advertised Mind* (2005), Erik du Plessis of Millward Brown's South African operations has pulled together a history of studies validating the argument that 'Advertisements that work are advertisements that are liked.' The evidence is based on researchers having correlated thousands of interview results with sales data. The sources include the Leo Burnett agency, the Ogilvy Center for Research and Development, and the Advertising Research Federation (ARF).

Du Plessis's extensive study of likeability has led him to refine a model that suggests the types of advertising that generally work or don't work. Granted, the model doesn't involve a tool to access the emotions fuelling consumers' responses. So Figure 6.8 shows an adapted depiction of this likeability model, including the facially coded emotions appropriate to each of the seven types du Plessis cites.

The point of sharing this likeability model isn't to suggest that these seven different types of advertising will work exactly the same way, every time, as depicted here. There will always be exceptions. Nevertheless, by seeing types, emotions and sales effectiveness together, one can get at least a general answer to questions often raised, like 'Which emotions are best to create in your audience?' and 'What kinds of ads tend to work best?' Yes, few people set out to create a confusing or alienating ad. But to discover whether a company's ad is truly entertaining or off-putting is why gauging emotional response is important.

Every button an ad attempts to push is designed to interrupt a potential customer's day-to-day routine and attract attention. But advertisers should seek to interrupt the imagery already implanted in the target market's collective imagination *judiciously*. Few people enjoy the effort of changing their minds. Dislodging what's already there is inefficient, and often threatens the happiness that hope builds toward. It's not by chance that familiarity is more toward the effectiveness end of the spectrum in the likeability model.

Figure 6.8   Adapted depiction of du Plessis's model with emotional responses added.

The location of each type of advertising style can be explained as follows:

- Positive: 1) Relevant news: delivering new ideas or opportunities is more important than pure information, which quickly grows stale. 2) Empathy: advertising that depicts a lifestyle or dramatization can pull us in. 3) Entertainment: since humour is so culturally dependent, entertainment may be liked without being effective.
- Negative: 1) Alienation: opposite of empathy, a depiction that fails to involve us. 2) Confusion: this type of advertising doesn't work because nobody likes to feel stupid while struggling to 'get it'.
- Neutral: 1) Familiarity: works best if there's a little bit of novelty. 2) Brand reinforcement: placement on chart not shown because it depends on what type of brand equity is being reinforced (positive or negative).

(Adapted from du Plessis, 2005.)

In short, advertising's goal should be to bring the promise of something new – but not *too* new – to the target market's mental doorstep. After all, advertising must work to reinforce, not demolish, its market's comfort zone.

That goal is more easily stated than accomplished, however, because even getting a chance to win somebody over has become a challenge. As Fallon copywriter Luke Sullivan notes, 'There is a high wall around every customer. And every day another brick is added.' Instead of welcoming advertising or even accepting it, consumers now experience growing intolerance in response to clutter and endless spin, as the statistics in Figure 6.9 make evident.

Figure 6.9   Growing intolerance of spin.
As is evident from the statistics, companies like BzzAgent are on the right track when it comes to spreading the word. The conventional wisdom that word of mouth advertising is the most successful has merit. Lowest on the totem pole? Ads put out by corporations themselves – proof that stellar brand equity matters (O'Brien, 2005).

Therefore, we now see the rise of alternative media and advertising phenomena like Marathon Ventures and BzzAgent. The former puts companies on TV by means of virtual product placements. The latter capitalizes on the fact that family members and friends rate highest as reliable recommenders. As a result, BzzAgent maintains a national network of 'volunteers' who create a buzz on behalf of offers they believe in, without a script, in exchange for rewards that include a sample of the offer.

The wicked irony is that, in this very tough climate, companies still need to understand whether consumers find their ads persuasive. The ability to attain that goal or an analogous aim like greater purchase intent as a result of exposure to advertising is, however, often difficult to discern. So it's no wonder that an agency and its client may clash regarding the validity and reliability of research measures.

Sensory Logic knows this contested territory only too well. Again and again, we've seen highly positive verbal response scores when a question about purchase intent or persuasion is asked. People at Procter & Gamble have told us that they've even mapped it as an artefact based on how close to the equator the country is. That's because places like Morocco, for example, consistently provide scores that prove to be vastly inflated compared with actual marketplace penetration once the offer gets introduced.

Sensory Logic hasn't tested in every corner of the globe yet. But a case that readily comes to mind is a test in which we asked subjects whether, after seeing a particular print ad campaign, they were now more inclined to consider the offer than they had been before seeing the ads. The result was an astounding 98 per cent 'yes', which if valid would have made it the greatest campaign in the history of advertising.

Clearly, companies should be cautious here. Asking people who are being paid to participate in a study whether an ad enhances their purchase intent – and trusting what they say – is just begging them to embellish reality. It's akin to your best friend asking, 'Isn't my new haircut great?' or a neighbour declaring, 'Isn't my baby adorable!'

We've found that the normative average for positive verbal responses regarding persuasion-type questions hovers around 65 per cent depending on the project. The rigorous method of facial coding puts that same number 10 per cent to 30 per cent lower. No wonder Jon Steel, formerly of Goodby, Silverstein and Partners, has written, 'If my life depended on picking which is more likely to be true, 1) what people say with their eyes, posture and attention, or 2) what they say with their words, I would choose one every time' (1998).

'Magic' versus the risk of message-itis

An over-reliance on rational messaging won't achieve persuasion

The Stage 4 decision phase is the launching stage to action. That is to say, it's the point in the awareness-to-action funnel where emotions serve as evaluators and consumers use their gut-level instincts in making their purchase decisions. The bottom line here is profoundly emotional in nature: does the advertised offer's value equation feel right to them?

In short, this is as far as advertising can go in terms of making the sale possible. From here on in, it's a matter of the media buy, the company's brand equity, the offer, its pricing, its distribution channel and, of course, larger marketplace factors like rival offers and how the economy is faring. Short of tracking sales against the timing of an ad campaign launch, it's also as far as market research can go in gauging effectiveness.

But given the pressure for advertising to boost sales, it's incumbent on agencies and their clients not to become so concerned about Stage 5 action that they undermine what the previous stage is really about. Always remember the need to leave enough breathing room within the advertising execution for subconscious, sensory-oriented processing to work its magic – joining up the imagery – while allowing emotions to play their role as evaluators.

What's the opposite of creating space for emotional 'magic' to happen? Encumbering ads with rational messages in an attempt to close the sale. To persuade consumers, companies often load up their advertising with extra messages. But that's a rational approach to what should be an emotional call-to-action. To include this reason and that one, this feature, attribute, benefit etcetera, and then some more, is asking consumers to work really hard – which is counterproductive to engaging their hearts.

It's difficult to set up more than one or two emotionally oriented value propositions in the short space of an advertisement. Instead, giving consumers a single, striking reason to care works best. Resist temptation and forego a wave of reasons that people will be left struggling to comprehend.

In effect, the problem of message-itis is akin to the feature-itis discussed in Chapter 5. Both offer design and advertising can become so complicated that nobody wins: not the company, the agency, the designer, the engineer, the marketer – or the consumer.

Overdoing the execution robs an advertisement of the opportunity to make a strong, clean emotional connection with the target market. And yet this error happens all the time. To understand more clearly why the error

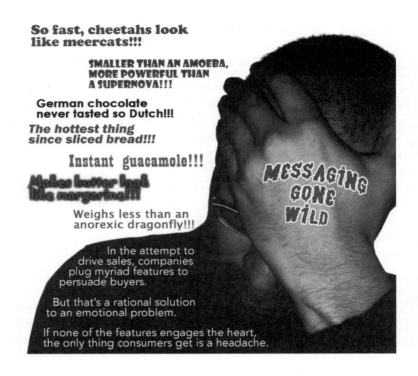

So fast, cheetahs look like meercats!!!

SMALLER THAN AN AMOEBA, MORE POWERFUL THAN A SUPERNOVA!!!

German chocolate never tasted so Dutch!!!

The hottest thing since sliced bread!!!

Instant guacamole!!!

Makes butter look like margarine!!!

Weighs less than an anorexic dragonfly!!!

MESSAGING GONE WILD

In the attempt to drive sales, companies plug myriad features to persuade buyers.

But that's a rational solution to an emotional problem.

If none of the features engages the heart, the only thing consumers get is a headache.

occurs and then what companies can do to guard against it, let's examine three specific reasons why companies have a message-itis tendency:

- The offer's origins. The ability to compete for earnings surely originated in bringing to market an offer, probably a product, that was functionally unique and superior.
- The company's goals. Faith that the offer will sell itself, on its own rational terms, is a factory-driven perspective that follows easily and naturally from a corresponding faith at the company headquarters that the offer is truly differentiated and relevant.
- A numbers mindset. A message bias is likely to be aided by a company mindset that focuses on production quotas and downplays or even disregards the emotional angle.

Two steps can be taken to help protect companies against message-itis, which is an undue focus on what is being said about the offer. The first is that, fortunately, the compensating strength of advertising agencies consists of *how* something is said. Part of their task is to remind the client that adding a consumer-focused element gives the offer an extra, emotional dimension that can truly lift sales. Given financial pressures, however, most companies are still likely to insist on trying to translate the agency's creative 'magic' into numbers of some sort, which is where the second step comes in.

Rationally oriented, verbal research invites subjects to, in effect, echo the messages in the ad copy. But what a company should really want to know is whether any of those messages break through, matter to consumers and lead to acceptance. Therefore, the second step should involve gauging the degree of emotional buy-in. Actions do speak louder than words. So companies interested in purchase intent can use facial coding as an alternative set of metrics based on the persuasiveness response evident on people's faces.

In a test Sensory Logic did for a financial services company, subjects viewed an ad, absorbed its official message, then gave the ad in question a healthy verbal response echo of almost 80 per cent positive. But they also took in an unofficial message – a feeling of being manipulated because a child actor was being used to sell a very adult offer. The facial coding outcome was a much weaker positive percentage, with emotional buy-in only half as robust as verbal approval (Figure 6.10).

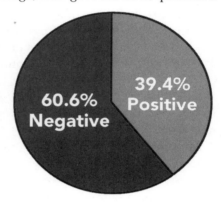

Figure 6.10   Facial coding results for a home mortgage spot.
Would anybody take advice from a horse on how to drive a car? Of course not. As it turned out in a test we did, people didn't really feel comfortable taking advice on home mortgages from a young child. Although their verbal responses were 80 per cent positive (after all, who can say cruel things about a cute little girl?), they felt differently. Their negative emotional response of almost 61 per cent informed us that while the spot was on-message, the use of the little girl was off-emotion because people felt manipulated and therefore lost trust.

Brand linkage matters

Introducing the branded offer should create a positive emotional response

Finally, to discuss persuasion fully requires taking into account the element of timing. The difference between feature-itis and message-itis is that with the latter the key isn't the offer but, rather, the *inherent* offer, namely what the offer will do for the consumers who buy. As a result, there's a future focus to advertising that puts extra pressure on it. Direct

TV aside, most advertising is meant to spur purchases that might be days, even weeks away. As a result, it's necessary for an ad to be easy to remember until the moment when the pertinent purchase decision eventually arrives.

Two factors are important here:

● First, the goal of being memorable is emotional in nature because our memory device, the hippocampus, resides in the emotional part of the brain. Only an ad whose content sparks a memory through an emotional hot-button connection or associatively relates to a memory already embedded in our brain will be retained.

● Second, an ad should aim not only to evoke an emotional response but also help consumers link the offer to the sponsor. For that to happen, at least some portion of the emotional response should happen in proximity to when the branded offer comes into view, especially in the case of TV commercials that take time to unfold.

After all, achieving engagement and likeability won't matter much unless consumers know whose advertisement they've found emotionally noteworthy.

Even research conducted using traditional means highlights the importance of creating brand linkage in order to enhance the odds of sales effectiveness. An independent research study involved 200 subjects seeing, among them, a sample of 800 commercials. Afterwards, the subjects were read descriptions of various ads one at a time and asked whether they had seen each ad. If they stated that they had seen it, the subjects were then asked to name the brand. Here's what this study found: only a quarter of the commercials benefited from a commercial/brand connection that could help to drive sales (Figure 6.11).

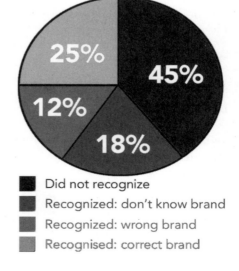

Figure 6.11 **Brand linkage testing results.**

When 200 viewers were asked whether they had seen a commercial, they gave answers that could be grouped in four categories. It turns out that brand recall only happened 25 per cent of the time (du Plessis, 2005).

Based on the low brand linkage scores that independent research has seen, the old saying, "Half my advertising dollar is wasted, but I don't know which half," runs the risk of being twice as optimistic as it should be.

What's the solution to avoiding the misuse of advertising dollars? It's to first look at when and where in an ad consumers get emotionally involved. Next, achieve brand linkage by getting the branded offer adjacent to some of those moments. Sensory Logic calls such instances *pivot points*. They're the places in an ad that exhibit the greatest concentration of gaze activity (according to the eye-tracking results), an unusually large volume of emotional responses, or a sharp and often prolonged shift in the impact and/or appeal score. There could even be all three results at once.

When those kinds of reactions happen in close proximity to when the branded offer appears, the potential sales outcome is golden. All that's needed now is for the final, net emotional response to be positive thanks to the offer's solution being a credible promise. If so, then the potential buyer has turned on, tuned in and been won over. Success means the offer and sponsor are closely enough linked in memory for the purchase decision to be triggered in the company's favour the next time it comes around.

To that end, consider the second-by-second emotional results of some Australian TV commercials (Figure 6.12). They provide a revealing look at good versus worrisome results, relevant to the volume of emotional response. Specifically, what should be focused on are the final seconds of each graph, which detail the impact, appeal and emotions present during the appearance of the brand and brand tagline in the commercials.

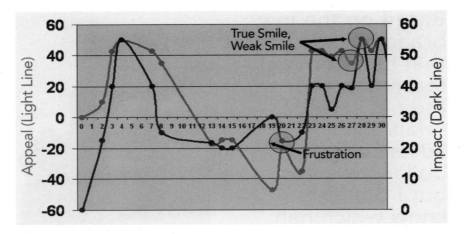

Figure 6.12   Emotions and brand linkage in contrasting spots.
The top chart shows how being on-emotion and having brand proximity to emotionally
engaging pivot points correlate to positive associations for the branded offer.
Meanwhile, the bottom chart shows how an off-emotion TV commercial fails to do this.
In a study Sensory Logic performed for some Australian spots, we found vast
differences in the emotional effectiveness of the placement of the branded message. In
the top chart, notice how positive pivot points present an optimal placement
opportunity for a brand tagline to appear in the final seconds of the spot. True and
weak smiles abound and provide a positive context for the branding. Conversely, the
chart below has an abundance of negative pivot points, and, while the spot ends with
some weak smiles, the impact they provide is not enough to overcome the negativity
and anxiety felt throughout the spot. To achieve positive branding associations, the
ideal approach is to correlate the branded offer, logo and tagline with emotionally
positive pivot points.

The top chart shows the results from an emotionally on-message commercial that managed to pull at the heart-strings of subjects. As you can clearly see, the final seconds show an explosion of both appeal and impact – and the emotions present at the pivot points that were revealed are comprised of true smiles and weak smiles. All in all, as the branding message was delivered, emotions ran high and happy – a perfect combination for brand success.

Conversely, the bottom chart shows the results of a TV spot from the same campaign. While emotionally stimulating, this spot just didn't have the positive oomph needed to create positive brand associations. Of the six pivot points that occurred, only one had a positive emotional response. And although it occurred during the final seconds of the commercial in synch with the tagline, the weak smiles that were elicited were not enough to create positive appeal. In order to achieve positive branding associations, you must correlate the offer or tagline with positive pivot points and end with positive emotions.

Finally, in regard to the shift in impact and/or appeal score rule, consider the best brand linkage Sensory Logic has ever seen. We tested TV commercials for a major US automobile insurance provider. One of the spots featured a tragedy-with-a-happy-ending in which a husband and wife crash into each other's cars in their home driveway, are mistreated by their current insurance provider, then turn to the advertised company for a better deal and better service.

The whole spot performed very well, with appeal appropriately dipping during the introduction of the problem and rising during the solution phase. The spot was on-emotion. But what stood out as a major pivot point was the ending. There, likeability skyrocketed just as the branded solution came on to the screen. Now that's a good sign that this brand will be remembered well and fondly enough to drive sales results.

Conclusion

When everything is said and done, what does 'persuasion' mean? As science has shown us, it's really about what resonates emotionally and can motivate behaviour. To bypass the emotional dimension is to accept the rationally defensible, good reason as gospel. The informed approach is to remember that priority will be given to ads that feel like they deserve our attention, acceptance and money. Consumers will want the rationally oriented intellectual alibi, but only as a means of justifying what they have already accepted emotionally.

Everybody is interested in the 'how-can-my-life-be-better?' story. Rekindling hope is what advertising is really about. To be effective, advertising must:

- Take the biological instead of the logical route. Be memorable by hitting an emotional 'hot button' in order to make a connection that reverberates. We remember what we internalize, and what we internalize is part of us – and what is part of us is an opportunity a company can sell us on again and again. Companies that are on-emotion don't need to buy as many repetitive placements to gain the audience's attention, thus saving money.

- Move past a statistical, demographic profile of the target market in order to gauge the audience's emotional profile. Then a company will know where to draw the necessary line between stopping power and offence, effective creativity and risky business. When using humour or sex, for example, be wary that the target market may become distracted or offended by the device meant to ensure stopping power. After all, in business what's better than a joke? A sale.

- Answer the question, 'How can we make our offer – and its story – as emotionally large and pertinent as possible in order to reach the widest target market in today's niche-markets?' The message-itis of rational benefits disengages consumers emotionally and exacerbates the problem of stretching both the creative and media dollars across many rationally derived segments.

An action plan

To make sure that the company's advertising is emotionally healthy, here are a few points to check when assessing effectiveness:

- Interest is emotional in nature, so play the emotion card to invite consumers in. To learn whether the company is in the game, discover whether consumers look forward to as well as internalize its advertising. The essence of great advertising is that it disarms the intellect and goes straight to the heart. So quantify the advertising's emotional response rate while also verifying whether it is evoking the desired emotions.
- Learn whether the company's advertising survives the key emotional filters – originality, relevancy, likeability and credibility – and has engaged the motivations that drive its target market's emotions.
- Sample current customers to see whether an advertisement for an offer they've already purchased reinforces its value and provides reassurance, thus reducing the risk of buyer's regret (sadness).
- Bear in mind Maslow's hierarchy of needs and examine, honestly, just how well the company's advertising addresses basic needs first, and then the progressively more complex emotional needs. We all pay attention to what is most necessary, then useful and only then nice to have.
- Gauge the emotional response to the key visual images in the company's ads. Since most consumers don't want to be sold to, and advertising is selling, the visual is the crucial element in getting past consumers' emotional filters and drawing them in. Secure proof that the visuals evoke the desired emotions, and then the company is at least half way home to a successful campaign.
- Reconsider how the company uses focus groups. Question the goal of understanding what consumers think. Very few really great creative advertisements will survive a focus-group study intact if the approach is, 'Look at this and tell me what you think.' The company has just asked the subjects to be rational. So they will try to 'look smart' or 'be safe' and the company will miss the emotional aspect entirely. Instead, make the goal to understand how subjects will feel.

7 Sales

How do prospects feel about being approached? This sign about sums it up. Nobody likes to feel vulnerable.

An emotionally savvy sales partner will make them feel like they're making a safe, beneficial choice instead.

Overview

Nothing in business relies more on face time and emotions than sales. Promoting likeability and trust is everything. How could it be otherwise when the selling process is really a buying process, thus placing a premium on establishing an emotional connection with a potential customer? To help salespeople do a better job creating the kind of rapport that will lead to greater success with prospects, this chapter will focus on:

- **Commitment:** like people, companies give as well as give off information about themselves. From the job interview through the introductory orientation and training, companies sometimes explicitly – but always implicitly – let their sales force know how they expect prospects to be treated. By adopting relationship commitment as a model, companies can ensure that their salespeople will ultimately be more effective. It is a relationship, after all. The average first sale takes seven calls to close, with 80 per cent of purchases coming after the fifth call (Davis, 1996; Coe, 2003). So let the sales force know how to treat prospects sensitively and build trust, which is emotional in nature.
- **Unity:** prospects are on the lookout for signs alerting them to the fact that the salesperson can't be trusted. Every other factor will pale in comparison to this gut-level judgement, which is primarily made on a non-rational basis. The salesperson's conduct must, therefore, involve no miscues. Everything should be consistent from start to finish during the process, with the seller's image and conduct aligning with the branded offer so that the whole package exudes steadfast integrity.
- **Interwoven rewards:** when sales directors take into account the need for after-sale customer support and healthy sales force team dynamics in their coaching and compensation methods, the opportunity for repeat sales is enhanced. That's because the team will feel like they're in it together and will thus aid the cause. To that end, it's essential that salespeople be incentivized on a broader basis, beyond sales volume alone, including factors like the satisfaction they create among customers and colleagues.

Now let's look more closely at how to honour the buying process, starting with how companies can develop sales forces with the right emotional aptitude.

Commitment: adopting a relationship model

Synopsis: Enacting a buyer/seller relationship model starts with hiring and cultivating a sales force with the emotional aptitude to build customer relationships, rather than 'strip mine' for sales. To help accomplish that goal, this section first discusses the opportunity inherent in building a sales force adept at relating to prospects emotionally. Then it highlights the three qualities found in superior salespeople so companies can reduce the costs, financial and otherwise, of salespeople who don't have what it takes to succeed.

Key take-aways

- Loyalty is based on attending to the emotional aspects of the relationship.
- Great salespeople are characteristically upbeat, resilient and caring.

Emotion and motivations.
Salespeople will be quietly consumed by **guilt** if they know the company's unofficial policy in treating prospects is exploitative in nature. Meanwhile, in motivational terms, they will find themselves pushed toward **acquire** by the company's goal of short-sighted and short-term sales profits, while left to **learn** on their own about possible conflicts between their beliefs and the company's.

Why a relationship approach is superior

Loyalty is based on attending to the emotional aspects of the relationship

The idea that salespeople should reorient their thinking and approach prospects using a relationship-based model isn't new. There's been talk about the problems of using a rational, functionally oriented, features-attributes-and-benefits sales approach for some time now. But the extent to which an emotionally informed relationship approach to sales has been adopted remains an open question. Without a more comprehensive understanding of why to change and how to proceed, companies will be tempted to stay with what they know, regardless of the disadvantages involved.

Thus the goal of this chapter is to give directors, managers and their salespeople the perspective and tools that will enable them to implement a true relationship approach. For that to happen, companies must change how they build their sales forces. What does this change look like? It involves procuring and further developing salespeople who are emotionally savvy. To move beyond a transactional approach, salespeople must understand the emotions relevant to buying.

In short, they must be alert to how sensory cues, emotions, motivations, and rationalized intellectual alibis all fit together for the buyer. Moreover, emotionally savvy salespeople are able to align themselves more fully with their prospects due to understanding both verbal and non-verbal communication.

For prospects, the sales process centres on one thing: **safety**. The safety of resources well spent. The safety of affirmation. The safety that they won't be taken advantage of. It is therefore the emotionally savvy salesperson's job to make sure that this overarching need is addressed.

Consider the essence of the buying process. From the prospect's point of view, the buying process begins and ends with a feeling that is pure gut reaction: *safety*. Everybody wants to feel secure, especially when being sold to by a relative stranger. We deal with people we like and we like to be in comfortable situations. So more often than not, prospects instinctively pigeonhole a salesperson as ally or predator. The psychological legacy of having ancestors who spent thousands of years on the savannah trying to avoid an early demise is that if the salesperson is a predator, intent on winning, the prospect must be the prey about to lose. As a result, the reality of sales is that every prospect is afraid of being ripped off and every salesperson is afraid the prospect won't commit.

Real change based on better emotional skills can bring success. An article in *Bank Investment Consultant* (Stock, 2005) profiled an innovative firm specializing in emotional training for financial sector salespeople.

The multi-week programme devotes the first 40 per cent of its time to teaching participants how to utilize emotional intelligence. The pay off? Numbers like these:

- In just two years, a bank's sales force enjoyed a rise in commissions from $16 million to $98 million, with only a relatively small increase in personnel (100 to 125 people) over that same time period.
- At another bank, the emotional intelligence training of new hires alone was enough to boost sales to a figure six times the original forecast – and did so within a single year.

These outcomes reflect the opportunity available to companies that broaden their sales emphasis from a purely rational or logistical approach to one that reflects the impact of emotions. In essence, there are two flawed assumptions that companies often make regarding sales that harm their potential for growth.

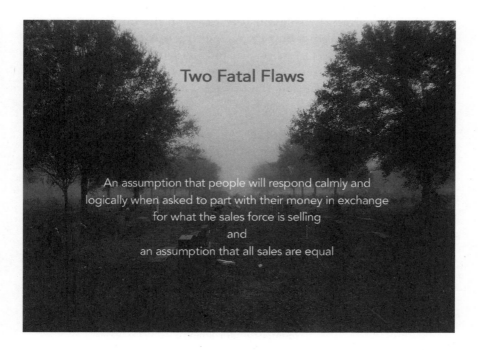

Two Fatal Flaws

An assumption that people will respond calmly and logically when asked to part with their money in exchange for what the sales force is selling
and
an assumption that all sales are equal

The first is an assumption that buyers respond calmly and logically when asked to part with their money in exchange for what the sales force is selling. A traditional, functional approach assumes that good techniques during a sales presentation will close the deal, or that the disclosure and manipulation of facts will bring success.

The second assumption is that all sales are equal. Long-term success in business depends on long-term sales. In other words, repeat sales hinge on fostering a sense of loyalty and partnership. In contrast, sales that are created by tactics such as pressure are short-term in nature and destroy long-term success.

Moreover, a short-term approach doesn't just hurt a company's relationship with prospects. It also hurts the morale of the sales force. Salespeople who know that it isn't their true goal to look out for prospects' best interests will be susceptible to guilt – thereby undermining their ability to stay emotionally sensitive in their jobs long term.

The solution is to establish a sales strategy based on identifying and understanding the prospect's emotions as a means of building relationships. Give prospects what they want, which is security and comfort. The best feeling for a buyer to have after a purchase is being at ease, without doubt or fear or anger. Nobody got sold anything and there's no sense of failure. Instead, buyers feel good about themselves and the offer.

Unfortunately, most companies approach the sales process from a seller's perspective. The solution is to focus on the buying process. To understand selling from a buyer's perspective, it is important to understand what the prospect's criteria are and the specific emotions involved as the process unfolds. Yes, every situation will vary to some extent. But in general, there are five steps in the process (Chitwood, 1996), as outlined in Figure 7.1.

Step	Buyer Decision Factors	Emotional Goal
Approach	Salesperson (company-offer-price-timing)	Comfort
Dialogue	Salesperson/Company (offer)	Respect
Presentation	Salesperson/Offer (company)	Assurance
Negotiation	Salesperson/Price/Timing (company-offer)	Fairness
Follow-up	Salesperson (company-offer-timing)	Security

Figure 7.1   The steps and emotional goals key to the buying process.
The typical buying process has five steps and also five factors that are not equal in importance. (Secondary factors, per step, are listed in parentheses.) What predominates? The salesperson whose personality and ability to create an emotional connection with prospects shapes the opportunity for success. All other factors get viewed by prospects through the lens of their gut-level impression of the salesperson.

What's noteworthy here? First, in stark contrast to a rationally oriented seller's approach, which emphasizes the offer, an emotionally oriented approach recognizes the prospect's emotions as central to the process. It's the emotional strength of the relationship between the salesperson and prospect that drives sales. Indeed, the offer doesn't even become a prominent factor until midway through the buying process. Second, it's important to note that the emotional goals cited in Figure 7.1 are all intended to alleviate fear. Yes, prospects want the seller to provide the offer. But even more so, they want assurance that protects and nurtures not only their safety but also their self-esteem.

Now that we have the buying process model in place, it's time to discuss what it takes to build an emotionally savvy sales force capable of honouring that model. Let's move on to the topic of hiring right.

Building a good team

Great salespeople are characteristically upbeat, resilient and caring

Adopting a relationship model based on the buying process requires you to focus squarely on the prospect and the prospect's emotions. Not everyone can do that well. After all, turning the prospect's fear of vulnerability into relief isn't an easy task. So a company may in theory decide to fulfil the model. But the more important question is whether the personnel hired to implement that model are up to the task.

In *Your Marketing Sucks* (2005), Mark Stevens asserts that 95 per cent of salespeople don't really have what it takes to be a salesperson. In fact, several national tests have shown that 50 per cent of salespeople failed simply because they didn't have the right attitude (Gitomer, 2003; Anderson, Hair and Bush, 1992). With the annual turnover rate in some sales forces near 70 per cent and the average turnover rate estimated at 18 per cent (Heide, 1998), it's hard to disagree: something is indeed wrong.

Part of the solution is to hire salespeople who are better at emotions, and for three reasons:

● The first is that hiring emotionally savvy salespeople makes sense because they will experience more success, stay longer, and therefore reduce the churn that damages the company/customer relationship. Not only do familiarity and rapport help short term; in the long term, continuity creates more credibility for the brand itself.
● Second, high turnover rates have an emotional cost on the salespeople who remain. That's because lots of churn damages morale and internal cohesion.

To create a great sales team, a company has to pick the best apples in the bushel. Making sure that the people who get hired are emotionally savvy is crucial. Facial coding can help ensure that a company doesn't pick a bad apple, thereby limiting its future profitability.

- Third, high turnover rates have a financial cost. Companies must invest time hiring and training new salespeople, depleting existing personnel resources to do so. (See 'The cost of bad hires' for details.)

The Cost of Bad Hires

According to estimates, each bad hire costs at least two times that employee's annual salary. Since the annual salary averages $30,000 in metro areas, a minimum cost per turnover is $60,000.

Therefore, it follows that with an average annual turnover rate for sales forces of 18%, a 100-person sales force has turnover costs of $1.44 million per year. The ability to reduce turnover by even half would save a company $7 million within a decade.

Now that we know the stakes, how can companies build a sales force that is emotional savvy? The first step is to acknowledge that emotions matter. Tom Reilly is on target in *Value Added Selling* (2002) when he notes that 'Selling is an emotional profession – and emotions play a major role in how salespeople do their jobs.' Relevant emotions for salespeople include pride in their company and what they sell, fear of cold-calling and rejection, and disappointment or joy, depending on how their sales opportunities turn out.

> Should one tell you that a mountain has changed its place, you are at liberty to doubt it; but if anyone tells you that a man has changed his character, do not believe it.
>
> Muhammad

While the first step is a matter of perspective, the key second step is incorporating emotion into sales force hiring decisions. Let's look at three emotionally based qualities that will have a huge impact on whether a salesperson has what it takes to succeed:

- **Upbeat.** A good salesperson is always 'up', because someone who exudes the right kind of confidence and success is likely to make a prospect feel 'up' too. Enthusiastic salespeople embody hope, which is contagious. Signs of it will also help prospects intuitively relax because a hard-sell approach is less likely to come from a person exhibiting buoyancy.
- **Resilient.** Being in sales and handling rejection go hand in hand. Anybody who can't be persistent and resilient when it comes to coping with adversity won't last long.
- **Caring.** Here the key is having the kind of empathy that builds rapport. Adroit salespeople make prospects feel as though they have an ally. There's no substitute for being likeable, caring and trustworthy.

Find people with those three qualities and the odds of success significantly improve. In support of that claim, consider the results of a study Sensory Logic did facially coding the emotional expressions of salespeople for a staffing company (Figure 7.2). The chart shows the differences found in facial response during those interviews. After the facially coded data was tabulated, the company's management revealed whether each salesperson we coded was an average or above-average performer. The results verify that tracking emotions in response to hiring questions is an excellent tool for recognizing successful sales candidates.

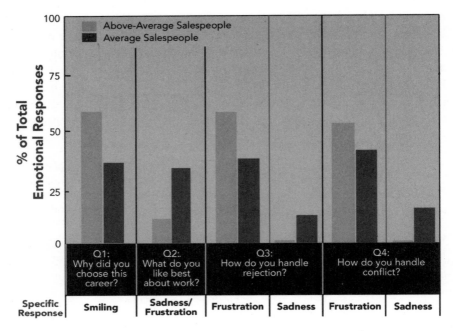

Figure 7.2 Upbeat, resilient and caring: the three qualities of a great salesperson.
This chart shows the results of facial coding salespeople for a staffing company. So what do the specific emotional responses tell us?

- **Upbeat:** Questions 1 and 2 capture optimism in opposite ways. For Question 1, a high level of smiling is present in the above-average performers. For Question 2, these two negative emotions are more than twice as high for the average salespeople, demonstrating their ambivalence toward the job.
- **Resilient:** Question 3 results reveal that above-average salespeople desire progress (hence high frustration) and aren't despairing (low sadness) because rejection doesn't faze them.
- **Caring:** Question 4 results map out similarly to Question 3 because above-average salespeople work through conflict (slightly higher frustration) rather than letting it get them down (low sadness). Here, understanding that disagreement shouldn't lead to a feeling of hopelessness is the key.

The verdict: facial coding does spot winners.

Even without the advantage of facial coding, it's beneficial to account for emotional temperament in hiring. The US Air Force had been dismissing 25 per cent of its recruiters every year because of their failure to meet enlistee quotas (Schwartz, 2000). Then the Air Force added a hiring test that screens for five emotionally related factors: assertiveness, empathy, happiness, self-awareness and problem solving. Within a year the failure rate for not hiring right had dropped to 2 per cent. As a result the Air Force began saving over $2 million in training costs annually while also enabling it to meet recruitment goals more effectively.

Ultimately, making the right hire and encouraging emotionally sensitive salespeople to use their emotional intelligence with prospects will ensure that a company's sales force is composed of capable people who enjoy what they do. That path will result in two big benefits: first, a feeling of pride within the company, and, second, feelings of confidence, comfort and reassurance in those who buy what the salespeople are offering.

Unity: staying in step with the prospect

Synopsis: Salespeople should always interact with prospects in a manner that builds equity. Then if difficulties arise, there's enough trust and rapport to keep the buyer/seller relationship viable. This section looks at how to handle that relationship, from the approach through the negotiation step in the buying process. Highlights include the Great Chain of Buying (how to gauge the prospect's interest) and the Bridge of Consideration (the factors that enable persuasion).

Key take-aways

- Ability and willingness to pay are, most of the time, emotionally based.
- The key to a successful presentation isn't the offer; it's the relationship building that's involved.
- The deep-seated explanations for prospect resistance are always emotional in nature.

Emotion and motivations.
Pride is only possible when prospects don't feel as if they were 'sold' or pushed against their will into a purchase that is unsatisfactory. The fear of being pressured causes prospects to put up protective barriers, which explains why **defend** is the key motivation here. At the same time, however, prospects also seek to **bond** with salespeople they hope are on their side.

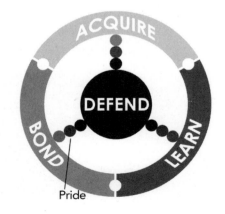

Pride

Approach and dialogue in the buying process

Ability and willingness to pay are, most of the time, emotionally based

Hiring and training people capable of emotional intelligence is vital. Why? From the prospect's point of view, the approach and dialogue steps are uncomfortable because change can be scary. During these steps prospects ask themselves, Why should I meet with someone new? Why should I change? Often their unconscious emotional response is fear.

Prospects may want to mask this discomfort, to both themselves and the salesperson, through intellectual alibis such as that it is not a good offer, not the right price, or the wrong timing, and thereby resist a meeting. Salespeople adept at alleviating fear are relaxed and upbeat. During dialogue they establish value and are seen as a provider, both confident and discerning. They guard their own time and energy by making both a rational and an emotional assessment in initiating the buying process. The overall goal must be to discern the prospect's ability and willingness to pay. Just as the prospects want to know about the company that stands behind the salesperson, so must the salesperson know what resources the prospect has available to draw on.

In the Approach and Dialogue steps, be careful not to plead for the sale.
As soon as that happens, a salesperson goes from *provider* to *beggar.*

Ability to pay is more straightforward, largely but not entirely a rational matter of budgetary resources and authority to spend them. Willingness to pay, on the other hand, may appear to reside in the neo-cortex, seemingly rooted in the rational, but is in reality emotional in nature. Of aid to a salesperson assessing the emotional aspects of winning over a prospect is what I call the Great Chain of Buying (see Figure 7.3).

So what is this Great Chain of Buying? It's a map of the buying process based on the fact that every offer for sale has a chain of greater or shorter length and heavier or lighter emotional weight. For example, a motor vehicle has a buying chain that's both longer and of greater emotional weight than does a banana. That's because a banana gets purchased more frequently and involves less financial as well as emotional significance than purchasing your next car.

The chain organizes the emotional attachment prospects feel toward their current situation, the status quo, into five steps depicted as the two cycles that together comprise the chain. Every offer has its own unique chain. But at the same time, every offer is identical in that a prospect moves through the five steps for any offer he or she considers.

Understanding the dynamics of the chain will help a salesperson understand the emotional realities for the prospect at each of those five steps in the cycle. The chain maps the emotional attachment and interest level a prospect feels towards the offer being presented. Simultaneously, it reveals as an emotional strategy a salesperson can enact to facilitate moving the prospect closer to the desired action: a decision to buy.

The two cycles of the chain intersect only at the purchase step, and from there a prospect moves either back through the cycle of opportunity or through the cycle of satisfaction. Both cycles have a distinct strategy for success. But they are linked by the reality that a purchase depends on aptly projecting the promise of happiness.

The cycle of satisfaction is short and in general terms isn't viable for new sales. That's because prospects either feel good about what they have bought or want to feel good about it, so as not to doubt their purchase decision. Emotionally, the distinction hardly matters. The bottom line is that these prospects won't be inclined to consider a new offer because they're emotionally invested in what they've already chosen. To tell them they've made the wrong choice is tantamount to threatening their self-identity (I'm a loser) as well as undermining their status in the eyes of others, so don't go there.

That being said, there are two stages to the cycle of satisfaction and they involve slightly different emotional realities. Here the **purchase** stage

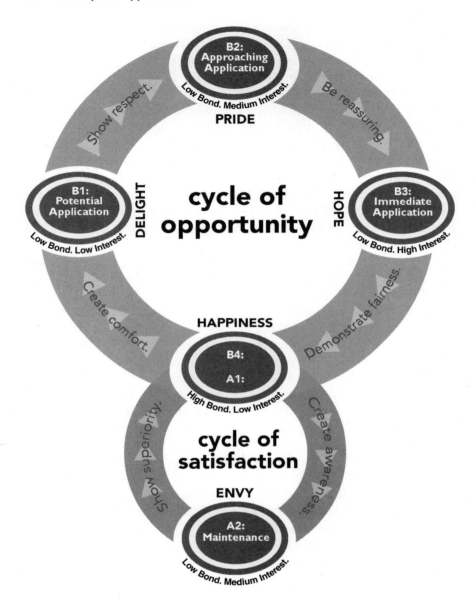

Figure 7.3   The Great Chain of Buying: stages and pertinent emotions.
In the cycle of satisfaction, people are financially and emotionally bonded to the status quo. For those who have recently purchased (A1), create awareness but try for no more. Maintenance (A2) is different. There, gently show the offer's superiority to inspire the envy that might just lead to a future sale.

In the cycle of opportunity, create comfort (B1), respect (B2) and reassurance (B3) in order to leverage emotional equity and close the deal (B4). Along the way, nurture delight, pride and hope in prospects. But be especially careful to demonstrate fairness so that prospects trust that their purchase experience will be a happy one.

(point A1) indicates that prospects have just recently bought an offer. So there's little to no chance that dissatisfaction has emerged yet. As a result, a salesperson can really only present the alternative offer, as an act of creating awareness, because emotionally there is no viable strategy other than to be generous and congratulate those prospects on finding happiness with an offer that works for them. In that way, the salesperson is being a friend and may accrue emotional equity for the future.

Only slightly more promising in terms of sales potential is point A2 in the cycle of satisfaction. The difference here at the **maintenance** stage is that some time has passed since the purchase. So while these prospects remain happy about their choice, they might be less emotionally committed to it because they have come to realize its limitations on their own.

A salesperson shouldn't induce disappointment. At the maintenance point in the cycle of satisfaction, the most a salesperson should be trying to achieve emotionally is to create a slight degree of envy in these prospects. They may sense that the salesperson's new, alternative offer could be superior. A hard sell shouldn't be attempted, however. Otherwise, the emotional outcome will be that the salesperson will have painted him or herself as manipulative (destroying trust) and as the bearer of the bad news that these prospects previously made a poor purchase decision (creating the sadness of buyer's regret). That's a dead end because people will avoid pain whenever possible.

In contrast, the cycle of opportunity is longer but far more promising in terms of the ability of the salesperson to emotionally connect on terms favourable to building a relationship and enacting new sales. Here the cycle consists of four points, based on the degree to which a purchase decision is imminent.

In this case, the end point, B4, is again the purchase stage. Once it's made, the question becomes whether the prospect turned buyer is satisfied with the purchase. If so, those prospects start to travel within the cycle of satisfaction. Salespeople who can take a prospect there have an excellent chance of getting repeat sales if they continue to attend to the relationship. But if satisfaction isn't rendered, then the prospect reenters the cycle of opportunity. Unfortunately, however, that opportunity will most likely exist for a different salesperson.

Prior to purchase, these are the other three stages in the cycle of opportunity:

- **Potential application.** On the left at point B1, prospects have either no immediate need and/or haven't yet separated themselves emotionally from an offer that didn't fully satisfy them. Either way, their goal is to feel comfortable during the approach step. An emotionally savvy salesperson will recognize that prospects at this point in the cycle are limited opportunities for now. Emotionally, the most that should be attempted is to inspire either delight in what the new, alternative offer can achieve or relief that a viable alternative exists.

- **Approaching application.** At point B2, prospects are emotionally prepared to go beyond the approach step and on to the dialogue step. They may need or want a new solution in the not-too-distant future, but they're not there yet. For now, what they want more than the offer the salesperson is selling is to be shown respect. In turn, they may then develop respect for the salesperson who is investing time and effort in getting to know them, thereby building the relationship, rather than simply trying to make a quick sale. Emotionally, the key here is to play to the prospect's sense of pride.

- **Immediate application.** With a pressing need or interest (B3), prospects can be taken right through the approach and dialogue steps on the way to the presentation. That's not to say the salesperson isn't an important focal point or that comfort and respect don't have to be established. Those factors matter. Nevertheless, the reality is that prospects will be open to learning more readily about the offer. Assurance that the salesperson, company and the offer all check out well and are consistently aligned will protect the hope prospects are inclined to feel.

Including purchase (B4), where prospects' faith in fairness is paramount while negotiating the factors of price and timing, those are the four stages of the cycle of opportunity. Note how those four stages also relate to the four first steps in the buying process. Furthermore, note the importance of preserving a feeling of yearning in prospects. That's the overall picture. But since the focus right now is on the approach and dialogue steps, two additional considerations should be introduced before moving on to the presentation step.

The first is the importance of asking questions (Figure 7.4). Yes, an emotionally savvy salesperson uses questions to readily discern where prospects are – in general terms – really at emotionally. But that same person will also use questions to unearth each prospect's specific pain. In revealing the problems inherent in the status quo, prospects become more likely to be emotionally alert to the possibility of finding a new, more fulfilling solution seemingly on their own. In short, good questions move prospects through the cycle of opportunity more quickly and accurately, as a latent desire becomes a vivid possibility waiting to be enacted.

Figure 7.4 The power of asking questions.
It's almost too late to ask questions at the point of negotiating a sale: the earlier, the better. Research indicates that good deal makers ask over twice as many questions as their less effective counterparts (Rackham, 1989).

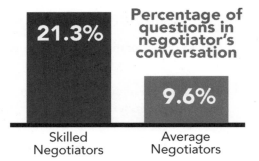

Percentage of questions in negotiator's conversation

21.3%	9.6%
Skilled Negotiators	Average Negotiators

Second, the speed at which prospects move through the cycle of opportunity will likewise be influenced by whether the emotionally savvy salesperson gets prospects to focus on their needs or their wants during the approach and dialogue steps (Figure 7.5). What's the difference between a need and a want? The first is more rational. The second is pure emotion. Guess which one prospects will pay more for? You're right, satisfying wants that involve aspirations.

Needs	Wants
Air	Blue Skies
Apartment	Mansion

Figure 7.5 Needs and wants are not the same.
What's the difference between needs and wants? Emotion. Which is more appealing: a shaker of salt or the lightly salted edge of a chilled margarita glass?

The bottom line during the approach and dialogue steps is to set up the first part of the formula that applies to the whole buying process:

Lead with wants.

Follow with value.

Close with price.

Whatever happens during the first two steps of the buying process, the emotionally savvy salesperson will remember one other truth: never try to create a need. Why? Because it takes forever. Prospects know their own circumstances best. Don't try force-feeding them. After all, that's not what we do to friends when building a relationship.

Now that we've discussed the cycle of opportunity, including in relation to wants, let's focus next on establishing value during the presentation step.

The presentation step in the buying process

The key to a successful presentation isn't the offer; it's the relationship building that's involved

The specifics of an offer are always overshadowed by emotional factors. So, given how they're often trained by their companies, salespeople make the mistake of rushing to emphasize the rational utilitarian aspect of an offer. In doing so they lose a valuable opportunity to better understand and thereby influence the prospect by listening to that person's concerns. Among those concerns is an emotional judgement about the degree to which the prospect feels at ease with, or wants to continue to interact with, the salesperson.

To put the presentation itself into this context, consider the six principles of influence outlined by the psychologist R B Cialdini (as outlined in O'Shaughnessy, 2003). Of the six, four are emotional in nature, while the other two are more rational. They will be examined later. Here are the four emotional principles:

- **Liking.** Prospects will initially focus on whether they enjoy the salesperson's presence, meaning whether they like the person they are with. Over subsequent meetings, if the interactions have been supportive and pleasant, familiarity will grow and the degree of liking will increase. But up front and at first, prospects are alert – even wary – and must be put at ease. Likeability is especially pertinent during the approach step, when establishing comfort for the prospect is vital.

The other three emotional influencers are compatibility, reciprocity and consistency. While emergent during the approach step, they mostly come into focus for prospects during the dialogue step. They consist of:

- **Compatibility.** Training programmes that tell salespeople to 'mirror' and 'match' the prospect's body language are half right. Ultimately, even more important is identifying and respecting the prospect's belief system. Remember that nothing is more innate or deeply emotional than a person's worldview. Reflecting a prospect's beliefs respectfully is imperative because people are comfortable with and like those who are like them.
- **Reciprocity.** Both liking and compatibility can be reinforced through favours or small signs of courtesy that invite reciprocity from prospects. Not only do people feel socially obligated to return favours, doing so makes them feel good. Through such acts of mutual generosity an emotionally savvy salesperson can add 'glue' to the budding relationship.

- **Consistency.** Consistency matters because during the first few encounters a prospect is still trying to figure out who the salesperson really is as a person. A consistent manner will help increase comfort in the belief that the personality on display will stay the same once the deal is signed and support services may be required. Consistency demonstrates integrity. As such, it also sets up the quality of assurance that will make the presentation itself far more effective.

Commercial copy:
"Hi! I'm Doug Harrison. My wife Suzanna and I started The SCOOTER Store because we believe that everyone has the right to enjoy life to the fullest."

What's analogous to a salesperson making an in-person pitch? A company spokesperson appearing in a direct response TV commercial. In such formats, body language that supports the message is imperative.

In work we did for The SCOOTER Store, the goal was to analyze viewer responses to commercials from America's leading supplier of scooters and power chairs for people of limited mobility. On camera at left is founder and CEO Doug Harrison aptly using his smile to project the enjoyment his company aims to bring customers by restoring their mobility and independence.

Sales presentations and delivery styles can likewise be critiqued with facial coding to identify what works best in achieving emotional buy-in from prospects.

Consider that asking your prospect to listen to your presentation and decide to purchase your offer has an equivalent. It's like asking him or her to cross a bridge that is perceived as being dangerous: an unlikely scenario, but a useful one to make a point. Faced with a decision like that, most people's instinct is to say no, unless there exists one of two circumstances. The first is that the bridge is the only means that exists to take prospects where they want to go. The other is that there is imminent danger and they must cross the bridge to survive.

Figure 7.6   The bridge of consideration and influence factors.
The bridge of consideration involves crossing from emotional factors to rational factors by way of the presentation. In order to successfully do so, a salesperson must adequately address all six influence factors (represented as cars) and manage to appeal to the emotional needs of the prospect (shown above the cars). If the salesperson can maintain emotional awareness throughout the whole process and make the prospect feel safe, he or she will gain a loyal customer.

The reason why this bridge metaphor (Figure 7.6) was chosen is as follows. Yes, the formal presentation of the offer is vital, the actual crossing of the bridge – the purpose of the presentation itself – is for the prospect an emotional decision that occurs quickly. Because this decision also happens intuitively, salespeople must not force a prospect to cross over before that person is ready. Once the bridge is crossed, however, that motion indicates you have built up emotional equity and your prospect is ready to listen to the rational alibis that so often are the only real aspects of a sales presentation.

The give-and-take of listening to and empathizing with a prospect (building trust) has a dual benefit. Not only does it help the salesperson to customize the presentation to the needs and wants of the prospect, it also begins to establish value for a prospect. Why is this? Far from being decided rationally, value is primarily an emotional proposition. Worth gets evaluated subjectively. The trust a salesperson has established in a prospect will migrate into establishing trust in the value of the offer. Moreover, placing the value of the offer within the framework of trust will help in the negotiations step to follow.

To protect customer-centric value and bolster the long-term customer relationship, the astute salesperson will stay focused on the prospect during the presentation. Doing so reduces errors in three ways:

- It minimizes the chance that prospects will tune out emotionally because the interaction continues to emphasize their wants and WIIFM (what's in it for me).
- It makes it less likely that the offer will seem like a 'stretch' for prospects, since their needs and ability to pay will have been kept front of mind.
- It helps to avoid negativity concerning rival offers, which will increase comfort levels. A long-term, viable relationship is based on positives. Going negative is a disconnect because it threatens to undermine the tone of respectfulness ideally created during the dialogue step.

Stay focused on the prospect's needs and wants

Remember that telling entails describing tangible features. It's overly rational. Selling entails touching the prospect's inner self with an offer's emotional benefits and doing so in personal terms.

All six of Cialdini's influence principles are crucial. So let's move past the first four that occur before the 'instant' emotional decision to cross over the bridge of consideration, and consider the remaining pair that comes into play after crossing over. These last two principles, authority and scarcity, are indeed more rational in nature. But in truth, the rational never fully separates from the emotional. That reality becomes evident by examining the end goal of a presentation: to generate belief in the offer. Belief involves justification, which is rational. But it also entails acceptance of the salesperson's authority, which is based on trust and faith and is therefore emotional in nature.

Lastly, scarcity also comes with a rational veneer. 'Limited availability' is the cry that plays on people's instinctive desire to acquire both for survival's sake and for the novelty of the new. Scarcity can be hinted at during the presentation. But it is most helpful during the negotiation step, which is examined next.

The negotiation step in the buying process

The deep-seated explanations for prospect resistance are always emotional in nature

Salespeople will be effective to the extent they realize that the longer the buying process stays primarily in the sensory and emotional parts of the brain, the better, and here's why. As discussed earlier in this book, most of people's thought processes are rooted in the intuitive, subconscious, nonverbal realm in which the two oldest parts of the mind specialize ('What'). Thus the heart of the matter is truly the heart of the matter. The longer and more often the salesperson gets close to prospects emotionally, the greater the extent to which a connection can be formed.

During the approach and dialogue steps, we saw that the focus of the prospect's attention is primarily the salesperson. Then during the presentation step, the focus expands to include the offer itself. And now during the negotiation step, the focus on the offer shifts again to include price and timing – though the underlying emotional issue is ensuring a sense of fairness.

Why should a salesperson avoid discussing price too early in the buying process? Price only has to be heard for the offer to be pigeonholed. Value has to be assessed.

The emotionally savvy salesperson recalls from Chapter One that in making something happen (a purchase), only the sensory and emotional parts of the brain drive muscle activity. So that same salesperson knows that looking for rational explanations when trying to understand resistance is less effective than looking for the emotional factors behind the resistance. When salespeople hear 'no' from their prospects, here are the three key emotional causes:

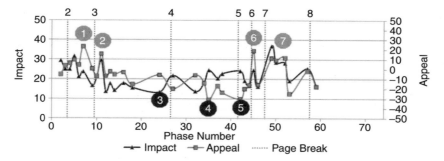

1	Phrase 8: "[The drug] possesses the efficacy."	HIGH APPEAL
2	Phrase 11: "today recommend treatment goals below 100 mg/dl"	HIGH IMPACT/ APPEAL
3	Phrase 24: "recently at the 2007 [Drug Convention] announced"	LOW IMPACT
4	Phrases 34–35: "and 26% of patients on [competitor]. / In comparison to [other competitor], the difference was even more significant…"	LOW APPEAL
5	Phrase 42: "With [drug] more patients than ever get the most effective LDL-C lowering available."	LOW APPEAL
6	Phrase 45: "You can achieve these dramatic LDL-C reductions and superior goal attainment"	HIGH IMPACT/ APPEAL
7	Phrases 50–52: "you have four choices / to get your patients to the goal value / Maintain their current [dose]"	HIGH IMPACT/ APPEAL

Figure 7.7 Linking second by second to a script.
This chart is from a pharmaceutical company study detailing the emotional response of doctors while listening to a sales script detailing a drug's benefits. Facial coding results can be time-stamped and linked to individual words or phrases, allowing for the most in-depth and accurate measure of subjects' feelings about particular segments of the script, thereby enabling specific improvements. In this case, more carnal, personal language and high-level aspirational statements worked better than in-the-weeds details.

- The salesperson has failed to establish his or her own personal credibility in the emotional influence terms of liking, compatibility, reciprocity and consistency.
- The salesperson has failed to establish the value of the offer in emotional terms.
- Finally, ironically enough, there is price itself, which may seem to be rational in nature, but in reality is imbued with emotion based on whether or not it feels fair to the prospect.

Now, granted, my earlier suggestion to close with price might seem strange. Not only does it raise the spectre of a discount, it would also seem that a prospect without funds would mean the end of the road. However, if the original meeting wasn't cut short after the due diligence of discerning

Figure 7.8   Money matters when the offer matters.
Negotiating about price means value has been established and the prospect is
interested in the terms of the offer. Serious negotiations then come down to three
conditions: the size of the need/want, the fit of the offer to the solution, and the
strength of the salesperson's relationship with the prospect. (Graph based on Rackham,
1989, used with permission from Huthwaite® and not to be reproduced. For more
information, visit www.huthwaite.com.)

true ability to pay, then both parties must have felt that the relationship
had potential. Indeed, the purchase may be just over the horizon. As
Figure 7.8 shows, price concerns arise when a deal is imminent.

So an initial 'no' related to price shouldn't be a big concern. Remember
that while 80 per cent of directly stated objections are price related, one-
half to two-thirds of sales supposedly lost because of 'price' are largely due
to other factors (Rackham, 1989).

That initial 'no' may simply be a prospect seeking a price break in order
to feel smart or to justify the purchase to the boss. Complaints about price
also provide a respectable, rational intellectual alibi, which is easier to
express than emotional concerns such as doubt about value or fear of an
offer that a prospect doesn't understand.

Assuming a real opportunity exists, what's the smartest emotional
means of handling 'No'? It's certainly not to attack fear head-on using
facts. That approach serves up a double whammy: increasing the
prospect's worry that the salesperson is a predator while also driving fear
deeper underground. The bottom line? Fear can't be eased logically.
Instead, an emotionally savvy salesperson should try to earn and retain
the prospect's trust. In other words, personal brand equity is really the
key because reasons don't persuade – people do.

Emotionally savvy salespeople can take two approaches in negotiations:

Hope means showing prospects that they can do more, be more and have more by acquiring the offer. On the other hand, fear is about making sure prospects don't forget the emotional pain and cost of their current predicament.

In preparing for a career in sales, people should take the initiative to examine both their own personal brand equity and the brand equity in the company they are considering for employment. As suggested in Chapter 4 on branding, which salespeople should also read, such a step entails understanding the character traits and the image associations most likely to accrue in prospects' minds over time. For instance, salespeople should ask themselves, 'What traits stand out about me, and how do they manifest themselves?' Moreover, 'Are the traits and associations being communicated consistently linking me, the company and the offer in emotional terms?'

Then during the buying process – and especially amid negotiations that have proven to be difficult – emotionally savvy salespeople have two approaches to rely on. The first approach is to guide prospects toward the emotion of hope: the dream of being more, having more, or doing more.

But since people tend to hear bad news more loudly than good news, the second approach is probably even more important: keep prospects focused on the emotional cost of the problem they are facing. Then re-establish the value of the solution you are providing. After that – since we don't rush our friends – sit back. Salespeople tend to like the chase. But in this case, they should cease chasing. Prospects must be given the time to feel for themselves the dire necessity of the change being offered.

The six truths faces tell salespeople

Salespeople seeking to anticipate prospects' buying motives, hidden objections and warning signs in time to influence the outcome of meetings and negotiations, should always be on the alert for these six specific signals:

- **Giving inadvertent offence.** Where's the fine line in challenging the prospect's ties to his or her current supplier? You'll know if you see the prospect tense up: the lower lip may tighten, for instance, or else the person's eyes narrow. Then you had better cross back over the line as quickly and smoothly as you can.
- **Coming on too strong.** Sales situations often involve fear: notably the prospect's fear of being cornered. How might you tell? The answer lies either in upraised eyebrows and wrinkles that emerge on the forehead, or else the prospect's mouth subtly pulling wider. Should you see those signals, slow down and try to get the prospect back into a selling atmosphere that feels more comfortable.
- **Failing to establish likeability or credibility.** Sometimes you can lose the sale almost immediately by not creating rapport with the prospect. Then you may see the nose wrinkle or upper lip rise in a sign that you've been rejected. Even more fatal: the corner of the mouth tightens in a sign of contempt because the prospect doesn't find your claims believable.
- **Ignoring lack of satisfaction.** Repeat sales and word-of-mouth endorsements are the surest way to build volume easily. But if disappointment surfaces, in the form of buyer's regret, the inattentive salesperson may not notice the corners of the mouth pulling down or the cheeks lifting obliquely away from the mouth in what looks to be a smile but is, in fact, a sign of sadness.
- **Seizing on opportunities for momentum.** There's a difference between a true smile and a social smile that plays mostly around the mouth. With a true smile, the eyes twinkle, the upper eyelid droops and the outer eyebrows may droop, too. Real pleasure as signalled in these ways should alert the salesperson to reinforce the statement or benefit that inspired it; to do otherwise is to miss an opportunity to enhance the volume of the sale, the profit margin or both.
- **Being deceived.** At least flat-out rejection by a prospect doesn't waste your time. Much worse are the maybes that are really nos. Be wary of smiles that don't have a natural rhythm or flow to them. Moreover, frozen smiles or Charlie Chaplin-like grimace smiles are actually a warning to move on.

Interwoven rewards: creating a 'we' mentality

Synopsis: Much depends on how the context for the buyer/seller interaction is set up by the company. Management should protect the opportunity for repeat sales by making sure salespeople are motivated to look out for the prospect even after the sale is made. To that end, this section focuses on the follow-up to a sale, when the salesperson and the supporting staff must stay committed. How to make sure that happens? In part, the answer lies in financial benefits structured to reward teamwork and customer satisfaction.

Key take-aways

- Sales forces interact best with the company when they don't get too isolated.
- Incentives should reward proven loyalty to customers and colleagues alike.

Emotion and motivations.

What makes **envy** the dominant emotion with regard to the follow-up step, and especially in terms of compensation, is more a matter of relationships within the company. Fellow salespeople and support staff may feel envious on seeing others do better financially, thereby harming teamwork. Colleagues and customers alike, however, will find their expansive desire to **bond** with the salespeople they know transformed into an instinct to **defend** their own interests if they sense an 'I've got mine' attitude.

The follow-up step in the buying process

Sales forces interact best with the company when they don't get too isolated

A common mindset in sales force management is to think of the salesperson as a conquering hero, who wins the war but doesn't have to worry about the peace because the money's been made. The problem with this scenario is that nobody else really wants the salesperson to be victorious. That's certainly true of prospects turned customers, and may even be true of general employees or fellow sales force members at the salesperson's own company.

Externally, the reason is simple: the salespeople who 'win' and make a show of their success offend customers who fear it means they've been conquered and may be abandoned. Nobody likes to feel as if he or she has been manipulated for monetary reward. Internally, there's also trouble. That's because money really does motivate people. Our need to acquire is driven by our fears about survival. Leading and less successful salespeople eye one another warily, concerned about the modern-day equivalent of survival: status. As a result, envy may surface as the dominant emotion within the sales force. The end result of this tension is that everyone ends up worse off, including the customers, whose paperwork and follow-up requests require the interaction of staffers and salespeople.

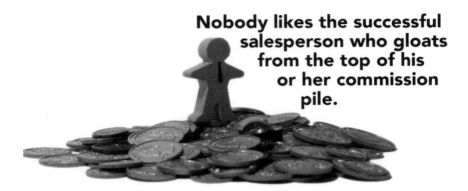

Nobody likes the successful salesperson who gloats from the top of his or her commission pile.

Consider survey results regarding the top five frustrations people have with salespeople. The first three are poor communication skills, lack of knowledge of the customer's company, and overly aggressive selling. But the fourth and fifth greatest aggravations both involve the crucial follow-up step: slow delivery or failure to deliver fully on what was promised (Davis, 1996).

To examine the impact of daily sales force management practices, let's focus on how the sales force is coached. The sales force leadership must remember that salespeople are looking to see whether the leadership walks the talk. A sales director or manager may encourage the sales force to get closer to both potential and repeatable customers out in the field. But if that same person does nothing to foster goodwill between the sales force and the staff in the home office, it creates an obvious disconnect.

As Figure 7.9 shows, that's the situation a homebuilding company in the Philadelphia area faced, as confirmed by Sensory Logic's sales force interviews. Diagnosed and confirmed through facial coding, the situation became clear to all involved. With crucial information in hand, the company was then able to move forward by stopping the flow of mixed messages.

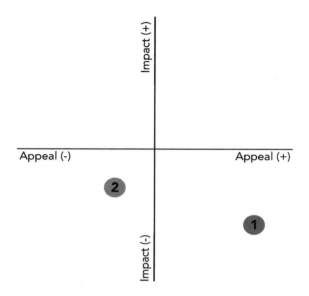

1 What is your reaction when a potential customer wants to tell you their side of the story?

2 How do you feel about your daily interactions with fellow employees outside the sales force?

Figure 7.9   Sales team split personality.
Being encouraged to be closer to prospects (Q1 results) while being kept isolated from and, therefore, at odds with the rest of the company (Q2 results) isn't a viable strategy. A sales force should intuitively want all the allies it can muster. Good sales force management involves implementing policies that show empathy for prospects while getting the sales force on the same page with supporting staff.

Retention and motivation practices

Incentives should reward proven loyalty to customers and colleagues alike

With regard to sales force management, motivation and retention practices should also adhere to the fundamental truth that emotions matter. Thus the basis on which performance is judged should look beyond sales volume alone toward efforts made to inspire feelings of loyalty among customers and camaraderie among co-workers. The sales force leadership should reconsider rewarding sales team members only with monetary bonuses in order to inspire potentially greater feelings of loyalty to the company.

Figure 7.10   The potential relationship gap.
Carole King sings, 'Will you still love me tomorrow?' In a similar vein the prospect wants to know, 'Will the salesperson still care after the sale is made?' Good salespeople know that they fulfil a customer service role if they want repeat sales (Owen and Miller, 2004).

Let's start with performance evaluation criteria. As Figure 7.10 indicates, the typical salesperson checks out the moment the sale is complete, figuring the deal is done. But that's not how it feels for customers. They're now committed and seeking support because, as Figure 7.11 indicates, they're often left struggling to learn how to use what they bought.

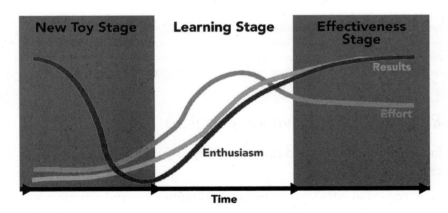

Figure 7.11   Stages of motivation and implementation.
As this charts shows, it is important to help buyers out. As they move past initial enthusiasm and into the nitty-gritty stages of actual knowledge and use, their amount of effort will yield less results than anticipated, leading to a drop in enthusiasm for the offer and purchase (salesperson included). On the other hand, as the buyers' results improve, enthusiasm resumes. (Graph based on Rackham, 1989, used with permission from Huthwaite® and not to be reproduced. For more information, visit www.huthwaite.com.)

Given the adverse, long-term impact that poor support is likely to have on the company's reputation, something more is needed to ensure that post-sale support is enacted. That extra step involves job evaluations and incentives based on multiple factors. Individual sales volume will of course be part of any evaluation. But it's also worth considering giving weight to the degree to which the salesperson interacts well with post-sale customers and fellow employees.

As to just what kind of non-monetary incentive or bonus a salesperson might receive for superior performance, one idea is a tangible reward like a desirable high-tech device or a holiday package. At present, cash rewards are probably more prevalent than tangible bonuses. But tangibles have psychological merit, as they provide the opportunity to incentivize a sales-person in a way that's more emotionally engaging than cash (Jeffrey, nd). For instance, every time a salesperson uses the awarded device or reminisces about a particular vacation, emotions will be rekindled. Such reinforcement is less likely to happen if the reward was cash, which might have been spent paying off a credit card bill or used in other ways that leave no traces.

As Figure 7.12 demonstrates, tangible incentives can be competitive with monetary rewards. In this case, one involving a major technology company's sales force, Sensory Logic determined that bikes and camcorders were either

Figure 7.12   Emotional response: cash versus prize.
In this test, two items were preselected as benchmarks. The emotional verdict favoured the bike but not the camcorder being presented. These results surely had to do with personal interest in the reward, and could be improved on in a real-life situation where a catalogue of choices would be made available. In comparison, the greater social comfort involved in telling a colleague about a tangible reward made it the emotional winner hands-down over cash.

ahead of or as well received as cash. Moreover, based on our emotional analysis, tangible rewards seem to be more socially acceptable than cash in terms of public discussion among the sales team. As a result, tangible rewards do double duty. They keep the heart warm over the long term and have more discreet social reinforcement value.

However salespeople are rewarded, it is important to choose and distribute rewards so that two results predominate. The first is that sales-people should be reminded that current work that builds on past sales relationships are important to management. (Therefore, those relation-ships are more likely to be valued.) The second is that the sales team remains a team, with members who are emotionally connected.

Conclusion

Prospects follow their gut instincts. Just as emotion comes before reason, feelings about the status of the relationship with the seller come before paying attention to the quality of the offer. Just as, inevitably, belief in the offer follows from trust in the seller. So to be effective, sales force direc-tors, managers and their sales teams must accomplish the following:

- Move beyond the common orientation that implicitly and unknow-ingly treats salespeople as heroes and casts the prospect as prey to be subdued through aggressive, rational arguments. Emotionally smart hires will be attuned to taking a truly relationship-based approach to sales.
- Make the buying process about the prospect at every stage, from approach through negotiation and follow-up. Salespeople should take the time to ask questions and clue prospects into the degree of pain they're feeling with the status quo, making a change to the new offer easy to consider. Then provide post-sale assurances that the purchase was wise, including documentation of good news concerning the offer and its implementation, to help alleviate any unresolved fears and cement the bond between buyer and seller. These steps will allow the salesperson to influence future decision criteria.
- Avoid buyer regret by addressing prospects' needs post-sale. Also be proactive about dissipating inter-company and inter-sales force envy before it becomes corrosive. Both initiatives will be more likely to happen if the right coaching and reward structures are in place. Ideally, bonuses should be determined by calculating not just complete sales but also the degree to which satisfaction exists in the hearts of customers.

An action plan

To make sure that sales force efforts are emotionally healthy, here are a few things to check when assessing effectiveness:

- Hire salespeople who can provide consistency not just in giving the pitch the same way, but who can also match the offer and their style of presenting themselves with the company's preferred image. They should know that knowledge about what they're selling isn't a substitute for learning their prospects' feelings.
- Train the sales force to recognize and connect rational explanations (the intellectual alibis) to what are essentially emotional motivations for purchase. A well-constructed pitch balances practical needs with emotional wants.
- Develop two emotional templates. The first involves the qualities any new job candidate must meet. The second concerns the emotions that prospects will probably experience. Besides wallet-based issues, what emotional factors influence the way various prospects respond? Identifying that framework will make it easier to handle resistance to purchase.
- Verify that the sales force believes in what it's selling so that prospects believe, too.
- Strive to build trust between management and the sales team as well as within the sales team itself. Otherwise, it's difficult to maintain a spirit of optimism and prospects will sense a lack of hope, which could be fatal to winning them over. The sales force members should enjoy a positive group identity that makes them feel like they belong to something that will nurture and protect them.

8 Retail and service

Were you satisfied? Nothing is more emotional for consumers or dangerous for companies than an unsatisfied customer. Why? When we are dissatisfied it's personal, and the transgression is announced to all who will listen. Delight, on the other hand, motivates people to spend more.

Overview

How truly satisfied are 'satisfied' customers? As chairman of the National Automobile Dealers Association, Alan Starling described the feedback system used by automakers as 'broken' and in dire need of fixing. No wonder the number of companies tracking customer satisfaction dropped by 26 per cent during the late 1990s (McEwen, 2004). And yet according to the Conference Board, the single biggest concern for CEOs is retaining their existing customers (Applebaum, 2001). Thus a more sensitive approach to consumers' retail and service experiences makes sense because what is loyalty, after all, if not an emotion? Protecting one's revenue stream is too important not to get to the heart of the matter. To help companies better gauge and reinforce consumer loyalty in the context of shopping, this chapter will focus on:

- **Respectfulness:** people prefer to do business with companies that make shopping and customer service experiences more convenient – for consumers. Showing respect means operating so people can see that a company values their time and energy. Eliminating inconvenience whenever possible enables customers to feel like they are being honoured instead of ignored, trapped or rebuffed. Respect starts with acknowledgment, as in being noticed. But it really means the right to achieve one's goals on one's own terms and as efficiently as possible.
- **Engagement:** because a desire for excitement animates the heart, curiosity is a huge part of why people like to shop. To satisfy people's urge to explore, merchants can gain an edge by playing to the senses. That involves creating an emotional connection by studying shoppers' experiences, identifying sweet-spot opportunities and eliminating sore spots. Meanwhile, customer service departments can do their part by ensuring that people get the opportunity to tell their tales of woe – but only once – to somebody qualified to provide a satisfying resolution.
- **Reassurance:** shopping lets people see how well they fashionably fit in, making just the right choices at the right prices. To make retail and e-tail more than just a price war – and to make stores and websites more than just battlegrounds – merchants must help customers experience a sense of community. Then shoppers can vicariously belong to the social groups to which they aspire, as well as interact and support each other with advice. But support alone doesn't eliminate the need for help from customer service representatives who are able to provide real assistance.

Now let's look more closely at how buying the offer and getting service related to it can lead to satisfaction and loyalty, starting with what happens when consumers initiate these activities.

Respectfulness: enabling efficiency

Synopsis: Nobody likes to be disregarded. Yet companies too often seem to be treating customers that way by failing to eliminate bottlenecks and facilitate a sense of control. This section will address the emotional cost of neglecting to give customers satisfactory access to service. What will follow next is analysis of the underlying psychological reasons why delays affect human nature so severely.

Key take-aways

- With customer service, what's really at stake is a person's sense of self-worth.
- A feeling of loss underlies customers' distaste for having inefficiency imposed on them.

'Can you hear me now?'

With customer service, what's really at stake is a person's sense of self-worth

There are two good reasons for opening a discussion of customer satisfaction and loyalty with customer service. First, of all the marketing mediums nothing else is more emotional for the consumer or more dangerous for the company than customer service. That's because service comes closest to affecting the customer's inner self.

After all, what concerns people most deeply? Hint: it's not the company they've bought from or even the offer purchased. Rather, it's their sense of personal worth and security. In a service situation, the company has customers' full attention because they've bought and are now typically trying to rectify a problem. Their purpose, however, isn't not only to salvage the purchase but rather, ultimately, to defend their belief that they made an informed purchase decision that benefits them. In other words, respectfulness from a company helps to protect customers' own self-respect.

Second, because shopping and customer service are typically self-initiated activities, they invite expectations of having it your way. But as we'll soon see, those expectations often run directly counter to the experiences people have shopping or seeking service.

As a result, Verizon's famous catch phrase – 'Can you hear me now?' – is unfortunately an apt place to start in establishing why the respectfulness

Emotion and motivations.
For weary or frustrated consumers, the context is as crucial as what gets bought – making **relief** the crucial emotional outcome. The difficulties consumers experience shopping or initiating customer service requests makes them want to **defend** their limited supply of energy and attention. But as the real purpose of shopping and service is to **acquire** something, and remain satisfied with it, defend remains relevant right through the customer service stage.

opportunity is so important. What the phrase highlights, in essence, is a lone individual trying to reach somebody else in real time, using technology meant to facilitate, not hinder, the communications process. As Verizon's phrase implicitly acknowledges, however, the reality is that technology doesn't always live up to its promise. Disappointment, even outright rage, can result.

> A lot of companies fall into the trap of believing that some new customer-service technology will take cost and management burden away and will eliminate the need to have very talented people on the phones and in their retail outlets.
>
> Dan Leemon, former chief strategy officer, Charles Schwab

Based on Verizon's catch phrase, people's attempts to contact a company by phone for service provides a natural segue into talking about, first, simply being acknowledged. For financial reasons, adequate staffing to handle all service calls doesn't seem to be on the cards. The expense would simply be too great. At least that's the official, rational explanation. But just how reasonable is it? Research indicates that it's five times as expensive to gain a new customer as it is to retain a current one (Desatnick and Detzel, 1993). Moreover, not only will 80 per cent of a company's dissatisfied customers do business with it again if the company can solve their problems quickly, they will also spend three times as much as other customers (Desatnick and Detzel, 1993; Gitomer, 2003).

So getting off on the wrong foot by failing to have attentive and available staff doesn't seem to be a patently sound business argument. Yes, protecting profitability by holding down costs is valid. But to date, the trade-off involved in terms of possibly sacrificing customer satisfaction and loyalty has been a strategic operating decision companies have made without the benefit of complete information. In short, you have to wonder: what's the trade-off in terms of dollars lost through negativity generated? To learn the emotional cost to companies of being disrespectful of their customers' time and efforts, Sensory Logic conducted a test. Our goal? To quantify the extent of people's displeasure with not getting their service needs handled immediately.

Figure 8.1 shows the results for various types of customer service delays, where waiting runs contrary to consumers' desire to have it their way immediately. The types of delays we tested for consisted of: 1) an in-person customer service desk (simulation of an airport delay: for instance, subjects were shown a videotape of people left waiting in line to get a question answered), 2) a call centre help desk audio recording with either background music or 3) a company's promotional 'spiel' played at discreet intervals, and finally, 4) a website that subjects were forced to wait to download.

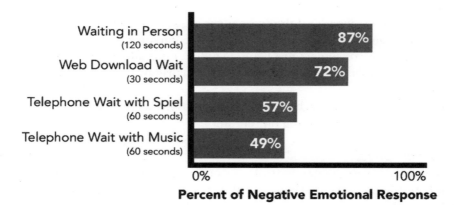

Percent of Negative Emotional Response

Figure 8.1   Oh, how we hate to wait.
Sensory Logic ran simulations to see how people responded to being forced to wait. This chart shows the results. Obviously, people are most offended when being forced to wait in-person. But none of the results supports the practice of keeping people 'on hold'. Only the wait with music option neutralized people enough to bring as many smiles to their faces as it did negative feelings like disgust and anger.

Obviously, any kind of wait rankles people. Hearing some music while waiting for help is better than hearing a spiel in terms of reducing negativity. But all delays sent people into a foul emotional state. Thus the overwhelming conclusion to be drawn is that it would be worthwhile for companies to invest more resources in handling wait times. They can do so with more staffing, or at a minimum, through even moderately pleasant distractions like music, that at least makes a nod at designing the experience to be emotionally more acceptable.

Why delays and inconvenience are so harmful

A feeling of loss underlies customers' distaste for having inefficiency imposed on them

Now that we can quantify the negative emotion felt as a result of waiting, what must companies do to overcome such negativity and create instances of customer satisfaction and loyalty? From a psychological and emotional perspective, there are three key reasons that delays and inconvenience matter so much to people and are, therefore, in need of being resolved by companies. From the consumers' point of view, they consist of:

- **Loss of control:** being forced to wait or otherwise suffer inconvenience against their will means that consumers have relinquished control.
- **Doubt:** delays and inconvenience lead to inefficiency that makes consumers wonder if the company is a failure in general.
- **Avoidance:** difficulty interacting with a company can create the suspicion that consumers are being avoided, especially when technology seems to serve as more of a shield than a bridge.

Let's briefly look at each of those three reasons as related to shopping, service, or both, depending on relevancy.

Loss of control

A desire to exert greater control over one's immediate environment is an innate human priority (Pooler, 2003). It's not hard to understand why. Without control people feel less secure and more vulnerable and, therefore, experience fear that is ultimately related to survival instincts. This control/fear syndrome readily applies both to shopping and service situations, though in opposite ways.

Why do people shop? Yes, for the functional benefits, of course: clothes to keep them warm, food to sustain them, etcetera. But another reason, pertinent to the problem of inconvenience, is in order to exercise control. As a self-initiated activity from which the other party – the merchant – can realize a financial benefit, consumers expect the clerks and the company in general to affirm their importance. In other words, the act of shopping gives people enjoyment and they expect a degree of deference to be shown by company representatives trying to satisfy shoppers' needs and wants. A chance to be in power and make decisions speaks to a desire to control one's own destiny, which is among the psychological forces driving the shopping experience.

Consumers want a shopping experience to be like on-demand TV: when they want it, on their terms and under their control.

In contrast, customer service situations aren't about exercising control but, rather, trying to regain it. What customer hasn't felt vulnerable, knowing he or she has spent the money and now hopes the company – a much larger entity – will still care about making the deal come out right?

Doubt

People naturally like to ally themselves with winners while avoiding losers. The same rule of thumb applies to shoppers, who would rather frequent companies that have their act together. Again, it's a matter of feeling respected and responding in kind. After all, consumers don't have to put up with inferior performers.

How important is ease of access and convenience in general? Consider a pair of research findings, which together cover both retail and e-tail:

- With regard to traditional brick-and-mortar retailing, a survey found that 64 per cent of consumers say they will leave a store if checking out takes too long. Meanwhile, 70 per cent say they make a point to shop at stores that don't waste their time (Ander and Stern, 2004).
- With regard to e-tailing, a study found that less than 40 per cent of shoppers consider the finding-and-buying process easy (28 per cent consider it tough). As a result, over 60 per cent of all virtual shopping carts are abandoned (Kotkin, 1999).

These statistics help validate two of the five key positioning options retail experts Ander and Stern propose in their book, *Winning at Retail* (2004). All five of those options are listed in Figure 8.2. While the other three positioning options will be discussed as the chapter progresses, the two relevant in regard to avoiding delays and inconvenience are quickest and easiest. Quickest is about timing and speed. At a deeper level, it is about avoiding the feeling of having been trapped: a claustrophobic sensation that human beings, as animals, instinctively dislike. In contrast, easiest is about not being forced to expend unnecessary energy to secure resources. When consumers are after the easiest way to get what they want, they are not necessarily looking to avoid traps so much as hassles they can do without.

Position	Rationalized	Emotional Goal
Quickest	Most Efficiency	Provide Relief
Easiest	Fewest Hassles	Provide Relief
Hottest	Newest Fashions	Create Delight
Biggest	Largest Offerings	Eliminate Fear
Cheapest	Lowest Prices	Eliminate Fear

Figure 8.2   Five positioning strategies relevant to shoppers.
The positioning options described here are those of Ander and Stern (2004), with the rational component implicit in their descriptions of each option. The feeling category – the emotional goal – is my own addition, and illuminates the emotional solutions the positioning options provide.

Avoidance

Consumers also naturally want to do business with respectful companies that help them, rather than avoid them or practise indifference by failing to make customer satisfaction central to their plans. The role that technology plays is a big factor. In a study funded by the Society of Consumer Affairs Professionals (SOCAP), 80 per cent of the people surveyed agreed with the statement 'I'm frequently frustrated by the way companies use technology to avoid talking to me' (Broetzmann, 2004).

The bottom line in customer service is that consumers want to talk to a live body in real time. That's because their essential dilemma doesn't involve an offer they purchased but, rather, their inner self.

In the end, the biggest problem in customer service isn't customers who give a company a hard time. It's those who abandon contact altogether, who give up and claim, 'I'm not getting what I want; I'm done.' At first, losing complaining customers might not seem so bad. But brand equity will take a nose-dive if enough customers jump ship. Lack of satisfaction harms the degree to which shoppers will consider buying from a company again, thereby rendering high awareness of a branded offer essentially irrelevant.

In summary, regarding the initial, approach stage of both shopping and customer service, companies should remember to safeguard respectfulness. That's because their relationships to customers are only partly economic in nature. A company's efforts to contain

As animals, humans instinctively dislike the feeling of being trapped.

costs are sure to backfire to the extent that they undermine a consumer's emotional desire for hassle-free experiences from access to checkout, in the case of shopping, and for more personalized interaction in the case of customer service. What do consumers want at this stage? To protect their time, their energy and their egos for the crucial engagement stage to follow.

A positive contrast: Nokia's successful focus on the guest journey

One company that is definitely getting it right in terms of the emotionally attuned choreographing of consumers' shopping and service experiences at its stores is Nokia. Using the term that Walt Disney first made famous, Nokia's philosophy is to help 'guests' feel close to their brand in as human and natural a manner as possible.

How does it manage that goal? The key is a five-step service approach:

- Connect: warm, genuine greetings are followed by giving the guest a chance to 'breathe'. Any reconnection comes at the optimal moment, using non-verbal signals from guests to know when the moment is right to offer assistance.

- Explore: restoring the art of listening enables Nokia staff to create a spontaneous guest profile. The subsequent options include offering a specialized store-tour, involving a specialist to help find solutions to a guest's specific needs, and directly assisting guests.
- Engage: demonstrations, inviting guests to play and experience the products on their own or providing guest tutorials are among the additional options. All demonstrations are based on Nokia's understanding that what their guests experience first-hand works better than relying on techno-speak.
- Deliver: again, attention to guests' non-verbal signals is considered the key to safeguarding the emotional value of the experience. The goal is for guests to be guided to the right solutions for them in ways that can create 'moments of delight'.
- Celebrate: people remember peak moments and the end of stories most of all. So Nokia is careful to facilitate purchase and/or activation, provide a personal farewell, and invite guests to future or ongoing events that match their guest profile.

The long-term business goal is to increase customer loyalty. Nokia does that by building rapport and trust based on having its service staff practise emotional intelligence on a daily basis. I've been in lots of stores, including for my emotional audit of Rodeo Drive stores on behalf of the *Wall Street Journal*. The bottom line? Very few companies enhance their emotional equity at the retail level as well as Nokia does at its flagship stores (Nokia).

Engagement: bringing back delight

Synopsis: Playing to people's innate desire for discovery and pleasure is fine, but then that desire has to be fulfilled. In the first half of this next section, the focus is on how companies can get high-quality attention. For retail shoppers, that means creating a sensory-rich store environment. In e-tailing, an engrossing plot is the key. The second half of this section is devoted to the service equivalent of pleasure. It's not so much about getting the problem solved but, rather, acknowledging and respecting the plight of the customer as a human being caught up in a problem.

Key take-aways
- The essence of therapeutic shopping is immersion in the experience.
- Great service means validating that the customer with a problem is important.

Choreographing retail and e-tail

The essence of therapeutic shopping is immersion in the experience

During their heyday from the 1860s to 1960s, department stores were glorious urban 'cathedrals of commerce'. But with the rise of mass-discounters and big-box category killers, shoppers typically endure no-frills warehouses of commerce instead. Why the shift? The likely socio-economic reasons include a shrinking middle class (hence a rise in cost-consciousness) and new forms of entertainment like TV, VCRs, DVDs, the internet etcetera, which have made shopping pale as an alternative.

Emotion and motivations.
The emotion to elicit is **delight**. For shoppers, it's done by creating experiences that balance comfort and allure. In customer service situations, it's done by connecting customers with caring and capable staff. Stores and even websites should be seen as sensory opportunities that consumers want to **learn** about and, if enjoyed, create a desire to **bond** with the merchant. In customer service, customers want to bond to the extent that service staff are interested in their predicament.

Delight

But whatever the explanation, the result is that the struggle to attract shoppers and to make shopping fun has reached near-crisis proportions. That's true for both traditional merchants and those selling over the internet. Their customer satisfaction and loyalty conundrum is, how to get the twinkle back into shoppers' eyes?

Of the five key positioning strategies outlined by Ander and Stern (2004), creating emotional engagement pertains to consumers seeking the hottest offers from the hottest places to shop. *Hottest* can be too narrowly interpreted. It refers not only to the newest fashions, for it is really much broader than that. Successfully capturing consumers who want the hottest involves not merely attracting their attention, but attaining quality attention. Doing so will be based on shoppers' experiences: first of the store's or website's general environment, then of the offer as specifically merchandised. In all, those experiences should ideally generate emotional warmth – most notably the blend of surprise and happiness that leads to delight.

In the old days, a store's display windows were the primary way to engage shoppers. But now the big-box retailers have typically dropped them altogether, or relegated this means of igniting an initial spark to the interior of malls and a few pedestrian-friendly retail settings like the stores on New York City's Fifth Avenue and on Michigan Avenue's 'Miracle Mile' in Chicago. In the 'old days', good display windows were like free theatre. They brought imagination into play in a way that car culture has all but obliterated.

In place of enticing window displays, brick-and-mortar retailers have two alternatives. The first is to rely heavily on advertising (Sunday circulars are the new window displays). The second is to leverage the entry area and the atmosphere inside. Thirty years ago, Philip Kotler (1973–4) recognized the power of deliberately designed environments and coined the term 'atmospherics' to describe a store's ability to entice and influence shoppers' buying decisions. As Kotler noted, people respond to an entire experience when shopping, not just to individual offers in a store's mix. Moreover, sensory atmospheric details serve as clues that talk to shoppers in exactly the silent, non-verbal language that facial expressions do, which is fitting since those clues both elicit and convey emotions.

Figure 8.3   If they don't look at it, they won't buy it.
What's the epitome of consumers wanting convenience? The menu board in a quick-service restaurant. In Sensory Logic's study for a company evaluating the success of adding a café to its convenience store operations, we found an inadequate degree of visual gaze attention being given to the café's menu board (see the minimal results above). What would be the upside of making some changes? A study commissioned by Coca-Cola found that, when mixed right, information, pictures and prices are the key elements on a menu board, with the inclusion of a photograph of branded cups, for example, capable of lifting beverage sales by nearly 10 per cent (Crawford 2006).

Of course, during the three decades since Kotler first emphasized atmospherics, much has changed. For one thing, the amount of retail space has tripled (to 21 square feet of space per person in the United States). Meanwhile, retail sales per square foot have dropped by nearly 25 per cent (Ander and Stern, 2004). Furthermore, e-commerce has exploded. By 2010, one estimate is that at least 30 per cent of all retail sales will be influenced by evaluations formed online in reviewing a company's website (Clancy, 2005).

E-tail's growth has brought with it a focus on encouraging engagement through five elements. All of them involve creating an experience for the visitor (Davenport and Beck, 2001):

- **Interactivity** means participation. Comment and response features provide one common approach to encouraging interaction. Allowing visitors to a site to vote or rank offers is another.
- **Competitions** such as games or quizzes take time and get site visitors involved.
- **High-production values** help turn e-tail's sight-and-sound atmospherics limitation into an advantage. For instance, Zappos.com makes browsing its online shoe catalogue easy, with a multi-view feature that lets visitors see any pair of shoes from all angles.
- Finally, while **entertainment** more or less speaks for itself, **narrative** is a special form of it. The co-creation of advertising by consumers submitting amateur videos is likely to be the next prominent form that will spill into e-tail. People can submit branded, offer-related 'stories' that utilize text, video, photos, questions and advice, which can then be posted to a website.

Science has now shown that 'retail therapy' is a matter of shoppers feeling 'high'. That happens naturally when the chemical dopamine is released in the brain because the person is experiencing something new and exciting.

At the same time, the importance of atmospherics with regard to traditional retailing has grown, creating increased competition. Now more than ever, merchants need to know whether their stores are eliciting the kind of favourable emotional responses that facial coding can measure.

That's because the right store environment becomes a strategic advantage, especially compared with e-tail. Smart merchants know they have the opportunity to engage shoppers by creating a sensory buffet that leads to immersive, emotionally enriching experiences.

Justification for making the effort and expenditure can be found in the payoff of shoppers making impulse purchases. Science has now shown that 'retail therapy' is a matter of shoppers feeling 'high', which happens naturally when the chemical dopamine is released in the brain. The trigger is that the person is experiencing something new and engrossing. What merchant doesn't want to provide therapeutic retail shopping sessions with exciting items available in a stimulating environment?

Nor does that therapy have to wait until consumers enter the setting. As evidence of the fact that entrances have real potential, consider the research Sensory Logic did for a high-end restaurant franchise (Figure 8.4). We assessed the emotional reaction of subjects to different areas and features of the restaurant. In this case, we actually found the entrance area to be best, overall, at generating a positive emotional response. A distinctive logo on the awning over the door and tastefully handled signage proved to be very appealing.

By contrast, once they got indoors the subjects found the main act – the dining room – less to their liking. Individual features, such as the lighting and art, worked well. But all in all, the dining room needed more emotional warmth, which the open-view kitchen exhibited well by

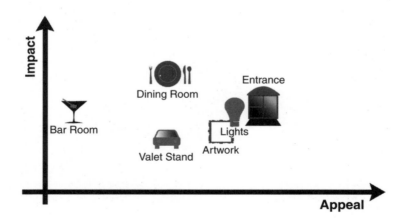

Figure 8.4 Facial coding results for upscale restaurant design.
Sensory Logic's study of emotional response to different areas of a restaurant revealed some interesting outcomes. The entrance was received well, with positive appeal and impact responses. But farther inside the restaurant, more negative feelings emerged. Management later confessed: the designer was designing for himself, instead of suiting their customers.

comparison. In short, subjects admired the setting (and management confessed to us that being admired was the designer's goal). But that type of emotional response wasn't enough. The designer's creation was leaving consumers feeling uneasy – and so management ultimately felt uneasy, too, left with spotty sales revenue.

For atmospherics to succeed, companies should design everything – especially the subtler aspects of the shopper's experience – according to the shopper's emotional needs and wants. In essence, not only make it quick and easy but also make it fun. In doing so, retailers enjoy the advantage of engaging a broader sensory bandwidth than do e-tailers, and should therefore leverage the natural sensory logic of see, touch, buy, own. It's eternal, innate logic that works again and again, making buyer and seller alike happier.

Co-discovery analysis and dream states: Saatchi and Saatchi X, shoppers and Sensory Logic

Saatchi and Saatchi X focuses on the hottest, most crucial new battleground in marketing: what happens in store, at the shelf set, including what kind of shopping experience is ultimately required to turn shoppers into buyers. To get to those insights, this agency throws the exploration net wider – and is now investigating with Sensory Logic the opportunities to apply facial coding in order to quantify the emotional peaks and troughs of the shopping experience.

Part of Saatchi X's effort involves analysing the role of the category, shelf set realities, the packaging and the brand, as well as shoppers' feelings and motivations related to the shopping environment and experience itself. A major insight tool is the shopping cycle. It identifies 12 key activity points that form the framework for any shopping experience, from the household context to the shopping experience itself and the occasions and rituals that individual shoppers employ around the moment of consumption back at home. After all, each shopping experience feeds into the next.

A second major insight tool is to engage in what Saatchi and Saatchi X calls 'co-discovery'. Captured through ethnography, in home, in store and in person-in-the-street type videotaped interviews, shoppers can see video clips of themselves and then narrate back over the top of that video what they were thinking about and feeling as the action unfolds.

INSIGHT

Emotional Rollercoaster. Shoppers simply can't leave the shopping centre without finding a novelty or bargain

Neutral

Looking for something different or special. A bit of a treat

Eating, drinking, meeting friends

Somewhere safe to bring the kids with easy parking and outside space

Pleasant, convenient shopping experience without the hassle

Aspiring to buy something a bit different. Trying stuff on

Actually buying something original, individual or unusual

Finding a bargain

Actually feeling positive / that you'd found a bargain

Cost / time spent travelling and value for money

Getting it all home. Post purchase satisfaction

APPLYING LOVEMARKS™ TO Shopping Centre X

MYSTERY → Feature unusual shapes, design, aesthetics and exhibits that arouse curiosity, draw people in and grab their attention

SENSUALITY → Create theatre, 'must have' excitement and engage the senses. Encourage people to look, feel, touch and interact

INTIMACY → Make people feel warm, special and welcome. Treat them like guests. Give them something they simply can't get anywhere else

1) **The challenge.** The self-reported emotional rollercoaster aptly shows that the low points come in regards to a) actually finding something original/unique, b) feeling positive about finding a true bargain, and c) effort and money spent versus the value realized.

The facial coding of a sample video supports and illuminates those concerns. When one young woman speaks of her desire to purchase something original, the first low point above, her face reveals anger (goal not realized). Meanwhile, the neutral data point regarding the desire for a bargain correlates to facially coded evidence of sadness on another young woman's face – she's feeling disappointment. Finally, the second low point above relates to the valve proposition of effort/value and a young man's show of disgust: a rejection of the shopping centre's current allure.

2) **The emotional pay-off.** Fortunately, the rollercoaster ends on a high, about post-purchase satisfaction. There's a nice true smile from a woman talking about hiding her packages from her husband, and a weaker smile from a man expressing pride about the replica/antique phone he found for purchase.

That's where facial coding enters the picture. After all, people filter – choosing what to say or hold back on, as well as quite likely not always being aware of how they feel. To the supplementary power of facial coding is that it's an intimate research tool geared to emotions. So aided by Sensory Logic, Saatchi and Saatchi X can now more effectively measure, analyse and help its clients manage the 'DNA of shoppers' experiences and expectations'. As a result, receptivity to the in-store communication of its clients' offers gets enhanced.

Saatchi and Saatchi CEO Kevin Roberts' *Lovemarks* and my previous book *Body of Truth: Leveraging What Consumers Can't or Won't Say* were linked on Amazon.com's website – and for good reason. We're coming from a similar place. As Saatchi and Saatchi X recognises full well, you can't get to reason until you go through emotion – that's a fact of brain function. Unless what you experience passes through emotion it's not even going to be integrated into logical decision making. Here's the problem: far too many stores and retail environments see themselves as places to demonstrate functional benefits, which doesn't make much sense.

For a start, eye-tracking research shows that shoppers only notice 50 per cent of what they look at, even standing in front of a shelf. This limitation is especially true in the critical first two-and-a-half seconds. If you don't catch their eye or enhance their shopping experience in a way that's emotionally and aesthetically compelling, the moment to win them over is gone in a flash.

Through tools like co-discovery and uncovering shoppers' emotional drivers through facial coding, it's even possible to investigate what Saatchi X calls the dream state. That's the ideal shopping experience – designed to be a more mysterious, sensual and intimate experience than previously thought possible.

The 'me-story' of customer service

Great service means validating that the customer with a problem is important

After finding a live body ready and willing to help, what do customers want? They want to find relief in telling their stories in order to restore their (anticipated) pleasure. And there's always a story. There's a pre-story about the customer's expectations of the company, and then there's the current me-story, meaning the story that spells out the customer's reasons for seeking vindication.

Vindication is important because, in terms of what customer service really provides, there are just two categories. There's what customers want and what customers don't want. They come to customer service wishing to get what they want and seeking assurance that they won't get what they don't want. As it turns out, vindication is really about validation.

What's the silver lining of angry customers?

A company has their full attention and a great chance to build a relationship.

What conclusions and feelings don't customers want to internalize? 'I've been cheated. I'm insignificant and easily ignored. This isn't right.' Any of those toxic responses fit the don't-want category. In contrast, wants go something like this: 'That was easy. Yeah! I got what I needed. People can be so helpful. I'm glad to find I wasn't crazy. Now I understand.' Those responses show how delight can be part of the customer service experience: let the customer's 'me' win (and do so graciously).

Disgruntled customers represent a wonderful relationship-building opportunity. That's because a company then has their full attention – a rarity in today's marketplace. And best yet, moving a customer from negativity to affinity isn't all that hard.

Consider a study Sensory Logic did evaluating shoppers' experiences at a big-box retailer, including the effect of employee behaviour on customer satisfaction. In this case, the study didn't focus on customer service representatives but, rather, on retail sales employees and their interactions with customers. To help us do our work, the client agreed to let us use a concealed video camera so that we could secure spontaneous, natural film footage. Then we showed the video segments to subjects to learn their emotional responses to both the store environment and various service situations.

In the results shown in Figure 8.5, the footage involved a checkout clerk handling one particular customer. What the second-by-second results show is both obvious and illuminating. More intent on talking to a co-worker than to a paying customer, the clerk violates the cardinal me-story rule: she fails to accentuate the customer's 'me'. As might be expected, subjects' collective emotional response to the indifference displayed by the clerk was a huge thumbs-down.

Service is a feeling. Don't give any feelings to others you wouldn't want to feel.
Jeffrey Gitomer

Figure 8.5 Consumer reactions to poor customer service.
The chart shows on a real-time basis the average emotional appeal response of
subjects to viewing a 73-second video segment of a checkout clerk barely paying
attention to the customer facing her at the cash register. Four time groups stand out
within the results:

- Group 1: the clerk is getting change with her back to the waiting customer. Appeal
  falls accordingly at second 26.
- Group 2: the only major appeal rise as the clerk acknowledges the customer's
  presence through interaction.
- Group 3: Appeal level drops as the clerk ignores the customer in favour of chatting
  with a co-worker while waiting for the receipt to print.
- Group 4: shows the response to the clerk handing over the receipt and saying,
  'Have a good day.' As the appeal results show, by this time the customer simply
  doesn't believe the clerk cares.

To avoid those kinds of situations, what can companies do? Training all
frontline personnel in how to read customers' faces is surely not financially feasible. But sales associates could be shown customers' reactions to
situations similar to those captured in the example just given. Doing so
would sensitize them to the impact their behaviour can have on
customers. Moreover, everyone on the staff could benefit from emotional
awareness training. It starts by understanding that customers want to tell

	Fear	Anger	Sadness	Happiness	Disgust
Pitch	High	High	Low	High	Low
Rate	Fast	Quiet	Slow	Varies	Slow
Range	Wide	Wide	Narrow	Wide	Wide
Articulation	Precise	Tense	Slurring	Normal	Normal

Figure 8.6 Translating vocal intonations into emotions.
How customers speak reflects how they feel. This chart shows what certain speech
patterns reveal about a customer's likely emotional state.

their emotional me-story first, before they're ready to accept rational, operational support. Meanwhile, for those customer service representatives on the phone, identifying and thereby reacting quicker and better to customers' emotional states through the assessment of vocal intonation will likewise improve outcomes (Figure 8.6).

Reassurance: proving oneself right

Synopsis: The topic here is providing ways to connect either with other consumers or with the company itself. As this section will first address, shopping is informed by consumers' instinct to belong. It's a social activity, a way to gain a sense of community. Second, shopping and service overlap in consumers' desire not to end up feeling like they bought foolishly. Consumers must feel like they have a supportive network to draw on for confirmation about their purchase decisions.

Key take-aways

- Shopping smart involves proving to the tribe that one has the right to belong.
- Good customer service requires overcoming the fears of everyone involved.

Emotion and motivations.

The operative emotion here is **fear**. The risk of being off-the-mark, socially or financially, is rooted in consumers' desire to be ahead of the pack, but not so far ahead that they are in jeopardy. With customer service, consumers wonder whether company representatives will approach the discussion as friend or foe. The resulting motivations are to **bond** – to affirm one's identity in relation to others – while still wanting to get the good deal that signifies superior ability to **acquire**.

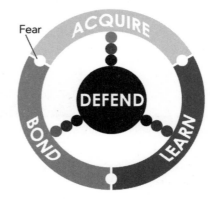

Fear

Honouring the savvy shopper

Shopping smart involves proving to the tribe that one has the right to belong

Just as control and curiosity are central to the aspects of shopping already discussed, ability is the key to the remaining aspect. More specifically, ability covers two related yet slightly separate applications with regard to retail and e-tail. The first is that shoppers want to demonstrate their ability to navigate style. They do so by being able to bolster their own unique identity while still being adept enough to fit in with their desired social groups. Second, shoppers also want to demonstrate their ability to secure goods on terms, including price, that give them a chance to practise and prove their 'hunting' skills.

In terms of the five key positioning strategies outlined by Ander and Stern (2004), the goal of being savvy, whether socially or financially, pertains to the two remaining options: *biggest* or *cheapest*. That's because wanting the biggest selection, for example, implies that shoppers have seen what's out there. They won't be caught on the down-and-out, socially or stylistically. Wanting the cheapest deal? That's code for wanting the right offer at the right price from the right place.

Now let's look at how the twin abilities of knowing how to navigate style and securing good terms function in retail practice. Let's start with style in relation to wanting to belong. Why do group dynamics matter so much? Surely, the reason is that through affiliating with others, consumers gain a sense of security (Pooler, 2003). So it should be no surprise that both retail and e-tail involve resolving shoppers' fears that they might be vulnerable and alone.

Of the two versions of shopping, brick-and-mortar has the traditional advantage of letting shoppers literally see for themselves how well they might be doing. Through comparison they can learn if their purchases make social acceptance more viable. In other words, they can look at their fellow shoppers in a store and observe for themselves the offers and styles in vogue and whether the stores they're frequenting attract the kind of people they aspire to associate with.

In that regard, stores with the biggest selections have at once both an advantage and disadvantage when it comes to satisfying a shopper's urge to belong. A large selection provides comfort. It implicitly tells the shopper: you're going to be wisely informed because you will have seen all the merchandise options. That's the advantage. But the disadvantage is that, in a marketplace where shoppers strive to feel special while also fitting in with their own unique groups, biggest can be socially empty. In effect, if everybody goes there, nobody goes there.

Additional positioning mixtures.
Other formulas are possible, of course. For instance, biggest can combine with another of the positioning options – hottest – in a paradoxically smaller, yet ultra-trendy boutique-type store that sifts through mountains of product, essentially performing the searching process for its customers. That type of approach can weaken a big-box store's advantage. That's because, when successful, the boutique only offers the socially or stylistically appropriate options for its devoted 'tribe'. Likewise, savvy could also involve a store with both the hottest and the easiest form of accessing merchandise, thus smart in terms of saving one's time. In the end, any store or website can satisfy most if not all of the major five positionings, thereby enhancing its odds of success. The trick is making sure that its identity and value proposition don't blur because it is trying to do too much.

So unless a store can also deliver on the social group shoppers want to identify with – in other words, the people option – it will miss out and default to being merely a pricing option. As a result, boutiques that address niche markets will often have an edge when it comes to fulfilling a shopper's desire for a sense of community.

Meanwhile, without any fellow shoppers in sight, e-tail has needed to be more imaginative in order to fulfil the urge to belong. How has that been accomplished? The answer is in part by providing an ever-increasing amount of personalized customization. Consumers can feel acknowledged not just by name but also by their procedure and content preferences. The other part is that e-tail has taken the lead over brick-and-mortar retailers by allowing more opportunities for the co-creation of content. By enabling users to add content to a site, e-tailers create the possibility for consumers to feed off the additions of others, thereby building and experiencing community via the art of sharing.

Why is that approach so emotionally smart and so appealing to the savvy shopper? The answer is that websites are emotionally alive to the extent that consumers feel that the sites are responsive and offer a home base when they're looking to connect with others.

The old model was for companies to provide content as an assumed, fixed value. But in today's business climate, it's not the content but the context that matters. The abundance of choices now available in the marketplace makes *how* a particular offer is used, and by whom, far more important than what that offer actually is (Grantham and Carr, 2002). In other words, value isn't a given. Instead, it gets created in the eyes of the beholder during the transaction process.

Now that's all very good, you might say, but why should merchants bother to address the urge to belong? Well, otherwise what's left to provide the savvy shopper other than going the cheapest route? In that case ensuring satisfaction and loyalty becomes a matter of delivering bargains. And without any more emotional buy-in from customers than that, being the source of whatever's cheapest becomes a tough positioning for all but the largest and most disciplined of merchants.

Website Emotional Results

Best Options Average Worst Options Average

Figure 8.7   Surfing the web for a gnarly page.
This example shows the emotional results from some research Sensory Logic did for a financial services company looking to change the homepage of its website. Among the four options being considered, whether subjects could relate to the people portrayed on screen proved to be the biggest variable. In rational terms, that difference wasn't apparent. Individually, none of the possible choices had a positive verbal response below 60 per cent. But when we used facial coding to look at the top two options averaged and the bottom two options averaged, it became clear that the rational responses given by the subjects didn't match up with the vast disparity in how they felt about the web pages. Only in some cases did they feel like they had anything in common with the people being depicted there.

Establishing better customer service

Good customer service requires overcoming the fears of everyone involved

As it turns out, the fear that motivates shoppers to both fit in socially and secure bargains so they appear smart applies to customer service as well. At a basic level, customer service is really all about the fears of three different entities: the customer, the service representative and the company at large. Here's what that statement means, one entity at a time.

Why do people need customer service? Truth be told, customers actually try to avoid having to deal with customer service. In fact, they may not feel like the two words go together. After all, people usually go to customer service when they've run into problem situations in which they, the customers, feel like they haven't received real service or else have bought something that wasn't of value. The reason customers resort to customer service is almost always problem-related, and human nature is geared toward trying to avoid problems.

Meanwhile, customer service representatives are likely to be equally fearful. They know the people calling or coming in think they have made a mistake. They know that those seeking customer service are probably feeling nervous about not getting what they expected and are therefore worried about starting from an inferior position. So what do consumers do? They over-compensate. They hide their fear through aggressive behaviour, and sometimes the nervous representative goes there first.

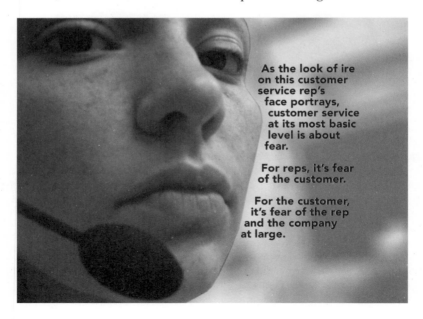

As the look of ire on this customer service rep's face portrays, customer service at its most basic level is about fear.

For reps, it's fear of the customer.

For the customer, it's fear of the rep and the company at large.

Likewise, customer service is something companies also seek to avoid. For companies, customer service isn't a profit centre; it's a cost centre. Thus the goal becomes containing the cost of customer service in order to protect profit margin. Most companies view it that way. They rarely, if ever, see customer service as an emotional opportunity to safeguard or even enhance value.

What's the way out of this destructive dynamic? Three major improvements can and should be made to demonstrate a company's ability to deliver satisfaction in terms of customer service.

First, *change hiring and retention practices*. It's hard for customers to feel well supported when the customer service departments they're interacting with suffer so much turnover that it seems as if nobody knows what anybody's doing. Fortunately, a solution exists. The employees most likely to be effective brand ambassadors already occupy other positions in the company. Internal transfers will work out best for two reasons. The first is that internal people already know the company. The second is that as veterans, they will also be more invested in its performance. Yes, staffing at least some positions with veterans instead of rookies will cost more. And the same is true of doing more to retain good employees. But the company will come out ahead in the long run, especially if it fills customer service positions with employees chosen for the job because they demonstrate an active interest in connecting with customers emotionally.

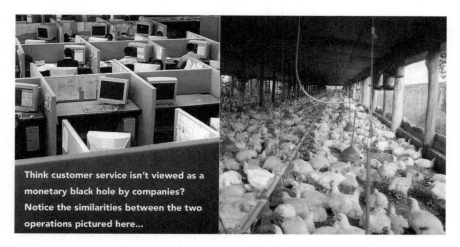

Think customer service isn't viewed as a monetary black hole by companies? Notice the similarities between the two operations pictured here...

Second, *make customer 'satisfaction' surveys more meaningful and insightful*. The typical surveys may measure the more rationally oriented, functional aspects of customer service. But they are woefully inadequate at gauging the emotionally charged me-story aspects of the customer service relationship. A decent half-step solution would be something like Gallup has done. Their approach? Shifting to more emotionally oriented satisfaction survey questions (Applebaum, 2001). Even better, however, would be to occasionally tap the emotional wells of customers using a more innately emotional tool like facial coding. If that's not going to be funded, at least make sure the first question asked addresses the issue or problem most customers would have – so they can quickly have their say. (A short, short, short form that's easy works best.)

Finally, *rethink customer service to see it as a valuable offer in its own right*. Bolstered by knowledgeable, committed employees and research that really grasps the situation, customer service departments would be better able to proactively design and deliver superior service experiences. The financial benefit is real. After all, research suggests that great customer service enables companies to enjoy a 10 per cent growth in their annual profit rates. That's in contrast to only 1 per cent for those with merely adequate service (Desatnick and Detzel, 1993).

There's no reason that the goal couldn't be to make customers who experienced customer service happier than those who did not. To that end, the question becomes: what does great service look like? Here are three examples by which to answer that question.

The first example involves Amazon.com, which treats customer service more like a research and development lab (Fishman, 2001). Every customer contact (that is, complaint) is monitored as another opportunity for improvement. In fact, one team does nothing but anticipate problems and develop solutions, while other service department members are part of every new launch.

A second example is that niche businesses are emerging out of the service problems that larger 'soft goods' retailers haven't been able to solve. These home-based businesses lure away the upscale merchants' most profitable customers simply by offering stellar, high-touch service through direct sales. For example, former personal shoppers at upscale department stores are now helping their former store clientele buy clothes by showcasing lines of merchandise in non-retail settings. A hallmark of this kind of service is that consultants track purchases and know style, colour and size preferences, sometimes even delivering new items to a client's home 'on approval'. This kind of attention and emotionally satisfying service have helped direct sales grow 79 per cent during the past decade (Kaplan, 2006).

Finally, a third example is the retail model offered by Apple, recently chosen by the readers of *DDI* magazine as retailer of the year (not bad for a company with zero retail presence half a decade ago). Yes, the ethereal white décor makes the merchandise seem heaven-sent. But the real stroke of brilliance was transforming the customer service desk into a 'genius bar', which casts the entire issue of customer problems in a more positive light (Sway, 2005).

> What companies really need to measure is emotional attachment – their real bond with customers.
>
> Paul Higham, former CMO, Wal-mart

Conclusion

The psychological reality of shopping and customer service is that the 'average' consumer doesn't exist. Each consumer's plea is always: understand me. To be effective, retailers, e-tailers and customer service providers must accomplish the following:

- Create easier access. Emotionally, the key is to welcome people.
- Reward curiosity. Connect with consumers through engaging atmospherics and empathetic interactivity so as to provide delight.
- Provide support. Help consumers feel secure by connecting them to their fellow shoppers or 'super agent' service veterans.

An action plan

To ensure that the retail, e-tail and customer service experiences delivered to consumers are emotionally healthy, here are a few things to check when assessing emotional effectiveness:

- Develop a strategy to increase shoppers' average lengths of stay in the company's stores or on its website (without frustrating them). To that end, try to separate shoppers' emotional experiences from their utility-driven activities of looking for what they came for. The more a positive emotional experience predominates, the more likely they will add purchases to the list with which they started.
- Prepare the store or site for different kinds of visitors. In doing so, provide a variety of emotional hooks for the target market. What are the shoppers after? Is it quality? Price? A deal? The satisfaction of comparison shopping to prove they're savvy? Have something for every key profile.
- Focus on the shoppers' emotional experiences when they interact with the company, and seek to remove or alleviate the barriers and frustrations they experience. Specifically, make it a priority to identify and remove barriers that elicit strong negative emotional responses. Similarly, watch out for service occasions in which customers feel as though they're being led or pushed through a series of activities. If customers react negatively, a company should change what it's doing.
- Do an emotional profile of both the offer and customer service experience to ensure they align. Ideally, service should be integrated into the offer and not merely tacked on.
- Make sure the service is no-fault to avoid evoking emotions such as fear and anger. Always remember that the optimal outcome is that both the person giving service and the person receiving service feel like winners. To that end, the service should be real and involve genuine concern about the outcome for the customer.

Part Three

Workplace applications

9 Leadership

The company's 'us' is composed of employees who bet their livelihoods that the house (the company) will win and in turn enrich them. A great leader has the qualities of a winner willing to share the glory.

Overview

When the *Wall Street Journal* runs front-page coverage about executives exercising stock options on dates that 'luckily' lead to windfall personal profits (Forelle and Bandler, 2006), you can bet people notice. But they take special notice of cases like that of one executive. His chances of having such fortuitous timing in exercising his options year after year was calculated by the newspaper's analyst as one in 300 billion. Was it 'blind luck', as the executive said (before resigning)? There's reason to doubt it, thereby reducing trust and making leadership a tougher, more urgent task. To help executives connect emotionally with employees, this chapter will focus on:

- **The greater good:** in joining an 'us', employees don't surrender their 'me'. Instead, they subsume it, believing that the greater 'us' will feed the 'me'. So company leaders should ideally be able to establish themselves as more than credible. They should also be unselfish, someone who looks out for the group. That profile gives followers faith that at the end of the day there will be something left for them, and indeed, more than they could attain on their own.
- **Clear vision:** there is a profound difference between leadership that looks ahead and leadership that simply manages the status quo. As Peter Drucker (2006) notes, 'Every product and every activity of a business begins to obsolesce as soon as it is started.' Therefore, successful leaders have clear visions of the future. Then they respond to change by providing direction in accordance with those visions. Moreover, because the inevitable need for change can be so traumatic to followers, leaders must also have the ability to paint a convincing picture of the future, and in doing so, motivate employees by preparing them for what's coming.
- **Cohesive culture:** to offset the risk of isolation, successful leaders don't just read the situation around them in emotional terms, they also foster a cohesive culture in which employees feel invited to participate and collaborate. To that end, they seek to surround themselves with talent. Thus, people will be as smart or smarter than themselves (both rationally and emotionally), and they will be recognized for their abilities and promoted for their good work. The outcome is a less stressful and more relaxed workplace, with all parts working in synch.

Now let's look more closely at how leadership conveys both competency and caring, starting with how best to demonstrate a sense of togetherness.

The greater good: why character matters

Synopsis: The key here is ensuring that the company's workforce views senior management as worth having faith in, and in best-case scenarios, even magnanimous and generous of spirit. In this section, we'll address how the CEO's character, as communicated to others, will determine the extent of employees' trust and commitment. Two specifics will be examined. The first is the need to close the emotional gap between leaders and followers to compensate for the financial gap between them. The second is how the emotions displayed on leaders' faces reveal their core personality traits.

Key take-aways

- Pay disparities require leaders with emotional savvy to offset the disconnect.
- Trust is based on a leader's honesty and generally pleasing emotional profile.
- In a complex, busy world, projected emotions are rightly taken as substance.

Emotion and motivations.
Alarm, the feeling associated with the risk of imminent danger, is a plausible response to knowing that a powerful leader could choose to act in his or her own interest. Employees see the leadership as embodied by the CEO, so there's an instinctive desire to identify and **bond** with that leader. At the same time, however, people commit their careers and livelihoods to the company, so an instinct to **defend** their own interests also exists.

Alarm

Getting people to follow

Pay disparities require leaders with emotional savvy to offset the disconnect

Whether it's political, religious or corporate leadership, the emotional dynamics of being in charge don't change very much. People will become ardent, true followers to the extent that they believe it's safe to do so; that victory is possible, if not outright imminent; and that they will get to share in the accomplishment and the rewards that come with success. Then a 'me' will join the 'us' and do so willingly – without coercion, without doubt, without questioning – because that person has forged an emotional bond and made an emotional commitment.

Unfortunately, creating a top-down 'us' in the business world has become harder than ever because of two major trends. The first involves the spotlight CEOs occupy and their related rise in pay. Until the wave of Enron-style scandals somewhat blunted this trend, the leadership type in ascendancy was the superstar CEO. Possessing the stature and political acumen to woo and wow Wall Street analysts, as well as the business media, this type could keep the all-important stock price from flagging (Khurana, 2002). In contrast, the understated, behind-the-scenes leadership celebrated in Jim Collins's bestseller *Good to Great* (2001) had begun to seem old-fashioned.

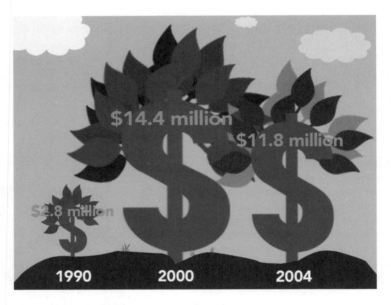

Figure 9.1   Average CEO compensation chart.
$27,000. That's what the average American worker made in 1990 – and what they still make today (adjusted for inflation). But CEO compensation in the US over that same period has been 100 to 400 times higher (Labaton).

The counter-response to the scandals and the whole celebrity CEO phenomenon has been a re-emphasis on the brass-tacks executive at the expense of the 'golden child'. But either way, the dividend-focused business world has driven compensation to unprecedented levels, putting leaders on an economic plateau far removed from those they lead.

What has the general response been? Recent surveys showing that 90 per cent of institutional investors believe that executives at most US companies are overpaid (*Chicago Tribune*, 2006), we can imagine how lower-ranking employees feel. Warren Buffett may not have been speaking only for himself when he said, 'Too often executive compensation in the U.S. is ridiculously out of line with performance' (Miller, 2006). Given the disparities in compensation, how can employees (and investors) not be inclined to feel suspicion and envy – even outrage – as the corner office continues to surpass the cubicle set by ever-widening margins?

Research indicates that in countries with pronounced income spreads, the inequality correlates to lower life expectancy rates. That's because such stark contrasts introduce stress into people's lives (Klein, 2002). In short, envy is divisive. What's the risk being taken by CEOs who have economically distanced themselves too much from the pay scale their average employee can relate to or accept? They've put their ability to forge an internal, emotional 'us' in jeopardy.

Even worse is the second trend: the ongoing wave of downsizing, outsourcing and other 'adjustments' like the demise of pension plans. In addition to widening the already-mentioned economic divide between top leaders and employees, these moves undermine employees' sense of security and well-being. To cite one figure, it's been estimated that over 10 per cent of all the jobs in America are at risk of being outsourced (Bardhan and Kroll, 2003; Center for American Progress, 2007).

Taken together, the two trends endanger the likelihood that employees will see their leaders as invested in a shared outcome. They also put additional pressure on the leadership to establish an emotionally solvent, personal connection with employees. What's the solution? It's that the degree to which leaders are economically divorced from their workers places a premium on having the emotional savvy to offset the disconnect.

Former GE CEO Jack Welch knew that emotions were a key part of running an innovative and profitable organization. The subtitle of his book affirms this perspective.

Therefore, to overcome perceptions of selfish indifference and get people to be emotionally on-board as followers, CEOs and senior leadership in general will have to add another dimension to the four leadership Es spelled out by GE's former CEO Jack Welch. What are Welch's four Es? They consist of having a competitive Edge, being a good Executor and being Energetic while Energizing others (Byrne, 1998). What's the new, fifth E? Emotional intelligence: a competency that two studies by the training firm Hay/McBer have confirmed to be what successful leaders have most in common (Goleman, 2000).

Aided by *Emotional Intelligence* author Daniel Goleman, Hay/McBer analysed the key characteristics that distinguish adroit leaders. What did they find? First, in a study of executives at 15 global companies, only one cognitive, intellectual skill proved to be a good barometer of success: the ability to sift through the big picture for patterns. All of the other core competencies involved emotionally based skills and characteristics like collaboration, political acumen and resiliency.

> Leadership isn't something you do writing memos, you've got to appeal to people's emotions. They've got to buy in with their hearts and bellies, not just their minds.
>
> Lou Gerstner former CEO, IBM

Meanwhile, in a related study that looked at executives at IBM, Coca-Cola and Pepsico, those people with a high degree of emotional competencies were in the top third of management, as reflected in salary bonuses for performance. So pervasive was the profile that it held true in more than 80 per cent of the various divisions within those companies.

The importance of hiring right

Trust is based on a leader's honesty and generally pleasing emotional profile

What's the message of the Hay/McBer research results? It's that people skills matter. They're not 'soft', although they're definitely emotional. Instead, they help a leader to connect with others – not through using emotions to manipulate perceptions, but by using emotional intelligence to understand where people are 'coming from'.

Corporate Board Member magazine has editorialized, based on Deep Throat's famous advice, 'Follow the money', that CEOs should spend 40 per cent of their time on investor relations (Khurana, 2002). But the audience that will help make the company's profitability actually possible is the internal 'us' of managers and rank-and-file employees, who must be emotionally energized to care.

What specific kinds of emotion-based traits should CEOs have? In perhaps the seminal study in this field, the leadership experts Kouzes and Posner (2004) engaged in research involving over 400 case studies and 75,000 people worldwide. What's their conclusion?

The key qualities people value in their leaders are, in order of importance: honesty, being forward-looking and inspiring

Why is honesty the pre-eminent attribute employees wish to see in leaders? Employees naturally want to know where a leader stands. So they'll ask themselves, 'Can so-and-so be trusted to look out for my security?' This question emerges from survival instincts. That's because as followers, they rely on a leader's ability to enhance their odds of staying alive and thriving (thus avoiding alarm).

For years now, *Fortune* 500 companies and other smaller firms have been relying on verbally based methods, including the excellent but expensive Hogan Assessment Systems survey, to probe the character and inner emotions of CEO job candidates to secure the best one (O'Donnell, 2004). Sensing the importance of a CEO's emotional profile, but looking for a new approach to measure it, an investment firm approached Sensory Logic a couple of years ago with a theory: the personality of the CEO affects the corporate culture, which in turn drives stock performance. Based on this theory, the firm wished to use facial coding as a supplementary means of assessing which companies to invest in. In other words, they were banking on facial coding to help them gauge a CEO's emotional make-up, thereby giving them an edge in identifying sound investing opportunities.

Our first assignment was to analyse the facial expressions of then current Hewlett-Packard CEO Carly Fiorina and Cisco CEO John Chambers. What emerged? Chambers lived up to his billing as 'Mr. Sunshine'. With expressions indicating a high degree of positive emotion, he was genuinely upbeat and conciliatory. In contrast, Fiorina's expressions indicated largely negative emotions. They betrayed the signs of a person already under siege. In a world where emotional competency matters, she rubbed a lot of people the wrong way, and presided over a 50 per cent drop in the price of HP's stock during her six years at the helm. (See Figure 9.2 for the comparison.)

The investment firm had its own proprietary system of determining which leaders to support based on eight key traits, with honesty getting a double weight. Emphasizing honesty makes sense for investors assessing a leader, as well as for employees. For most of us in life,

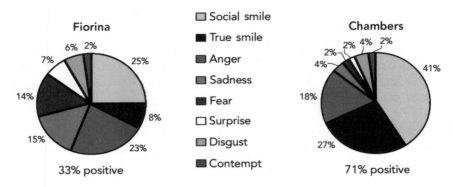

Figure 9.2 **CEO composure comparison.**
We analysed videotaped interviews of high-powered CEOs John Chambers (right) and
Carly Fiorina (left). Over a quarter (27 per cent) of Chamber's facial activity involved
true smiles – a phenomenally high percentage. In comparison, Fiorina vacillated
between social smiles (25 per cent), anger (23 per cent), sadness (15 per cent) and
fear (14 per cent).

honesty comes first. If we don't believe we will get something at least
approaching our fair share, then the odds of our hanging in there –
emotionally, and not just physically as merely another 'warm body' at
work – will decline severely.

Related to honesty, Sensory Logic also conducted another, separate
study in which we looked at
the responses of employees
whose companies had recently
undergone dramatic organizational changes, such as a
merger or acquisition. In that
case, we asked among other
questions: did employees trust
their leaders, and did they
believe what their leaders had
told them about the changes?

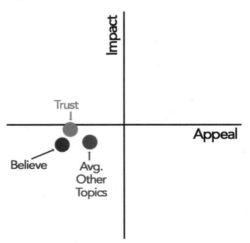

Figure 9.3 **Employees not on-board.**
The two questions that revealed the emotional concerns of employees amid change
most clearly were 'How much do you now trust the leaders of your company?' and
'How much do you believe what you've heard from the company about the change
your company recently experienced?' Our research revealed that faith had been
broken, imperilling the 'we' culture necessary for success.

What did our results uncover? (See Figure 9.3 for details.) When subjects were asked the belief question, anxiety in the facial coding activity reached the highest level in the study: 22 per cent. That's illuminating and here's why. Anxiety signals fear and, along with surprise, fear makes up the alarm employees are likely to feel when confronted with reminders that their leaders are powerful enough to brush their concerns aside. Put another way, change may bring with it concern, even suspicion, about whether one's leader will be a faithful guide during the struggle ahead.

In it for the long haul

In a complex, busy world, projected emotions are rightly taken as substance

The investment firm's approach of wanting to analyse emotions through facial expressions was smart. Furthermore, its emphasis on traits when assessing good leadership was astute. After all, personality, traits and emotions are closely related concepts (Howard, 2000). *Personality* refers to the set of predictable behaviours by which others recognize us as ourselves. These specific behaviours are often called traits. Repeated, commonly shown emotions are, in turn, a means of assessing traits, which is why, for example, we say so-and-so is a 'hot head' when he or she gets angry quickly and often. How do we know that person is angry? The answer is in no small part because of facial muscle activity that reflects and communicates people's feelings.

Since the core of an emotion is readiness to act, analysing a person using facial coding can provide a means of gauging both their core personality and related behavioural tendencies. To that end, I looked at the exhibited personalities of Ken Lay (the former CEO of Enron) and Martha Stewart (who had been accused of insider share dealing) for *Fast Company* (McGregor, 2004). What I saw was the contempt both showed for the legal proceedings to which they were subject, and the fear displayed by Lay. I also critiqued the 2004 US presidential debates for the *New York Times* (Tierney, 2004), National Public Radio (Feldman, 2004) and BusinessWeek.com (Dunham, 2004) in order to better understand how the public might respond to George W Bush's smiling smirks and John Kerry's deadpan expressions.

More recently, Sensory Logic studied the facial expressions and, therefore, the personality of 10 famous CEOs (see Figure 9.4). What emerged from our analysis of videotaped media appearances from this set of leaders? First, the majority of these leaders exhibited a predominantly positive personality, with approximately two-thirds of the leaders

CEO Facial Coding Results

● Bezos	■ Gates	◆ Buffett	▲ Dell
– Ellison	● Knight	▣ Murdoch	◆ Oprah
▲ Trump	✖ Jobs		

The Personality Traits of Strong Leaders

Faschingbauer and Rubenzer created a cumulative personality profile of the best presidents and the average president in their book *Personality, Character, & Leadership in the White House: Psychologists Assess the Presidents.* The formula gave a percentile value to each of the Big Five personality traits according to their importance in the personality of a quality president.

Similarly, the same type of formula can be applied to successful CEOs. Professors Steven Kaplan, Mark Klebanov and Marten Sorenson identified key personality traits of 225 CEO hires. The study followed the performances of the CEOs and used the most successful ones to determine which personality traits are most prevalent. Their study found that conscientiousness and extraversion were the most important of the Big Five personality traits for a successful CEO.

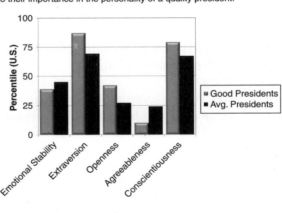

Figure 9.4 Appeal and impact – ten top CEOs.

What is perhaps the best combination of feelings for a CEO to exhibit? True and robust social smiles, since people buy hope, combined with just enough anger to keep people on their toes about making progress. What's the worst combination? It's probably dislike (disgust and contempt) combined with anxiety (fear), because a condescending, scared leader has cut him or herself off from others.

landing in positive appeal territory. Second, as our separate emotional profiles revealed, some leaders – like Rupert Murdoch and Ralph Ellison – are notably hard-driving individuals whose most characteristic emotion is anger, signalling a frustrated desire to make even greater progress than they already have. Third, Phil Knight, Jeff Bezos and Warren Buffet are among the 'happy campers', those leaders most likely to be enjoyable to work for in that they exhibit happiness, even delight.

Figure 9.5   Creation of personality traits over time.
What are traits? They're actually emotions embodied over the long term, and like beliefs, represent the influence of emotions at their most sustained level.

What's the bottom line here? Executives shouldn't underestimate the value of facial expressions in helping them understand how audiences will respond to them. One CEO who understood this value had Sensory Logic review three of his public appearances: two consecutive annual meeting addresses to employees and a one-on-one interview at a business club function. Notable were three findings:

- During the annual meetings, this CEO only showed codeable activity every other minute while on camera: a relatively low degree of expressiveness. In the more intimate club setting, however, the CEO opened up and was more expressive. The implication? The CEO was likely to make a stronger emotional connection with workers in venues like breakfast meetings or smaller, department-size sessions where he might convey his feelings more vividly.
- Previous coaching to encourage this CEO to deliver his message in a more upbeat style was succeeding. The latest employee meeting data was far more positive than the earlier one. The implication? Without undercutting a CEO's integrity, it's possible to train leaders to improve their body language and, thereby, convey more warmth and hope.
- Overall, this CEO was sending mixed signals. The good news was that a complete absence of scepticism verified his authenticity (he never

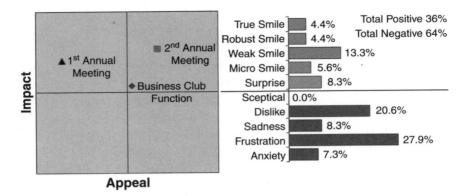

Figure 9.6   Analysis of CEO's emotional display.
The left-hand chart shows that the second annual meeting had the most positive result.
The right-hand chart shows the average emotions shown by the CEO across three
public appearances. It also defines trouble spots. The first is that most of the positive
emotion is from less lively forms of smiling. The second is that dislike (including
contempt) is prevalent enough to be possibly off-putting to employees.

used a social smile to mask a negative comment). His expressions of
frustration were also authentic and understandable because of the
slower than anticipated implementation of new initiatives. The bad
news? This CEO could be undercutting his goals by displaying
contempt, an emotion that employees could interpret as an inability
to please him. The implication? In situations where a positive
outcome seems remote, human nature is to give up – thereby robbing
companies of the effort they need from employees in order to cope
with a changing, competitive marketplace.

In the end, leaders aren't leaders just by title or power alone. They must
have followers who pledge their loyalty, talent and energy based on the
belief that they'll get something back. Therefore, a CEO must protect his
or her credibility above all else. That's because people expect to believe
their leaders and want to feel that their leaders care about them. People
follow people they like, and unless he or she is deemed trustworthy, the
probability that employees will truly like an executive and strive on behalf
of achieving success for the greater good is close to zero.

Change is fundamentally about feelings. The new management paradigm
says that managing people is managing feelings. The issue isn't whether or
not people have 'negative' emotions; it's how to deal with them.
                                                    Jeanie Daniel Druck

Clear vision: forward thinking and feeling

Synopsis: The next key criterion for success is reassuring employees that they will be protected by astute, decisive leadership that knows how to keep the company not just abreast but ahead of the curve. Here, the CEO's strategic instincts – as communicated to others – will determine the extent of employees' confidence and support. In this section, we analyse how executives must negate stress and reach out to employees in times of change so that their visions are realized rather than resisted.

Key take-aways

- Looking ahead is about providing hope while also alleviating fear.
- Amid change, leaders must negate the stress that causes productivity to implode.
- Change is aided by identifying and understanding the resistance involved.
- The emotional dynamics should be factored into change management planning.

Aspirations lead to inspiration

Looking ahead is about providing hope while also alleviating fear

Why should the quality of being forward-looking or visionary come in second overall, behind honesty, in Kouzes and Posner's leadership survey results? George Bush (the elder) half-dismissively called this quality 'the vision thing', trying to escape comparisons to the Reagan revolution. So why is it something employees prize? And why might an executive's being forward-looking translate into feelings of confidence in employees?

Emotion and motivations.
A vision for change that affirms for employees that new opportunities are plausibly attainable can inspire **pride**. Given an understanding of why the change is necessary and how it can be reached, employees will want to **learn** more in order to **acquire** wealth and prestige. Of course, the downside is that change enforced without inspiring pride will battle with fear and perhaps lose.

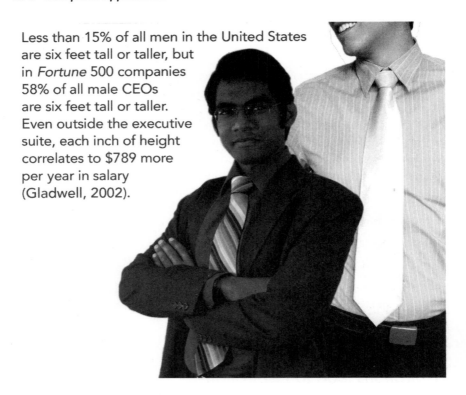

Less than 15% of all men in the United States are six feet tall or taller, but in *Fortune* 500 companies 58% of all male CEOs are six feet tall or taller. Even outside the executive suite, each inch of height correlates to $789 more per year in salary (Gladwell, 2002).

In the most basic terms, the answer is at least hinted at by how our brains are hardwired through evolution. Here's the kind of intuitive, associative thinking that leads to tall CEOs. Being visionary, forward looking, physically tall, and therefore literally able to see better than others: again, the logical and the biological come together. After all, what would have forward-looking literally meant on the ancient grasslands? What physical characteristic might have been helpful out on the savannah many thousands of years ago? Could it possibly have been being tall so that one could see farther across the horizon – a helpful attribute for hunting wild animals and spotting approaching danger? Couldn't there be something to the joke that diversity in senior management often consists of including a short white guy?

In other words, are we really so sophisticated and advanced as a society? Or is it that we've just held on to that physical attribute – height – as a proxy for another equally desirable quality in our leaders: the ability to envision (see) and enact a better future for all?

Instinct suggests that deep down, subconsciously, the first answer is 'no' because the second answer is 'yes'. Height and strength: these are correlatives that indicate the ability to win the battle for resources. That's the game. And it is profoundly emotional in nature for two reasons.

First, a visionary executive who gives employees a cause that distinguishes them from others provides the opportunity for both hope and pride. Many of a company's best workers will be explorers by nature, eager to conquer new lands. Second, being given a sense of direction by such an executive soothes anxiety and brings relief to all employees, who can then focus and get excited about the possibilities ahead.

Nobody saw more clearly the need for executives to be forward-looking than the legendary Drucker, who urged companies to embrace 'creative destruction' since 'today's certainties always become tomorrow's absurdities' (Drucker, 2006). Embracing that same spirit was Samsung's CEO Kun-Hee Lee. Yes, he may not be literally tall. But Lee was a giant when it comes to being visionary, having transformed Samsung into the world's fastest-growing brand during the past half decade by emphasizing the need to spark people's emotions with elegant, human-centred design (Breen, 2005).

Vision, then, is part of being a true leader. But a successful leader must also make vision translate into action by being able to communicate convincingly what direction is being taken, and why, in order to get employees emotionally on-board. Followers have to accept emotionally, not merely rationally, that it is in their best interest to join in an endeavour. Because the immediate reality of change is often quite negative, the reasons given for them to accept the change must alleviate concerns and provide relief. Otherwise, a sense of hopelessness and toxic fear sets in for employees, a scenario executives must strive to avoid.

Leadership amid a M&A or major reorganization

Amid change, leaders must negate the stress that causes productivity to implode

Effective leadership is a visionary and process-oriented combination: executives focus on what will be, while their managers receive guidance in order to handle what is. But as statistics show, in times of great organizational change, that combination will get derailed if employee emotions are not also recognized and handled adroitly. Amid change, boosting employee pride is vital because the emotional alternative – engendering fear – is so destructive to a company's productivity and, therefore, ultimately its profitability. It's a causal chain that starts with the announcement (or, usually first, rumour) of change, followed by anxiety, stress and a slump in productivity.

To understand why the sequence gathers such momentum, let's look more closely at how change, fear and business results correlate. The two yardsticks will be physical and financial in nature, starting with the physical.

Boosting employee pride is vital because the emotional alternative of fear destroys productivity and profitability

As biologically monitored, how does the experience of change affect the body? The technical answer is that people's heart rates, blood sugar levels and cortisol hormone levels all shoot up (Boyatzis 2006). Meanwhile, the underlying, psychological answer is that this trio of physical changes indicates stress. Changes in a person's (work) environment are causing the body to go into overdrive in order to cope with adversity. Moreover, this trio of physical changes corresponds exactly to those that have been measured when people experience the emotion of fear. So it's no wonder the estimate is that only 25 per cent of employees willingly accept change (Brill and Worth, 1997).

Yes, in the short term those physical adaptations make peak performance possible. They're nature's way of helping people rise to the occasion. But typically organizational changes take time to unfold – and in the process the very same biological tricks that make peak performance possible start to undo it. For instance, over time high cortisol levels prove to be toxic and capable of dulling the mind's receptive capacity.

In short, biology helps, then hurts. Anxiety starts to eat people up, as lingering change proves to be a major physiological and psychological, body/mind distraction that lowers employee productivity.

Now for the financial yardstick to bring that point home. For starters, let's note that fear is powerful enough that no amount of corporate planning has ever proven equal to that emotion. It's been estimated that organizational change can cause a decline in work productivity *at levels approaching 75 per cent* (Childre and Cryer, 2000). More specifically in relation to financial outcomes, the dismal track record for merger and acquisition activity can be found by examining Figure 9.7 (Carleton, Klein and Lineberry, 2004).

Underlying the financial troubles companies often experience amid change is emotional trouble. Think of the movie *Jaws*, specifically the scene in which the mayor urges residents and tourists alike to get back into the water because 'It's safe.' Nobody leaves the shore. Inherent to any significant change in any company is a sense among employees that there's a corporate shark circling, with the likelihood of blood in the water imminent. All employees will feel emotionally and perhaps even physically vulnerable – given the stress involved – because it's easy for them to imagine that the blood could be their own.

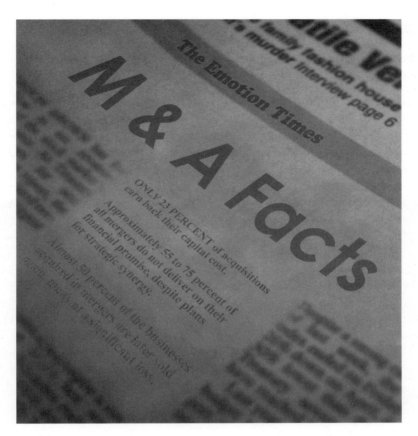

Figure 9.7   For those who put the deals together, M&A activity can be sweet.
After all, the pendulum that swings between advocating 'synergy' or a 'pure play' to
undo a failure involves heavy commissions. But for the employees of the affected
companies, dread, not glee, is the far more common emotional response.

To avoid company-wide paralysis, executives must take the lead to quell
the fear that sets the causal chain of fear leading to lost productivity in
motion. Moreover, they must do
so as quickly as possible – before
the physical toll of stress so saps
the workforce that a corresponding decline in the company's
financial performance follows.

Like seeing a shark's fin in
the water, reorganization,
including mergers and
acquisitions, instinctively
puts people on edge.

Employee response to change

Change is aided by identifying and understanding the resistance involved

Curious to follow up on the estimate that only about 25 per cent of employees willingly accept change, Sensory Logic studied the emotional response of employees at companies amid dramatic organizational changes. The result was that we found the estimate to be, if anything, a little too optimistic based on our research findings.

7 reasons for emotional resistance

Insecurity
Economic concern about job security is obviously the place to start. People wonder if they will be able to make ends meet. They feel vulnerable and, therefore, anxious about entering the unknown.

Powerlessness
Not only does change bring chaos, it also can create or reinforce the realization in employees that they lack control. Their influence may wane or the access they previously enjoyed to somebody with power may go away. In large scale change, the events are bigger than the people involved and may cause them to retreat or otherwise collapse in on themselves.

Dread
Somewhere deep in the psyche in response to organizational change is dread. It comes in response to knowing that the final change in life is death. Being reminded of the ephemeral nature of existence generates some of the sublest and yet most profound anxiety in employees during a time of company change.

Betrayal
Employees have emotionally formed a pact with the status quo, sometimes fully, sometimes half-heartedly. But at whatever level, they feel attached to the familiar. Now they may say to themselves, 'I didn't ask for this. I thought things were going so well. Who let us down?'

Exhaustion
Change requires effort, and especially when sapped by the nerves of waiting for 'the other shoe to drop' any extra push might be hard to give. Expending energy to understand and adjust, first to the disruption and loss of comfort, then to the new, simply isn't welcome.

Defeat
Bad news falls on deaf ears as survival instincts will tend to shut it out. Employees may feel as if the change is a result of failure, theirs or the company's, with the stigma of losing attached. The sentiment: 'We had to do this because we're not good enough.'

Injustice
With most change, there are clear winners and losers. Given human nature, employees may feel passing sorrow for unknown 'losers' while being consumed by jealousy for the winners. Grievances will grow if employees don't perceive much of an advantage for them personally.

Figure 9.8   The seven reasons behind emotional resistance.
One or more of these reasons may come into play for employees actively or passive-aggressively resisting a change brought about by a company's senior management (Jarrett, 2003).

Among other questions, we asked, 'What degree of resistance do you expect leadership to face from remaining employees?' The subjects gave the issue a verbal rating that tied for the most positive, which would indicate little resistance. But the emotional acceptance tied for second lowest in the study. In other words, a large say/feel gap was exposed – with what employees said and what they felt being dramatically different (Figure 9.9).

Combining the acceptance estimate of 25 per cent with our own results of 14 per cent, it's no surprise that the number of organizational transformations that work is no higher than 30 per cent (Carr, 1997). With such a low success rate, a new approach must be found.

The place to start is by establishing a firm understanding of why people emotionally resist organizational change. Figure 9.8 details seven reasons that employees become emotionally resistant to change in the workplace. A tool like facial coding could be a crucial advantage in situations where leaders are trying to identify and understand the nature and depth of the resistance they might be encountering in their efforts to move the company forward.

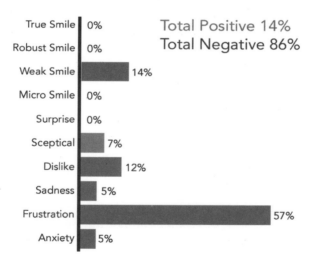

Figure 9.9   Employee emotional resistance.
Given that these emotions were elicited from employees in response to a question about the degree of resistance leaders should expect from remaining employees, things certainly could have looked better for senior management. Clearly, people have a tendency to dig in their heels when confronted by change.

As part of that analysis, it's worth remembering that there are really four types of workers. First up are the winners – those employees most likely to benefit from organizational change and to feel pride at the prospect of an enhanced company identity – for whom some of those seven reasons may come into play. But those reasons will be felt far more strongly by other employees. In addition to the winners, there are three other de facto worker groups that emerge during change:

- **The switchers.** These high achievers can readily go elsewhere, and may not have the patience for the turmoil and paralysis that comes with change. That's especially true if this change seems wrong-headed to them.
- **The survivors.** Employees who will do anything to hold on, for reasons varying from trying to protect a pension to lacking the energy or talent to go elsewhere.
- **The losers.** Those badly affected by the change may turn into the walking dead because of a loss of hope combined with increased fear or even anger. They can harm the winners, motivate the switchers to go and make the survivors even more bitter. Therefore, this group must be removed from the company ranks as quickly as possible to avoid infecting others with their negativity.

Proactive executive response

The emotional dynamics should be factored into change management planning

To bring about progress during major organizational change, executives must plan in financial, legal, operational *and* emotional terms. Now, including the last part might seem obvious. But during the planning stage prior to implementation, the odds are that companies locked in rational mindsets will not have devoted much time or thought to the emotional dynamics of change.

In part, that's because of lacking enough time to do it all. But in all honesty there are other factors involved, too. For one thing, outside resources like lawyers and consultants aren't likely to have a good feel for the company's internal dynamics. Aptitude may be lacking, too. Finally, neither they nor senior management may have the stomach to contemplate in human terms the possibly wrenching changes involved.

As a result, a company's senior management may focus on the logistics of change. But they will be blind to the human dimension and inevitable emotional fallout that accompanies the announcement of a merger, acquisition or reorganization. Furthermore, as noted by Carey and Ogden in *The Human Side of M&A* (2004), these transactions are often done in haste. So change happens 'without the required know-how to assess the people and to get a clear window into the organization'.

Focusing only on the logistical issues of a merger or acquisition can cause the human element to remain blurred in the background.

Given the likelihood – even certainty – of employees giving lip service answers to survey questions related to change, facial coding can be of decisive help. In Sensory Logic's study of the emotional response of employees in companies amid dramatic organizational changes, one outcome especially intrigued us. We wondered whether employee response would be determining whether their feelings about being part of a winning team would surpass the uncertainty that comes with the change.

What's the good news here? The employees we studied had a sense of being victorious and proud amid change. That response overshadowed the ambiguity of the situation. When asked, 'Does the change feel like a win, loss or draw for your company?' the subjects showed a 30 per cent higher degree of positive response than they had to the question, 'Has the uncertainty that came with change bothered you?' (Figure 9.10). In contrast, the verbal self-report ratings responses for the two questions were a tie.

Without a doubt, more reliable insights into employee feelings can aid executive planning. To quote Carey and Ogden again: 'Most mergers – even those that are ultimately less successful – sounded good on paper. Yet in many cases, the highly variable human element – the softer side of the deal that is not as obvious or easy to quantify – was not accounted for.'

Even without benefiting from the scientific rigour of facial coding, however, executives must do better during the planning stage. Incompleteness is the primary problem. Too often, the planning remains exclusively rational and lacks input from people more intimately aware of

Figure 9.10   Victory versus uncertainty, emotionally.
Two keys to navigating change successfully are not to let employees feel like losers or to drag out the pain of uncertainty. These results show a split verdict. Despite a negative total of 56 per cent for the win/loss/draw topic to the left, the companies in this study were actually doing fairly well in terms of establishing hope for new opportunities. However, those same companies were not doing a good job moving employees through the uncertainty that comes with the change (evident in the very high negative total of 86 per cent for the topic to the right).

the feelings and attitudes within the company ranks. Adding middle managers and seasoned employees to the planning mix can help. That's because they will broaden the company's knowledge of the emotional environment in which the change will take place.

Next, in preparing the case for change, senior management must identify the various rationales they might use to explain the change to employees. They can then test-drive the persuasiveness of those rationales by gauging the likely emotional acceptance of them by employees. This step is crucial. Executives who are not in touch with the emotional pulse of the company, but still seek change, will find themselves in a predicament equivalent to driving a car with the emergency brake on.

The most important rationale to identify and communicate successfully to employees will be the risks of sticking with the status quo. People's emotional desire for security will motivate them to accept change if they understand the consequences for failing to change. At the same time, however, hard truths should be delivered softly so that people don't panic, freeze or surrender. Simply saying, 'It's safe to go back in the water,' isn't good enough. The picture of the future has to be vividly clear and exciting – stressing the company's move into a superior position in relation to the competition, if it's to be successful in retaining the switchers.

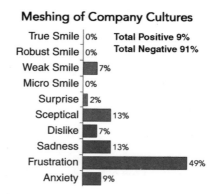

Figure 9.11 Protecting hope and struggling to mesh cultures.
The left-hand chart shows the limited emotional 'hope' of employees at companies undergoing M&A activity. The chart on the right shows the response of those employees to the meshing of corporate cultures. Clearly, companies could use some more help to ensure that productivity improves rather than sags under the weight of negative emotions. But emotions can't be managed if they can't first be measured. Quantifying employee emotional responses during change can inform leaders of the type and extent of intervention required.

In officially communicating the case for change – in front of employees and not through email, memos or a video – executives must explain credibly how change will deliver more benefits to employees than the emotional turmoil incurred. To make the case clear, leadership should focus on emotional benefits. Invoke a sense of victory, greater job security or a fresh new direction, along with a clear synopsis of facts and data. Rational analysis alone doesn't motivate employees. They must grasp a 'truth' that touches their feelings. The delivered message should therefore be simple, heartfelt and aligned with the current emotional climate within the company.

Moreover, in their delivery executives should be careful about their non-verbal signals. That's because people dance to music – not words – with regard to what they accept most deeply. Remember that the sensory and emotional parts of the brain preceded the rational brain, where verbal abilities reside. So employees will trust the CEO's body language more intuitively than anything that gets said.

Finally, in selling and enacting change senior management must account for the fact that there are, of course, always two channels of communication in a company: the official channel and the grapevine. Leaders must leverage the former. But they should also be wise to the realities of the latter, which, contrary to its reputation, research has found to be 75 per cent to 90 per cent accurate (Conniff, 2005). In enacting change, leaders must bear in mind the physiological data pointing out how anxiety eats people up over time. As a result, there's real value in getting big changes over quickly – before the emotional and financial trajectories dovetail downward.

Cohesive culture: bringing everyone along

Synopsis: The other mark of a great CEO is the ability to build a company in which employees feel they will be invited to participate, collaborate and be recognized for achievement in ways that promote good work. As this section shows, this attribute is a matter of establishing the right emotional tone first. Then it's a matter of building a leadership team whose emotional intelligence makes it possible to foster an entire corporate culture capable of inspiring employees to give their best effort.

> **Key take-aways**
> - The CEO's personality looms large in a company but works best close up.
> - A beneficent CEO is inclusive and able to draw on the talents of female leaders.

Emotion and motivations.
A good leader makes everybody believe they can get ahead, thereby fostering the comfort and confidence that are the underpinnings of **hope**. Employees will look to the leader, and also to one another, to **learn** the appropriate behaviour for the culture they are part of. If they like what they see and feel, then the desire to **bond** will manifest itself and lead to a more cohesive, dynamic company.

Creating goodwill

The CEO's personality looms large in a company but works best close up

The third key leadership quality in Kouzes and Posner's worldwide survey is an executive's ability to inspire. As with honesty and being forward-looking or visionary, valuing inspiration makes sense. Honesty comes first because employees need to know whether they trust their leaders enough to follow them. Being forward-looking comes next because employees feel more secure knowing the direction they will be heading (provided that they're convinced it will lead to a good outcome).

Then to round out the list, there's being inspiring. Now the question becomes: do employees feel motivated enough by leaders to adhere to the direction that's been set and the pace being asked of them?

The term that sometimes gets applied here is 'charisma', although that term is misleading. Being inspiring doesn't involve a magical, magnetic charm. Instead, it centres on a leader's ability to inspire goodwill and hope. Right on the mark is the argument made by Daniel Goleman, Richard Boyatzis and Annie McKee in *Primal Leadership* (2002). They write that, above all else, executives must 'prime good feeling in those they lead', because 'resonance – a reservoir of positivism that frees the best in people' – is what's required to make a vision come true. In other words, the sooner executives embrace the fact that they should focus on emotional uplift, the sooner their plans will be realized.

To support their argument, Goleman and company cite numerous examples, including:

- a study of 62 CEOs and their top management teams which corre-lated positive emotional outlooks and interaction with superior busi-ness results;
- a study of 19 CEOs and their direct reports at insurance companies, where the emotional climate accurately predicted high rather than low profits and growth.

What's the authors' overall conclusion, based on a score of case studies? The emotional climate within a company may account for as much as 30 per cent of its performance. Furthermore, over 50 per cent of that climate gets predominately established by the CEO.

Perhaps more riveting than a pile of statistics is to provide a single dramatic instance. Let's look at the success of General Electric's former CEO Jack Welch (Byrne, 1998). His nickname, 'Neutron Jack', came from the way he focused on downsizing by sacking weaker performers.

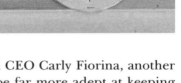

The emotional climate within a company may account for as much as 30% of its performance.

Furthermore, over 50% of that climate gets predominately established by the CEO.

But in contrast to former Hewlett-Packard CEO Carly Fiorina, another hard-driving executive, Welch proved to be far more adept at keeping more people emotionally on-board and helping GE reap the resulting financial benefits.

What's the difference between the two leaders? In a nutshell, it's probably Welch's love of interacting with employees. The guy was famous for spending half his time on people issues. So he took the extra step of devoting hours to being in 'the Pit' at the GE training centre at Croton-on-Hudson.

There Welch demonstrated accessibility in his management development courses. Seeing his personality and leadership style up close, people could judge for themselves the man who took GE's market value from $12 billion in 1981 to around $300 billion almost two decades later. Welch understood that spending time with employees face-to-face in the Pit and in other everyday interactions within the company could really work wonders. A corollary to Welch's success is that to connect emotionally with employees, a leader can benefit from both exuding and generating an element of enjoyment.

In contrast, consider the cautionary tale of an isolated CEO, whose new vision for the company was at risk of losing employee support. Sensory Logic became aware of this situation when asked to perform research involving two different positioning statements, each consisting of three one-word descriptors. The goal was to learn which statement (the CEO's preferred version or an alternative) would be best accepted by employees (Figure 9.12).

What were the results? The CEO's key descriptive term came in last among the six terms. What was his reaction to this news? Rather than defensively dismiss the findings, the CEO magnanimously accepted the alternative brand positioning statement developed by his staff. In that way, he provided the company's employees with a positioning statement they could believe in and act on as part of an effort to update the company's image to better fit a changing business-to-business marketplace. All in all, he knew that without employee support and emotional buy-in, his strategy was dead on arrival.

Figure 9.12   Employee emotional buy-in.
Facial coding revealed true buy-in that verbal input alone was not able to measure. Without a more incisive tool, the company could have taken the wrong path. Not only was the CEO on a different page from his employees regarding which brand positioning statement they would favour, his favourite descriptor generated a positive emotional response of only 23 per cent.

Leading, but not alone

A beneficent CEO is inclusive and able to draw on the talents of female leaders

In truth, as top dog the CEO inevitably sets the emotional tone for the company. Or perhaps I should say top ape. That's because research involving primates demonstrates that it's laughably obvious how much others in the tribe look to the alpha leader for guidance (Conniff, 2005). Why should it be surprising then that in a variety of settings – from speeches to press conferences, negotiations or testifying in court – the character and temperament on display in CEOs' faces can help predict the outcomes?

That being said, CEOs can't – and in effect won't – build hope and cohesive corporate cultures on their own. They need good, emotionally intelligent members of senior management to round out the top team. Here's where the willingness of a corporate leader to share the glory can really pay dividends. After all, what aspiring, talented junior-level executives wouldn't be tempted to join a company whose CEO feels secure enough and generous enough to allow them to exercise their abilities and reap the rewards?

To create a positive, unified culture, a leader must commit rationally to being emotionally vulnerable. As a result, emotionally savvy leaders won't be afraid of being usurped because they realize that they and the company at large will benefit from not hindering the professional growth of others.

What we are ultimately talking about here is nurturing, instead of holding people back. It's about motivating people to want to do their best. They will be grateful to the CEO for being a servant leader (Greenleaf *et al*, 2003), the kind of person who helps others achieve their potential because everybody benefits in the end.

Now, given their acknowledged skills at emotionally oriented core capabilities like relationship-based communication and collaboration – among other things – shouldn't women get more of an opportunity to lead? To prove the point, consider these findings:

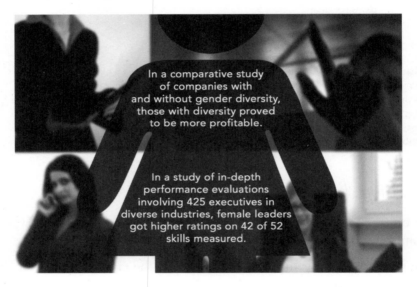

In a comparative study of companies with and without gender diversity, those with diversity proved to be more profitable.

In a study of in-depth performance evaluations involving 425 executives in diverse industries, female leaders got higher ratings on 42 of 52 skills measured.

- As summarized by Douglas Elix, head of IBM's Global Services Division, women are often superior at thinking through decisions, and they tend to interact more collaboratively and seek less personal glory. Instead of being internally focused, women are often more driven by 'what they can do for the company' (Sharpe, 2000).
- Elix's view is seconded by Professor Rosabeth Moss Kanter, author of the 30-year-old management staple *Men and Women of the Corporation* (1977). Her research has found that 'women get high ratings on exactly those skills needed to succeed in the global Information Age, where teamwork and partnering are so important' (Sharpe, 2000).

Yet there are remarkably few women in senior leadership positions. This gap curtails the opportunity for them to help make their companies' cultures more emotionally inviting and capable of bringing out the best in people.

Just how few? In 2005 women held just 16.4 per cent of *Fortune* 500 corporate office jobs requiring board approval – a measly increase of 0.7 per cent from the level documented in 2002. As of 2005, women also comprised only 6.4 per cent of the top five earners among corporate officers. Women of colour were represented even more poorly. They held but 1.7 per cent of the corporate officer spots and were 1 per cent of the *Fortune* 500 top earners (Hymowitz, 2006).

Those low numbers can't be because there aren't any openings or available candidates. Gallup reports that, for instance, during the first four months of 2005, 441 CEOs of companies of varying sizes left their jobs (Gerber, 2005).

Potentially ready to move up, women comprise 49 per cent of those in the professional and managerial ranks. Nor does that number alone give full justice to the talent pool available. Get ready for two more statistics. Consider the fact that not only are 40 per cent of all small businesses in America women-owned, they also employ 35 per cent more people than the entire *Fortune* 500 does worldwide (Barletta, 2003). Often feeling stymied and sidelined without profit-and-loss responsibilities, women in the United States are launching small businesses at more than twice the rate of men (Hymowitz, 2006).

Finally, the low number of women in senior leadership positions also can't be because the status quo is working so well that their skills and emotional intelligence aren't required. One dirty little secret about senior management is that companies are often saddled with unhappy, unproductive leadership. *USA Today* reports that only 49 per cent of top executives are engaged by their jobs. On the other hand, 9 per cent of top executives are actively disengaged (Jones, 2005).

Another study shows that 40 per cent of all newly promoted executives and managers fail within the first 18 months of their promotion. That's because they don't build strong teams or reach out to colleagues and peers (De Koning, 2005). What are the odds that the majority of the leaders who struggle to involve others are men? Pretty high, given the earlier statistics indicating the greater likelihood that women will be collaborative in nature, demonstrating emotional intelligence in the process.

Surely, a better way forward exists. CEOs need good teams supporting them, people who can communicate and emotionally connect.

So why not give women, proven to be highly skilled in both of those skill sets, the chance to exercise them? The essential masculine code of the strong, silent type calling the shots downplays the emotional factor. In contrast, women tend to be more conversant and emotive. Indeed, Sensory Logic's research results indicate that they are more emotionally expressive, on average, than men are.

Our research also shows how important women's less combative, less winner-take-all approach can be in fostering a cohesive culture. What I remember most from conducting an interview with two male employees at a recently acquired company in Denver was the yelp of one employee when he realized the other employee – from the acquiring company – saw the Denver operation as a conquered entity. Not surprisingly, in our study of companies amid change, the ability to mesh corporate cultures exhibited the lowest percentage of positive facial coding results (see Figure 9.11).

Given the emotional intelligence women bring to the job, companies would be wise to promote more women into top-level positions. After all, to compete in the global marketplace they need a diverse leadership team that can relate well – with emotional sensitivity – to diverse employees and customers alike.

Conclusion

Leadership must always remember two realities that showcase the importance of emotions. The first is that it's the human side of business that consumes most of the operating costs. So a failure to be emotionally adept is very counterproductive, even suicidal. Second, it's the employees at a company who turn the CEO's dream of progress into more than just a strategic plan by becoming emotionally committed to that plan. To be effective executives must, therefore, accomplish the following:

● Create faith in a 'greater we' by establishing themselves as real people, rather than merely as the holders of big titles, big offices and big salaries. Part of the reason why it's important to be more personal is that nowadays leaders must also establish themselves as honest. Only then can they generate the emotional momentum necessary to push through change.

● Have a vision that instils pride in employees. Otherwise, the hidden costs of negative feelings such as envy or fear can undo a company during a period of change because emotions are highly contagious. Remember that emotions are, indeed, a hyper-effective means of communicating without words. So disengagement by employees is a leading emotional indicator that executives aren't doing their job well.

● Use face time to make the journey of an unknown future, as a result of corporate change, emotionally acceptable to employees by being willing to meet in person and ask for and accept advice. Unless very poorly handled, those meetings will reap emotional benefits because, in general, greater familiarity leads to greater appeal.

An action plan

To make sure the leadership style on display is emotionally healthy, here are a few things to check when assessing effectiveness:

- Do employees and investors believe the leadership's goals and interests align with their own? Do customers believe that the company, and therefore its leadership, has their best interests at heart? The psychological equivalent of the Bermuda Triangle, in which ships disappear from sight, is the emotion fear, the motivation to defend and the actions of avoidance and denial. Using a scientific, objective tool like facial coding ensures that a company's executives truly know where they stand with key audiences.
- Leaders with a mission must appear to be confident, unafraid and the equal or superior of every other leader in companies similar to their own. People being people, employees will inevitably make comparisons. So it's best to be seen as top dog (or ape) through body language that conveys assurance but stops short of arrogance, because if caring isn't projected by leaders, their employees won't buy in.
- Deliver bad news early and clearly (without using legalese or financialese). When employees and investors receive bad news later rather than sooner, they will feel betrayed. Be timely when delivering news; get it out there before people make up their minds emotionally about what they're going to hear.
- Senior leadership should appear to have unity within its ranks, and any newly hired leader should be justified to employees in an emotionally relevant way. In other words, employees need to answer easily the question: why was this person the best choice to safeguard everybody's interests? Never forget to offer hope about how employees' lives will improve as a result of initiatives or changes.
- Develop communication plans that identify formal and informal points of contact within the company. Emphasize the latter in order to learn more – especially during a time of change when sincere as well as frequent opportunities for employee input and feedback are necessary. Senior leaders with training in facial coding will be able to understand how employees feel before, during and after a change by reading their spontaneous expressions during small group or one-on-one meetings.

10 Employee management

To create the foundation for a great workforce, companies first have to identify and hire emotionally adept individuals. Then they must build on that potential through emotional engagement and training.

Overview

Managing employees is the single most emotional component of the business world. It's a real-life, working relationship between a boss and the staff in which the interaction is ongoing and sometimes intense. Crunch-time crises will happen, and misunderstandings or disagreements will creep into the daily relationship – affecting morale and trust. Inevitably emotionally charged 'moments of truth' will come to dominate the relationship, subtly overshadowing rational components like company goals and specific work assignments. To help managers and staff enhance their working relationships, this chapter will focus on:

- **Compatibility:** gauging the emotional aptitude of job candidates is crucial. Knowing credentials and skills isn't enough. What's missing? Intangible factors like personality, energy level and inter-active abilities. Assessing those 'soft' factors requires emotional tools that will enable companies to determine a candidate's real fit and value in a job. Only then can companies form a realistic under-standing of the candidate's compatibility with the manager and the organization at large.
- **Reciprocating trust:** there's nothing flashy about making a manager/employee relationship work. It depends on both sides being able to feel that the other party is looking out for everyone's best interests. A strong connection only happens when there's an aura of respect and trust – in a word, authenticity. The two parties don't always have to like each other. But they must be able to share both rational and emotionally oriented information to avoid the paralysis that comes with mutual alienation.
- **Mission critical:** authenticity is tied, in turn, to employees being able to enjoy the work at hand because it's meaningful. Feed the heart, feed the spirit and the company's bottom line will be fed. What's required here is a mission-critical sensibility, not in the sense of requiring nerve-wracking deadlines but, rather, by helping employees avoid stagnation. Managers can gain emotional leverage by letting the staff plug in and prove their capabilities. Often the best way to do this is to organize employees into effective, emotionally satisfying teams.

Now let's look more closely at how to build stronger work relationships, starting with getting the right person on-board.

Compatibility: identifying what works

Synopsis: Trying to change people is impossible. The wiser route is to identify their patterns and tendencies – their emotional profile – in the interview process. Then the right personnel get put into the right positions. To aid in that outcome, this section opens by examining flaws in the interview process and why new hires go wrong. Next, it looks at the role of emotional intelligence in selecting new hires who work well with their bosses and colleagues. The section then concludes with a discussion of personality types. Brought into play is how generational diversity is making workforce compatibility a tougher challenge.

Key take-aways

- Rational hiring criteria miss the large role emotion plays in the outcome.
- Compatibility is rooted in gut-level judgements like comfort and credibility.
- Long term, emotions show up most in character traits and belief systems.
- New, shared experiences help overcome generational conflicts.

Emotion and motivations.

A mixture of happiness and sadness, **yearning** is the key emotion here as job candidates try to discern how they may end up feeling about the available position. They seek happiness, but may also suffer doubts based on previous work experiences. In motivational terms, from the job candidate's perspective the pertinent drivers are to **acquire** and **learn**. Potential employees seek to acquire power and status through an entirely new job or promotion, thereby simultaneously gaining opportunities for growth and discovery.

Interviewing: the age-old dance

Rational hiring criteria miss the large role emotion plays in the outcome

Any relationship, professional or otherwise, is built on the character traits that individuals bring to the party. How are companies doing in their search for suitable talent? In truth not very well, as the following statistics make clear.

A study has found that nearly 50 per cent of new hires will fail within 18 months. Poor interpersonal skills are primarily the reason. To be specific, of those who fail 26 per cent will do so because they can't accept feedback, 23 per cent because they aren't able to understand and manage their emotions, 17 per cent because they lack motivation, and 15 per cent because they have the wrong temperament for the job. Way down in fifth place, among the reasons why so many new hires don't succeed, is a lack of the necessary technical skills, at 11 per cent (*Expansion Management*, 2005).

How can companies improve on these kinds of results? The feeding of CVs into a machine coded to look for certain key terms, qualifiers etcetera, may serve as an adequate tool in screening for certain more technical, rationally oriented skills. But another step is needed in the process to lift the success rate for new hires. That's especially true given the importance of emotions in general, and specifically, the degree to which interpersonal skills are lacking.

What could that step be? If not the outright use of facial coding to help evaluate the personalities of candidates, then at least interview inquiries or exercises geared toward ensuring emotional compatibility are in order. After all, it's false to imagine that interviewing isn't inherently emotional in nature. How could it be otherwise? The people doing the hiring are human beings, with their own preferences and biases, their own way of filtering the information they're hearing from candidates. The question isn't whether the hiring process will be influenced by people's emotions or not. Instead, it's whether the individuals involved in the job interviews will realize and accept the role of emotions in the process and do something to incorporate that reality into the proceedings.

To that end, remember that people do business with people they like. We like and often hire someone with whom we can easily relate. Meaning, we tend to hire ourselves. So a company runs the risk of lacking diversity with regard to race, gender and age as well as subtler factors like work style. This emotionally driven, often unacknowledged inclination can reinforce a company's narrow perspective – and that's just one of the holes in the usual, supposedly rational hiring model.

Here are the others:

- Talent gets overrated in relation to character: a company needs to know what's going on inside the job candidate to know whether things will work out in the long run. Talent is a great advantage. But research indicates that the inabilities to manage emotions or accept feedback combine to account for 49 per cent of the reasons new hires fail. So an emotionally savvy route to screen for those factors should be part of the mix.

We tend to do business with people whom we like, people like us who share our beliefs. In effect, we tend to hire ourselves.

- A candidate's interactive skills (or lack thereof) are simply overlooked: people are social animals and business requires people to get along with other people. One survey found that only 40 per cent of employees were deemed able to work well with others (Harris Interactive).
- People spin, deflect, hint and hold back: skills and levels of experience listed on CVs tend to be inflated, despite the irony that they may not be central to what determines success on the job. Often candidates will say what they know they're expected to say to land the opening. Therefore, assessing their non-verbal signals becomes the avenue to securing greater veracity.

Why are these issues so prevalent? One veteran of the personnel placement industry has used his experience to outline his top 10 hiring 'hot buttons'. Seven of the 10 are emotionally oriented: initiative, self-confidence, leadership, compatibility (personality and behaviours), attitude, social skills and integrity (Straits, 2006). These are the types of qualities that companies too often neglect assessing throughout the hiring process. In the end, failing to identify the presence or absence of those emotional qualities leads to the hiring traps listed above.

Sophie **deflects**, **hints** and **holds back** on her CV...

Hmm...
Burger Quick drive-thru worker
or COMMUNICATIONS MANAGER FOR
A NATIONAL
CHAIN RESTAURANT!!!

Hire for emotional intelligence

Compatibility is rooted in gut-level judgements like comfort and
credibility

For starters, companies should first consider what research has unearthed
about how traditional, rationally oriented job interviews work best. More
specifically, studies regarding the predicative validity of various job interview techniques have identified the three techniques that, when combined
with a basic general mental aptitude (GMA) test, provide the best opportunity for combining core validity with increasing the validity of the GMA test.

Personnel Measures	Validity (r)	% increase in validity
GMA	.51	–
Work Sample Tests	.54	24%
Integrity Tests	.41	27%
Employment Interviews (structured)	.51	24%

(Schmidt)

Figure 10.1   The job interview techniques that combine to work best

As outlined in Figure 10.1, those three additions are works sample tests,
integrity tests, and conducting structured employment interviews. In
comparison, unstructured interviews have 13 less validity and add 16 per

cent less validity than a structured interview. Moreover, such common approaches as reference checks, years of job experience or years of education have barely half as much validity as the three supplemental techniques shown in Figure 10.1, and provide only one-third as much of an increase in validity.

Even more effective will be to devise an emotionally oriented version of most of the techniques in Figure 10.1. For instance, the GMA can be paralleled by including a test that gauges emotional intelligence (EQ). Meanwhile, both role-playing work sample tests and integrity tests involving hypothetical ethical dilemmas at work could be videotaped. Then they can later be facially coded to understand the degree to which the candidate is emotionally up to the job.

In their book *What Happy Companies Know* (2006), Baker, Greenberg and Hemingway observe that companies can improve the hiring process by screening for both intellectual and emotional intelligence. The authors define the latter as actively managing both 'thoughts and feelings to bring out the best ... abilities and to create positive interactions with other people'.

But how can companies identify and screen for emotionally smart people? To see how precise and beneficial facial coding can be in making a hiring decision, consider a slightly tangential though relevant example. In this case we were asked to help a pharmaceutical company's advertising agency decide which actors to hire for a new ad campaign. The offer was controversial in nature, for the target market feels a clannish loyalty toward fellow members seeking to kick the smoking habit. Therefore, the actors to be chosen not only had to be likeable and have stopping power (stage presence), they also had to be highly credible as authentic members of the target market.

In this case, the subjects were shown brief, videotaped excerpts of 14 actors ad-libbing about the special nature of the offer. The subjects became, in effect, the hiring managers, and the actors the job candidates. The actors' taped appearances were the equivalent of the answers job candidates give when asked, 'Why do you want this job?'

As shown by the results (Figure 10.2), clear preferences emerged. The subjects recruited to fit the profile of the target market gave less than half the actors a positive response. And of those viewed favourably, the subjects clearly preferred two actors. Only that duo were able to consistently embody a personality that the target market would be likely to accept. How do these results relate to the hiring situation? While comfort isn't everything – remember: hiring people we like can undercut diversity efforts – to do entirely without it won't work, either. Here emphasis was placed on gauging credibility through facially coded responses to the actors. That's similar to the workplace because without trust there's no viable, long-term working relationship between a boss and an employee.

		Appeal	Impact
A	Male	9.96	13.47
B	Male	1.16	14.95
A	Female	13.91	9.07
C	Male	12.95	9.39
B	Female	4.35	12.99
D	Male	3.56	13.66
E	Male	-10.93	19.88
F	Male	-12.06	17.6

		Appeal	Impact
G	Male	-8.84	15.4
C	Female	-1.19	13.47
H	Male	-3.81	14.22
I	Male	-9.39	15.81
D	Female	-15.33	18.63
E	Female	-6.15	13.79
▲	Average	-0.072	14.6

Figure 10.2   Facial coding results for casting call.
Audience reactions to potential spokespeople are analogous to an interviewer's responses to potential employees. In other work situations, an alternative approach is to analyse a job candidate's expressions to learn what they reveal about that person's personality and suitability for the job.

Tools for gauging an appropriate fit

Long term, emotions show up most in character traits and belief systems

Human resource leaders are becoming increasingly aware of the value of hiring job candidates who are good psychological fits for the company at large as well as for the specific positions to be filled. The idea of adding emotional assessments as part of the job hiring process is catching on, and for good reason. Breakthroughs in brain science have shown how central emotions are to people's intuitive, immediate behaviour. But in combination with psychology, neurobiology has now also revealed that personality traits are linked to characteristic emotional displays. Two deeply entrenched, ongoing manifestations of the power of emotions are personality traits and belief systems. Both of them prove to be highly relevant to the job candidate evaluation process.

Let's look at personality traits first. These largely fixed, enduring characteristics will come into play across a wide-ranging set of situations should the candidate be hired, affecting productivity and assignment outcomes. Fortunately, much of what is likely to manifest itself on the job can already be apparent during the initial interviews, making wise hiring choices more feasible.

An ideal vehicle for assessing a candidate's personality type is again facial coding. It's emotionally oriented, scientific and capable of gleaning more than can be readily gathered from the candidate's more conscious, verbally delivered responses. Barring that route, however, here are other specific tools that also exist to help companies improve their hiring odds.

One is the well-known and often used Myers-Briggs test. But it's so transparent in what it measures that its validity gets undercut in the process. A second option is the Hogan test mentioned in Chapter 9, which is highly acclaimed but expensive. A third option with both critical acclaim and financial feasibility is Costa and McCrae's 'Big 5' factor model (Figure 10.3). It arose from the rigorous computer modelling of over 4,500 factors related to personality traits (Howard, 2000). Unlike Myers-Briggs' four-factor model, Costa and McCrae's version of assessing personality includes neuroticism – the second most heavily documented personality dimension.

The Big 5 Factor Model

Extraversion A significant, pronounced tendency to engage with the world. Extraverts are talkative, high-energy and assertive. Natural sales people.

Agreeableness A concern with cooperation and social connectivity. Agreeable people are sympathetic, kind and affectionate; good customer service qualities

Conscientiousness An ability to be self-disciplined and thorough. Conscientious people tend to be organized, thoughtful and are plan-oriented. This makes for great strategies and implementers.

Openness A creative, imaginative approach to problems and the world. Open individuals have a wide range of interests and are both imaginative and insightful – a profile often found in top-notch creatives.

Neuroticism A tendency to experience and dwell on negative emotions. Neurotics tend to be tense, moody and anxious. Good leaders in high stress jobs will have low neuroticism.

Figure 10.3   Costa and McRae's model of the key personality traits

A number of tests are available for measuring the Big 5, including the International Personality Item Pool (which is in the public domain) and the NEO PI-R, a 240-item inventory (packaged as a commercial offer). These could be given not only to the job candidate but also to the manager involved to ensure compatibility.

The other deeply entrenched emotional variable human resource leaders and hiring managers should address is the belief systems embraced by all parties involved. Talk concerning the candidate's need to acclimatize to the corporate culture can be vague. Of greater, more action-able help in engineering a good fit between the company and a potential employee is identifying what values the company cherishes. The next step is to learn whether those same values matter to the candidate. Facial coding can be used to make an assessment of emotional buy-in to those values. Proof of concept is that companies like Endo Pharmaceuticals and the public relations firm Waggener Edstrom have been adept at making a values linkage part of their hiring process.

Generational diversity

New, shared experiences help overcome generational conflicts

For a while now, companies have been wrestling with the emotionally charged topics of gender and racial diversity in the workplace. Slowly coming into sight, however, is another obvious division among employees: relative age (Dychtwald, Erickson and Morison, 2004). The

Clearly, America's workforce is ageing – leading to new, emotionally charged issues that current and future managers will have to resolve (Dychtwald, Erickson and Morison, 2004)

labour pool is ageing. Although companies continue to downsize and outsource, they will soon face the new dilemma of finding enough skilled workers once the Baby Boomers start to retire en masse.

Age diversity brings with it both of the two deep-seated emotional elements just discussed: personality traits and belief systems. While the relative mix of the Big 5 factors is likely to remain stable in a person over time, they do tend to fluctuate based on maturity (Figure 10.4).

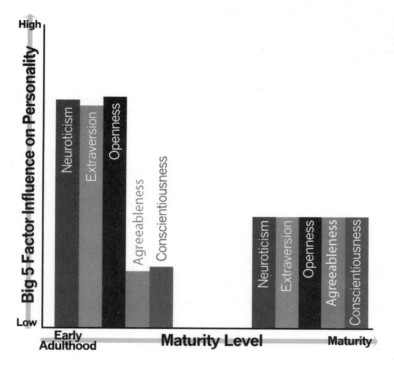

Figure 10.4 Changes in personality due to maturity.
As we grow older, wiser and more experienced, our personality tends to even out. When younger we tend to be more outgoing and open to new ideas, but also more concerned with setbacks and challenging the world. Over time, we begin to find our place in the grand scheme of things and develop a more even outlook (Howard, 2000). Companies benefit from having employees at all stages of life, so as to have a richer range of dispositions.

In contrast, the dynamics of belief systems involve interpersonal rather than intrapersonal differences over time. With an unprecedented four generations of workers – Traditionalists, Baby Boomers, Gen-Xers and the Millennials – great potential exists for emotional, value-based conflicts. After all, employees now have frames of reference stretching from the aftermath of the Second World War to the iPod. If some portion of a company's employees don't feel respected and understood, then the whole effort to be effective in the workplace is at risk because being emotionally in synch is vital to the enterprise.

From Dust Bowl squatters camps...

to the digital era...

the workplace now consists of over three generations of experiences and different ways of comprehending the world around us.

The solution is to recognize that different frames of reference involve different experiences that reinforce generational conflicts. Employees' belief systems won't readily change. But it's possible to ensure that colleagues from different eras find themselves integrated into collaborative team efforts. Then new, common ground experiences can supplement – and at times perhaps even supersede – the memories of other experiences that separate the generations.

Is it important to make that kind of effort? Absolutely. Only 51 per cent of employees believe different generations work well together. More critically, 19 per cent of employees report experiencing frequent intergenerational miscommunication (Cummins, 2005). Clearly, there's plenty of room for improvement. Hiring employees with greater emotional aptitude will make the issues involving an age gap that much easier to navigate. That's because they'll be able to read and respond to the emotions of others not only more quickly, but also with greater ability.

Reciprocating trust: avoid disconnects

Synopsis: Contempt kills relationships. Fortunately, managers and employees can develop a good, sustainable working relationship with rapport built on mutual trust and respect. In the pages to follow, we'll confirm how emotional the workplace really is. Then we'll look at why the bulk of formal training doesn't work and why manager-led training is superior. Finally, the link is made between constructive performance reviews and improvements in morale and retention that lead to greater productivity and lower turnover costs.

Emotion and motivations.

A mixture of anger and sadness, **sullenness** is the key emotion here because the danger of the manager/employee relationship breaking down is high. That fate can be avoided through a shared sense of mission, with pride of sharing in a great outcome the better emotional result. But managers must be able to protect against the sadness of resignation and the anger that arises from wishing to control the process. Both sides have a tendency to **defend** their own emotional interests, with the drive to **bond** sure to suffer unless the relationship can become and remain robust.

Sullenness

Key take-aways

- Alleviating employee concerns makes the working relationship feel right.
- Knowledge-based training ignores how emotionally driven idea retention is.
- A constructive job review is really about developing a path for self-growth.
- The more emotional morale issues become, the more hidden they're likely to be.

The emotional stakes involved

Alleviating employee concerns makes the working relationship feel right

Once the new hire is in place, the question becomes: how best to ensure that the manager/employee relationship develops and sustains itself effectively. As background, consider an exhaustive study conducted by Gallup. It involved over 80,000 managers in over 400 companies (Buckingham and Coffman, 1999). Winnowing down to those questions that best diagnosed the core elements required to attract, focus and retain valuable employees, Gallup cast aside many wrong-headed – and yes, wrong-hearted – notions about how success is achieved.

Out the window went the criteria used in the annual study, *The Hundred Best Companies to Work For*. Why? Yes, factors like on-site daycare facilities, vacation time, profit-sharing and training are important. But those benefits failed to address the pivotal importance of a good manager/employee working relationship in relation to its impact on employee performance.

Likewise, good pay didn't prove to be crucial. Nor did the organizational structure. Nor did the efforts of senior management. Those things matter, but don't prove to be the critical, causal factors leading to superior employee performance. Instead, the quality of the interaction with a manager and whether the worker had a positive emotional regard for the manager were the keys to loyalty and success. That's because, as stated in Buckingham and Coffman's *First, Break All the Rules* (1999), 'people leave managers, not companies.' Put another way, employees stick with somebody who alleviates their concerns, and respects and values their efforts.

In short, Gallup learnt that emotions matter. Without a strong tie to the manager, employees lose heart and give up, resulting in plummeting productivity.

Nobody knows the importance of morale better than middle managers. The push to realize ever greater productivity makes them both the object and agency of change. Under stress to perform, they're probably the first to understand that pursuing low wages and low prices is a race to the bottom that only one company per sector can win. For everyone else, the goal instead must be to craft a functional corporate culture and, on a daily basis, foster successful manager/employee relationships. Putting those elements in place brings out the best in workers so that the company can, in turn, provide its customers with offers and service that give it a fighting chance.

To that end, only part of providing good value can realistically come from hard knowledge. The rest will have to be facilitated by better emotional interactions that capitalize on the fact that, as noted at the start of this chapter, managing employees is the single most emotional element in the business world. Without good attention to the emotional dynamics of that working relationship, where is the 'steam' of unresolved stress likely to go? Into undermining the manager/employee bond, that's where.

Here is proof of the inevitably high emotional stakes involved in the manager/employee relationship. Sensory Logic conducted a study for a fast-food company (Figure 10.5). We normally see emotional response rate levels around the 40 per cent mark for projects involving offer design, advertising, etcetera. But in this case, where we were testing for employee satisfaction, the average was 50 per cent.

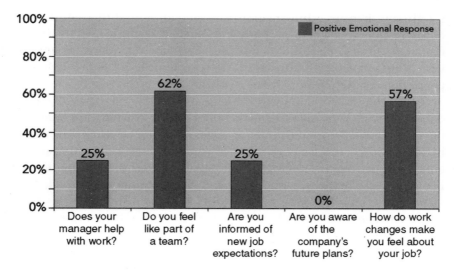

Figure 10.5   Fast-food workforce's endorsement of managerial style.
In a study Sensory Logic performed, the two highest positive responses also had the
highest emotional response rate levels. We concluded that the workers at this particular
company truly feel like part of a team and appreciate changes that seem to improve
their daily work. But the low degree of positive response to the other three questions
points to a lack of communication and interaction between managers and employees.

Fortunately, the two inquiries that netted the most emotional responsive-
ness (that employees felt part of a team and that they felt the changes
underway were beneficial) also had the most positive emotional
outcomes. Therefore, employee concerns were being addressed and alle-
viated. But the next three issues that got employees worked up the most
were about what they felt wasn't going well: 1) controlling the work flow,
2) knowing what their roles were, and 3) knowing more about the
company's future plans. Since these are areas where employees felt the
greatest concern, they are also the problem areas in which we recom-
mended management could and should make improvements.

Post-hire: training and coaching

Knowledge-based training ignores how emotionally driven idea retention is

Ultimately, in bottom-line terms, employee management is about
creating a working relationship in which performance thrives. It's no
surprise that a recent survey sponsored by the International Association

for Human Resource Information Management found that 96 per cent of the respondents cited 'performance' as their top priority. To achieve that goal, those same respondents then cited 'learning management' (by which they meant linking training and on-the-job knowledge to performance) as their next highest priority.

On first blush, that sounds good and certainly logical. After all, better output through knowing more makes sense. What won't work, however, is the usual, rationally oriented training and 'knowledge' development. That's because it fails to engage employee hearts as well as their minds. Consider another result from the same survey. It found that only a little more than 10 per cent of the survey respondents saw their companies as presently 'well aligned' with respect to skills, abilities and goals. Meanwhile, other findings estimate the amount of training information that gets retained and put into actual use at barely 10 per cent (Baldwin and Ford, 1997).

That low estimate sounds plausible. For starters, classrooms are rarely places that make people comfortable. Trainees tend to fall into three groups: vacationers (time away from the office), prisoners ('Do I have to be here?') and the eager beavers who actually liked going to school as a kid.

There are three types of trainees...

| Vacationers | Prisoners | Eager Beavers |

But there's a much more profound reason why formal training can only do so much, and it returns us to brain science. Remember that people are 'hardwired' through evolution to *feel before they think*. That's why any formal training that emphasizes rational thought over feelings isn't a substitute for providing more emotionally intimate, more emotionally meaningful guidance. After all, as is true of all memory formation, idea retention during training is primarily a function of striking an emotional chord. To be especially effective, alternative training must come from a source:

● to which employees will be emotionally alert;
● that the employees respect;
● with which the employees feel comfortable.

Two options exist for meeting those three criteria. The first is potentially the employees' bosses. They have the advantage of heightened relevancy, thereby strengthening the odds that employees will pay attention and take the opportunity to learn. At the same time, however, those bosses may not always enjoy the employees' confidence. Moreover, they may be emotionally 'tone-deaf' and know their stuff but be unaware of the little non-verbal signals they're sending. Then the likely outcome will be that they win the battle of minds while losing the war involving hearts.

As a result, a second option exists. Good training requires providing real knowledge both of the 'facts' and of the needs, wants and beliefs of employees. Recognizing that context is decisive, Sensory Logic's new European training partner is the Dutch-based firm, Performance Solutions. Informed by the approach taken by Michael Johnston, Performance Solutions considers its staff to be guides, not trainers. Their mission? To promote permanent changes in employee behaviour requires moving participants from 'have to' to 'want to' by connecting on an emotional, employee-centric as well as customer-centric basis.

More specifically, an employee-centric approach involves emphasizing why/who, the context, over the traditional how and what dimensions. Otherwise, if meaning isn't established first in a way that will talk to employees' values and beliefs, then over time employees will fall back to their usual, default behaviour mode.

Context	Process	Content
Surrounding	Procedures	Knowledge
Framework	Standards	Information
Reason for being	Systems	Data
Identity	Skills/competences	Results
Being	**Doing**	**Having**

Context is the company. Its heart and soul. The starting point. Only by creating a context that addresses who they are and what they stand for as employees, can a company achieve such goals as a permanent culture change, optimizing performance or designing and implementing new concepts and systems.

Secondly, effective, emotionally oriented coaching of the type that Performance Solutions champions also involves making an emotional connection with customers as part of any company's core business model. Thus as shown below, focusing on the desired guest experience – the emotional outcome – takes precedence over merely delivering in functional terms the product and/or services being offered.

Process is leading ———▶

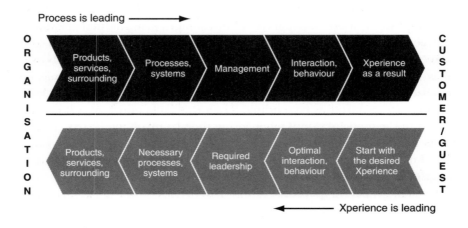

◀——— Xperience is leading

In orienting its employees to the job at hand, too often companies adhere to a traditional, internally focused process in which the product or service offering takes precedence over concern about customers' emotional take-away experience. In Performance Solutions' Reverse Thinking Model, priority is given instead to, first, the desired guest experience of the company and, next, how the behaviour of staff can ensure a favourable experience. Leadership, processes and the offer itself take secondary, support roles rather than helping to dictate a company-centric approach.

Either way, or through a combination of an emotionally attuned manager and training firm, the ideal approach will take into account the advice of Nigel Nicholson in a *Harvard Business Review* article (1998). There he wrote about the implications of evolutionary psychology in relation to management practices. Evolutionary psychology draws on academic fields like cognitive science, evolutionary biology, genetics and neuropsychology in order to foster a better understanding of the basic human condition.

As discussed in Chapter 1, neurogenesis means that new neurons and new mental connections form throughout our lifetimes. Nicholson's key point is that this plasticity or opportunity for growth and change in individuals must be balanced with the understanding that there are distinct limits to just how much basic human nature can be remoulded. Therefore, emotionally wise managers won't despair and forfeit their desire for improvements. But at the same time they won't set themselves up for disappointment by failing to recognize these truths:

● People usually think most creatively when they feel safe. They're unlikely to absorb something new if on edge.
● People have a tendency to be overconfident in their abilities, and may underestimate the difficulties they face.

As a result managers can make employees aware of their mental blind spots. But they must do so gingerly because experiencing a sense of failure (bad news) won't make employees feel very safe or supported. A difficult balancing act arises because employees will resist change unless personally dissatisfied with their performance. Yet they may not be capable of acting on what they've heard from a manager if they're not confident.

In other words, the difficulty involved in simultaneously maintaining employees' sense of safety while also getting them to pursue improvements in performance explains why managers who aren't emotionally skilled often falter. By psychologist Richard Boyatzis's calculation, only about 12 per cent of managers are really good at their jobs. Why isn't the percentage higher? The primary reason is because most managers lack emotional smarts.

Is there hope for the almost 90 per cent of managers who aren't especially emotionally literate? Yes, awareness and practice will help. Moreover, there should be other resources for managers who struggle to deliver both knowledge and rapport at the same time. For example, one of the really progressive programmes belongs to Caterpillar Inc. Its Cat U has been honoured as one of the best training programmes by the American Society for Training and Development, the Corporate University Exchange and the International Quality and Productivity Center. What makes Cat U so great?

- It's an ongoing programme integrated into daily business practice (rather than being another flavour-of-the-month exercise).
- The knowledge network the programme draws on is broad and flexible. It includes trained programme facilitators, advisory board members who serve as strategic partners and, most importantly, access to experts from across the company.
- The programme is also flexible with regard to timing. Coaching is available at short notice, and collaborative sessions enable those who participate to post questions and share presentations to gain quick input (Caterpillar Inc, 2006).

Feedback and performance appraisals

A constructive job review is really about developing a path for self-growth

If there's ever a point in the year when it all comes together – the employee's, the manager's, and by extension even the company's, hopes and concerns – it's the periodic performance review (White,

2006; de Koning, 2004). Talk about an emotionally loaded situation. To avoid having lingering sullenness as an emotional outcome, especially on the part of the appraised employee, the following checklist of objectives should be pursued through careful planning and execution:

- **Clear goals.** Too often the periodic review is a subjective discussion that doesn't feel fair to those on the receiving end. Employees are unable to anticipate how their managers view their performances and they approach the reviews with a defensive mindset. To counteract that possibility, even likelihood, the review should be based as much as possible on quantifiable outcome-based metrics tied to sales, customer loyalty, financial returns, quality measurements, complaint levels, etcetera. Done well, performance reviews become a positive developmental activity that enables the employee to feel that pride and hope are plausible. Expansive goals should map out the path for the employee's self-growth. Avoid narrow, short-term goals that seem to be selfish in nature. In those cases, managers who are merely trying to feather their own caps before moving on to new assignments damage the integrity of the entire performance review process.

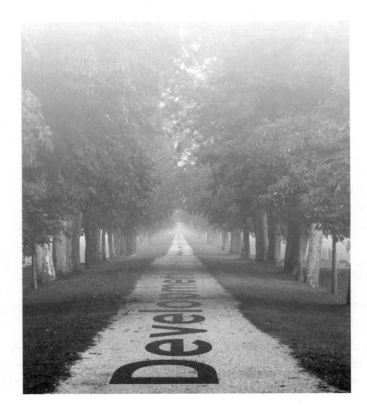

- **Authentic buy-in.** Emotions turn on and propel action when people sense relevancy. So employees should be authentically empowered to take ownership of goals, rather than feel like they are just handouts from management. At the start of a review period (but separate from the previous performance review meeting), managers and their employees should sit down to discuss performance expectations and agree on specific targets and desired outcomes. Done well, those one-on-one sessions will lead to employees believing that the goals to be pursued are legitimate, real and worthy of their efforts.
- **Credible, complete assessments.** While it should go without saying that managers will have a broad understanding of their employees' actual performance levels, too often that isn't the case. Distracted and harried managers risk appearing clueless at review time. Those managers don't know themselves how the employee performed and may fail to incorporate insights from that worker's peers, clients or other managers, all of whose input can help them arrive at a big-picture view. Specific examples are crucial for employees if they are to learn in ways that 'break the mould'. The mind must be able to *envision* what the boss is talking about for the heart to follow.
- **Clear developmental path.** Engaged employees are interested in improving their skills and advancing their careers. The goals cited earlier must be strategic, not merely small tactical steps that won't take an employee anywhere long term. Too often, managers neglect to help out, creating the disappointment that leads to employee sullenness. Either as part of periodic performance reviews or in separate meetings, managers and their employees should discuss strengths and areas for improvement. Then they should jointly create developmental action plans that will enable progress, without merely resorting to a list of training classes as a proxy for growth.

- **Genuine pay/performance link.** When the review process is founded on appropriate and meaningful metrics, the link between pay and performance is typically self-evident. Still, even the best system can break down if the company's short-term financial results are seen as an excuse to shortchange an employee's compensation. Then the performance appraisal becomes suspect, creating an emotional disconnect for the employee that is bound to show up in future performance levels. Should that result come as a big surprise? No. The financial *and* emotional bottom line here is that the salaries of good workers aren't the place to fix the company's bottom line. Period.

- **Focus on learning.** Another guideline for ensuring constructive performance reviews is to make sure they serve as significant opportunities for learning. What's the big distraction here? It's a bottom-line focus on the question that's inevitable even when not spoken aloud: 'How much more money am I going to get?' The problem is that fear and hope get affixed to learning the answer, instead of a more proper emotional focus on creating the yearning to improve. The solution is for managers to handle the money distraction on a separate occasion. In performance reviews, focus on creating dialogue that gets workers to really emotionally internalize and accept opportunities for growth.

- **Engaged follow-up.** Finally, let's touch on the critical need to maintain ongoing dialogue and feedback. Long term, managers need to stay in steady but not overwhelming contact with employees to have the emotional equity required to endorse or coach with regard to behaviours that are contributing either to successes or problems. In the short term, the approach should be to circle back a couple of days after the review. A follow-up discussion provides an opportunity to affirm the positive take-aways, quell confusion and air any issues if there's a bitter aftertaste from the review. Not to do so is dangerous because negative feelings won't go away and will only fester. For a manager not to be proactive by circling back around isn't rational. Instead, it's behaviour driven by fear and avoidance, and it will most likely make the whole review process that much messier and unproductive the next time around.

In summary, the performance review process doesn't have to be an emotional time bomb dreaded by managers and employees alike. When appraisals are handled well, employees feel like they're part of a fair, honest, open system, and therefore the process has the potential to improve their morale, commitment and effectiveness.

Morale and retention

The more emotional morale issues become, the more hidden they're likely to be

Even the best, most sensitive managers will have a hard time knowing what's really going on at the crucial emotional level in their daily interactions with staff members. After all, little can be learnt if training, coaching and appraisals occur too deeply in the shadow of the hierarchal relationship of boss to subordinate which tends to suppress the upward flow of information. Why does that tendency exist? Hardwired into everybody's psyche is the realization that danger may be involved for those in the powerless position.

Therefore, even sincere, good-faith attempts by a manager to learn how it's going for his or her employees are unlikely to result in candour. And the more emotional, often negative, the situation becomes, the more morale is likely to be adversely affected even as the employee goes through the motions of pretending otherwise.

A case in point with regard to hidden, unexpressed feelings is a study Sensory Logic conducted for a major company in the financial services sector. As a follow-up to its usual annual survey of employees, we secured volunteers from a smaller sample of workers. Then we videotaped them so that traditional verbal input could be compared with what they really felt, as revealed by their facial expressions, about a select number of the survey topics. Here are the topics chosen:

- **Development:** Opportunities exist for me to learn new skills that can help further my career growth.
- **Support:** My manager makes it possible for me to succeed.
- **Satisfaction:** I'm able to find meaning and a sense of progress as a result of my work assignments and outcomes.
- **Life/work balance:** The demands of my job aren't overwhelming my commitments at home and adversely affecting the quality of my life.

For the purposes of this test, all verbal responses to each topic were categorized as essentially positive, neutral or negative. The analysis of the comments was then compared with the facial coding results that quantified the degree of positive emotional response or buy-in to these four assertions in the survey.

What emerged in the results? Not surprisingly given that people's livelihoods could seemingly be vulnerable if evidence of negative attitudes became apparent, what our subset of employees said was often very different from what they felt. As Figure 10.6 shows, verbal responses, regardless of topic, were always at least 50 per cent positive. In contrast, in three of four instances the percentage of positive facial coding activity was less than half of the percentage of positive verbal input. Clearly, a huge gap opened between what employees were verbalizing and how they emotionally responded to the survey's affirmative assertions.

The key lesson for managers here was that morale looks vulnerable. Not only was just one score positive – the one related to future opportunities – the others were very low. Normally, we might see scores as low as 35 per cent to 40 per cent positive when facial coding analysis uncovers resistance. But here the other three scores are all below 30 per cent, and low enough to indicate that while the future may hold promise, the emotional reality is that at present workers are struggling to find enjoyment.

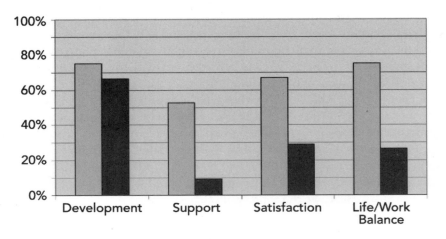

■ Positive Verbal Response   ■ Positive Emotional Response

Figure 10.6   Emotional addendum to annual employee survey.
By contrasting the percentage of positive verbal and emotional responses, Sensory Logic found that employees at the company honestly saw opportunities for advancement, but not much else.

How do companies end up with sullen employees? When workers lose hope. Sullenness results from a combination of rising frustration and sadness (regret and resignation), which simultaneously lowers the energy levels available to deal with work situations. Companies that do not identify and turn that predicament around run the risk of losing morale, then momentum, and finally, employees – especially the top performers with the best prospects for moving on. As noted in Chapter 7, one estimate suggests that every staff turnover costs the affected company at least $60,000 and often much more. That sizeable sum is based on the required training and orientation for the replacement worker, among other factors.

So losing all but the most mediocre employees is obviously not the way to go in building a financially and emotionally sound company.

To make the link between emotions, morale and retention statistically clear, note the results from three separate studies (*HR Focus*, 2005; Business Wire, 2003; Frost, 2003):

- One found that, among employees with intensely negative feelings, 28 per cent are actively looking for new jobs. In contrast, only 6 per cent of those who are happy are on the look-out for other opportunities.
- Another calculated that up to 40 per cent of employees who believe they are being poorly supervised consider departing.
- A third concluded that workers who dislike their bosses are four times more likely to leave the company than those who rate them as excellent.

Figure 10.7   What good workers want.
By being able to evaluate what's wrong, and not just who's wrong, emotionally smart managers improve the odds of creating a productive working relationship in which employees remain open to learning and innovation, rather than succumbing to fear and resignation.

Without question, managers who can keep employees emotionally on-board are invaluable. To that end, what good workers want is apparent (Figure 10.7), and tied to all of the core motivations except acquire – indicating that a truly good job isn't just about money.

By providing employees with all three items from the Bill of Wants, companies will get plenty back in return. Emotional engagement makes positive outcomes possible in the workplace. Moreover, study after study confirms that there is a direct link between employee satisfaction and customer satisfaction. Finally there exists another series of links between employee satisfaction and higher levels of productivity, profitability and employee retention (Baker, Greenberg and Hemingway, 2006; Boyatzis, 2006).

Mission critical: inspiring a questing mentality

Synopsis: In effect, mission critical refers to eliciting more effort and better outcomes from employees who can find real meaning in their assignments. This section will address the need for nourishing company cultures, whether within the company at large or in smaller, team-based settings in which employees feel the kind of camaraderie that makes greatness possible. The section ends by examining the emotionally based qualities that enable a team to exceed expectations.

Key take-aways

- Employees work better in smaller units and with a healthy dose of encouragement.
- Great teams enjoy a sense of mission and are able to draw on everyone's talents.

Emotion and motivations.
Pride is the key emotion in play here. It occurs when happy employees feel just enough anger and desire to break through barriers and achieve results. No matter how good the working bond with the boss, employees may experience pride best in peer-based teams more likely to encourage uninhibited action. The primary motivations are the urge to **bond** with co-workers combined with the opportunity to **learn**.

Pride

Getting to the right size

Employees work better in smaller units and with a healthy dose of encouragement

Everyone at a company is subject to the company's general culture. No manager or employee is immune to its influence. It would be great if most workers regarded their corporate cultures positively. But unfortunately, the statistics aren't promising. As reported in *USA Today* (Jones, 2004), a Booz Allen Hamilton survey found that apparently one in three Americans believe they work for a passive-aggressive company, where smiling without actually being in accordance serves as the dysfunctional norm. (Figure 10.8 depicts the survey's full results.)

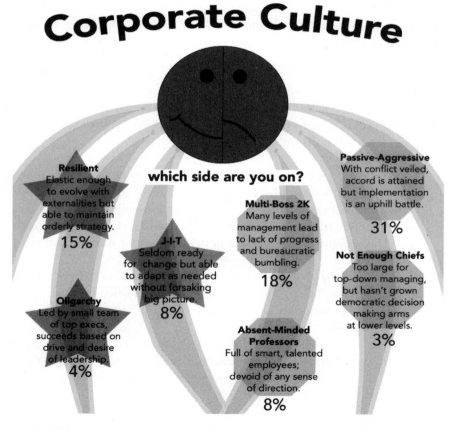

Figure 10.8   Only 27 per cent of American workers respect their workplace.

That picture fits the estimate that there might be as much as 40 per cent in 'untapped productivity reserves' at the typical company. Why such a loss? Because it's emotionally dysfunctional (Jones, 2004). Hamstrung by an unhealthy culture, managers and employees alike begin to feel as if qualities like comfort, excitement and nimbleness are but a distant dream.

How best to find a solution? A constructive approach is to look back at historical human nature to find the way forward. Have people thrived best in groups or alone? What role do emotions play? What group size has traditionally worked well for people? Hint: it isn't the mega-corporations that exist today. In contrast, it's believed that for most of recorded history – 99 per cent of it – human beings lived, hunted, then began farming in small groups of no more than 10 to 50 fellow members (Baker, Greenberg and Hemingway, 2006).

From sports teams to military squads, the core unit rarely exceeds a dozen members. It's a size that has traditionally proven to deliver the best opportunity for social and emotional cohesion, thereby creating the best opportunities for positive outcomes. Yes, the whole can be greater than the sum of the parts.

So what's believed to be the ideal team size in the business world? For optimal effectiveness, a team should have no more than six members. As Tom Peters jokes, a team should never, ever be so large that it can't be fed by two big pizzas. The rationale pinpointing this group size comes from two different angles (Conniff, 2005):

- Every extra person in a group exponentially increases the number of one-on-one relationships. As a result, larger groups place more emotional and cognitive demands on their members. While a six-person team involves 15 different pairs of relationships, each requiring attention, for a seven-person team that number balloons to 21.
- A listener should ideally be within five feet of a speaker to hear well. If there are six inches of shoulder-to-shoulder distance between team members, no more than seven people can sit next to each other in a five-foot diameter circle.

Clearly the second point – being able to hear what's going on – is functionally advantageous. But it's the first point that establishes the core reason small groups work well. Without a rich sense of undistracted intimacy, team members can't bond with one another, feel supported and produce desired results. To accomplish its mission, the co-workers on a team must be able to form good individual relationships. Then self-disclosure doesn't seem risky and affirmation can take on a personal glow.

A decade-long study of management teams at Ross Perot's old company, EDS, is illuminating here. It came away with hard and fast numbers regarding how important emotional support actually is to forming a successful team (Conniff, 2005):

- The 15 high-performance teams in the research project averaged 5.6 positive interactions for every negative one.
- In contrast, the 19 lowest-performance teams had a positive/negative ratio of 0.4.

The study also concluded, however, that being too positive can be bad. At more than a five-to-one positive to negative comment ratio, teams get lax and begin to grow ineffective. It's a classic case of cause and effect. If emotional support begins to feel inauthentic because every effort gets praised, such empty praise will cause the team's output to suffer.

The qualities that drive great teams

Great teams enjoy a sense of mission and are able to draw on everyone's talents

Like its common counterpart (namely the staff or project meetings led by managers organizing the goals of their direct reports), a well-functioning, specially convened team should stick to a pair of basic rules.

First, to get the best from people, members – and especially team leaders – must avoid embarrassing others. Remember that many people fear public speaking more than practically anything else. Therefore, public humiliation of any kind will undermine that person's ability to function in the group. Fear always comes before the opportunity for pride. One study found that an amazing 28 per cent of employees said they typically feel uncomfortable in meetings (MacIntyre, 2005), which means that open, full participation won't be easily coaxed from them.

Yes, their reason for discomfort is fear of being put 'on the spot' during a discussion. But they could feel uneasy for perhaps an even more justifiable reason: boredom. Meetings should always have genuine purposes and end with clear calls to action. A meeting is a story: it should have a beginning, a middle and an end.

Unfortunately, most meetings have beginnings that drag on and on. So a second basic rule is that if no clear, decisive action will be taken as a result of the meeting, don't meet. Boredom is an emotional cancer. It leaves department staff members and specially convened teams both mentally and emotionally bed-ridden.

Those are just ground rules, however, to be followed so as not to inhibit potential. Of greater interest is to learn what really makes a team a great team. The question is intriguing, and the answer is primarily emotional in nature.

A case in point is consulting work that Sensory Logic did for a company seeking greater cohesiveness within its ranks. For a group of directors and their staffs, we conducted a study involving half a dozen questions that could serve as a springboard for discussions about how best to improve working dynamics. As is evident from the results in Figure 10.9, everybody involved was emotionally on-board with the general belief that the company was characterized by a 'we' mentality.

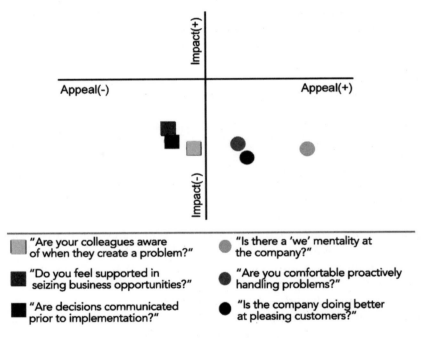

Figure 10.9   Company culture claims versus practice.
The subjects emotionally endorsed the idea that the company has a 'we' mentality. But the degree to which it is all-encompassing comes into doubt because of weaker responses to specific issues involving how people at the company interact.

But that was more at the conceptual level. When the questions got down to specifics, the picture changed. Then the subject's emotional responses revealed that, while specific problems were handled proactively and well, larger, company-size initiatives were falling by the wayside. For instance, the subjects felt assured that customer needs were being addressed. They didn't have the same emotional confidence, though, regarding their own needs when it came to cooperation, communication and pursuing business growth opportunities.

Great teams – which is what this small company's management group aspired to be – take care to get the essentials right. Let's review what they are (Bennis and Biederman, 1997).

The first essential has to be the composition of the team. Talent matters. But just as important to the successful functioning of a team is that its members fit together well, emotionally and in terms of personalities. Don't impair a team from the off by establishing the wrong emotional mix. Here are three routinely ignored selection criteria:

- **The right level of status diversity:** team members should be relatively equal in status within the company, since lower-downs usually defer to higher-ups. Mixing status can rob the team of intellectual input and emotional commitment.
- **Gender parity:** there needs to be a good mix of men and women so that the team can benefit from the different emotional skills typical of each gender.
- **Personality diversity:** there can't be too many A-types in the group since they will tend to struggle with each other instead of with the issues the team was formed to address. A critical mass of B-types can serve as a good counterweight to the A-types' influence.

The second essential, team size, we've already addressed.

The third essential is that the team must have a true leader. Often a leader is imposed on a team. But a great team doesn't gain its leader that way. A great team is emotionally wise enough to recognize that the drive to lead is inborn. It also knows that the drive and ability to lead can depend on circumstances, a would-be leader's location in his or her professional life cycle, the way the team's project fits with a potential leader's interests, and the way the project suits the company's needs. For instance, at IDEO, where innovation rules (it leads the list of offer-design firms year after year), employees choose their teams and then the teams choose their own leaders. From such spontaneity can grow the kind of results a great team dreams of delivering.

Speaking of dreams, that's the fourth essential. Great teams enjoy a real sense of mission. They have a purpose and often an 'enemy' that helps to mobilize their energies. This enemy could be a rival company, whose offer a team regards as inferior and yet is currently dominating the market-place. Or this enemy could even be the company bureaucracy in which the great team operates, struggling to prove its potential as an 'underdog'.

The fifth essential is that, when blessed with a mission, a great team knows how to swing into action. It knows how to leverage everybody and every resource on the team so that dreams can emerge fully realized. To that end, a successful team will deliver a what's-in-it-for-me (WIIFM) to each and every team member. The team will also let everyone feel as though he or she is in it together and can influence the outcome. Great teams are their own reward, and everyone on them has a job suitable to his or her abilities.

Finally and perhaps most crucially, a great team is so emotionally fuelled that it lives on hope, not reality as narrowly defined by a set of deliverables. In other words, the members of a great team find satisfaction throughout the process – not just in completing it – because the experience itself is intellectually and emotionally rewarding. Yes, great teams ship – they deliver – but they do so by meeting standards that exist in their hearts, not on slips of paper. The contract they really have is with themselves.

To avoid violating this list of essentials, there is, finally, one crucial anti-rule regarding teams: don't ever form one if it's merely a cover-up for not taking real action and seeing changes through. The vitality of great teams is dependent on their authenticity. Cease to make them a vehicle for fresh, truly open thinking and actionable outcomes, and management poisons the emotional groundwater that makes them such a valuable addition to a company.

Ultimately, companies that tap into a great team's inspirational, emotionally fuelled potential day by day – and make it possible – will get the results they long to have. In increasingly flat companies where self-directed work is likely to become the norm, instilling pride isn't some 'nice to have' platitude. Instead, pride, hope and emotional engagement, in general, have become a business necessity in order to be highly productive and competitively viable.

Conclusion

Positive, constructive employee management is the heart of most successful businesses. Unfortunately, in the day-to-day distractions of running a business, the emotional components of employee management often get overlooked. To be effective and robust, management must accomplish the following:

● Make the right hires. Companies that know themselves and understand the types of people who will flourish within their ranks are more likely to make the right hiring decisions. The opportunity open to any and all companies is understanding their own emotional components. Then they can better take into account the job candidates' personalities, values and interactive abilities.

- Build rapport. Because the manager/employee honeymoon is fleeting, it's important to establish good habits early. The key one: given a choice between under-communicating and over-communicating, always select the latter. That's especially true when appraisals and other forms of feedback or coaching become necessary as a result of setbacks. In those instances, rapport helps provide the emotional equity that sees the working relationship through.
- Don't pen people in, otherwise they will wilt emotionally. Good employees will want room to operate (while still having their managers or team leaders establishing realistic boundaries). Rhetoric about empowering people, coupled with lots of limitations, is asking for an outcome that doesn't exist in nature. It's like trying to breed a cross between a lion and a sheep.

An action plan

To make sure that the company's employee management is emotionally healthy, here are a few things to check when assessing effectiveness:

- Hire people using a process in which multiple employees meet the job candidate in as casual and social an environment as possible. Build in opportunities for storytelling, both by candidates who can reveal themselves in action and by company representatives prepared to be candid. This way, both sides can address not just the rationally oriented skills required for the job but also the personality and values best suited for the situation. (In relation to fit, cancel the interview if the manager the candidate would be working for can't make it to the session.)
- Ensure that everyone feels welcome and the company's commitment to diversity feels believable and not just like window dressing. Nobody can perform well if they're not emotionally comfortable and at ease. In today's society, the company should be growing more, not less, diverse by race, gender and sexual orientation.
- The processes by which the company operates should feel fair and legitimate, not rigged. They should also feel human and personal rather than seemingly being delivered in a unidirectional, cold, distant voice.
- The company should be sensitive to the way employees' emotional needs vary as they go through their life cycles of service at the company. New hires will be more anxious about unknowns, while younger but established workers will look for expansive futures, and veterans will seek both steady situations and new challenges.

Afterword

So what now? What does the future hold for emotions?

The science-fiction crowd may not be far off. As technology progresses in its ability to replicate human characteristics, we may be standing on the precipice of emotionally aware robots that respond to their owners' feelings.

The Irish poet William Butler Yeats believed that history doesn't repeat itself so much as form a spiral staircase, with repetition but at an ever higher level. In that case, it shouldn't be surprising that back in the 18th century Adam Smith created not only the 'dismal science' of economics but also took a pioneering role in the 'sentimental science' of psychology. Today, Smith's twin study of money matters and emotions looks ever more prescient. His two favourite disciplines are intersecting again but at a much higher, more sophisticated level than ever before thanks to the ongoing, futuristic force of technology.

Some of that technology involves the fMRI brain scans that have been providing striking evidence about the essential role that emotions play in the decision-making process. At other times, however, technology goes beyond confirming the importance of emotions to exploring new possibilities.

For instance, consider the techno toys joining our world. A relatively simple example is Playmates Toys' invention, 'Amazing Amanda', a baby doll capable of showing a small range of feelings that her face emotes electronically while she speaks (Marriott, 2005).

At the same time, functional, semi-emotionally-literate robots have begun to appear. After fluffy little robots called 'Furbies' came Sony's AIBO Entertainment Robot (Norman, 2004). With the programmed capacity for the six core emotions of facial coding – happiness, sadness, anger, surprise, fear and dislike (disgust) – Sony's robot adapts its emotional state and behaviour based on external stimuli, just like human beings do in real life.

Our lives are being 'wired' in all sorts of ways, so it is inevitable that emotions have become part of the changes afoot. Indeed, robots replacing humans and capable of doing everything people do – only better, including showing emotions, responding emotionally and even reading the emotions of others – is what many artificial intelligence initiatives are really all about.

Writing for *Scientific American*, Microsoft's chairman Bill Gates provocatively titled his article, 'A robot in every home' (2007), then backed it up with the estimate that nearly 10 million personal robots will soon be in use. By 2025, the personal robot industry is expected to be worth over $50 billion in annual sales, as robots keep tabs on home security, do domestic tasks and care for the bedridden elderly, among other forms of assistance to their owners.

Even without the use of robots, the confluence of economics and emotions originated by Adam Smith is well on its way to reaching new and higher formats. Video games are a major sector already, with characters engaged in highly animated movements and displaying a large variety of facial expressions. Perhaps these games, as well as company websites and even camera-enabled cell phones, may soon bring us interactions in which our feelings are read, then reflected or responded to accordingly, in an attempt to heighten our enjoyment or directly modify our purchase decisions.

Does that sound too futuristic? Then consider the fact that the business of emotion detection, using speech analytics, is already a $400 million industry (Shin, 2006). What is being done through tracking volume, pitch and the categorization of transcribed words and phrases will sooner, rather than later, become a reality in regard to facial coding too.

Ekman's FACS system was created based on individual facial muscle movements, which makes it ideal for computer generation; it is a codified system to accurately and completely represent physiological actions. This ability has allowed game engines, such as Half Life, to model realistic facial movements that transfer across any model for certain actions. As games are capable of rendering graphics more realistically, the need for realistic actions becomes even more pronounced. The realistic rendering of human appearance without the realistic modelling of human behaviour creates a completely unbelievable representation. The most well-known occurrence of this lapse is probably *Final Fantasy*, a movie beautifully rendered in exquisite detail, but which lacks believable interaction, thus preventing viewers from reaching the point where they can suspend their disbelief of the situation.

In short, programming machines to display or interpret emotions is going to transform both the marketplace and the workplace, enabling companies to get closer to consumers and reinvent offices and factories in ways that were never imaginable until now.

Why emotions win every time

In the end, it's really quite simple: to achieve success, companies must follow nature. Given that emotions process sensory input in one-fifth of the time our conscious, cognitive brain takes, reason will always depend on emotion to define what is vital to us. The evolutionary process gave us feeling before thinking. Solving the emotion puzzle originates with quelling fear and the related motivation to defend ourselves. Because of this, *Fear Factor* isn't just a TV show; it's the essence of a sound emotional business strategy, as reflected by the old, but true, adage that 'trust is the emotion of business'.

Further breakthroughs in brain science are occurring at an increasingly fast pace, making it difficult to come to a close on the information contained in this book. It is an exciting time for new developments in consumer and employee insights. On an almost daily basis, I find news stories that affirm the guidance I've sought to provide in this book.

One day it's the *Wall Street Journal* reporting about fMRI scans that show different neurological reactions to strong and weak brands (Helliker, 2006). Another day it's the AP wire services detailing a study that shows women get paternal clues in men's faces (WCCO, 2006) or the *New York Times* reporting on research indicating that men are better than women at detecting an angry face in a crowd (Bakalar, 2006). Within days of each other, the *Economist* (2006) made 'Happiness (and how to measure it)' its cover story, and *Strategy + Business* (2006) named Fisher and Shapiro's (2005) *Beyond Reason: Using emotions as you negotiate* as one of the best new books.

But the most significant news story in terms of what Sensory Logic does to help companies measure and manage emotions came to me via the BBC News ('Face expressions "hereditary"', 2006). This story further validates Charles Darwin's original work on facial coding – and in particular, the universality of facial expressions – because it is a dramatic study by a team of Israeli scientists who found that the facial expressions of family members are closely aligned. In particular, their research found support for Darwin's belief that facial expressions are innate. In analysing the expressions of 21 volunteers, some of whom had been blind from birth, along with those of their relatives, the scientists discovered that facial expressions were strikingly alike. The revelation that facial expressions are inherited and have an evolutionary basis furthers the hunt. The next step? Looking for the genes that influence facial expression.

Meanwhile, armed with the emotional knowledge provided in this book, readers can begin to see and identify the intellectual alibis that are present everywhere. Read faces and, by and large, it's possible to know where people stand. Changing people's beliefs is hard work: selling them on what they already believe and feel is far easier. My advice is to connect emotionally and then provide rational support. After all, the 'facts' are malleable but our gut instincts are unyielding.

References

Ackerman, D (1990) *A Natural History of the Senses*, Vintage Books, New York

American Optometric Association (1991) *An Assessment of American Education*, Harris Education Research Council, New York

Ander, W N and Stern, N Z (2004) *Winning at Retail: Developing a sustained model for retail success*, Wiley, Hoboken, NJ

Anderson, E and Simester, D (2003) Mind your pricing cues, *Harvard Business Review*, September

Anderson, R, Hair, J and Bush, A (1992) *Professional Sales Management*, Wiley, New York

Applebaum, A (2001) The constant customer, *Gallup Management Journal*, 17 June

Atkin, D (2004) *The Culting of Brands*, Portfolio, New York

Baig, E C (2005) Why are tech gizmos so hard to figure out? *USA Today*, 2 November, pp B1–2

Bakalar, N (2006) Men are better than women at ferreting out that angry face in a crowd, *New York Times*, 13 June [online] www.nytimes.com/2006/06/13/health/psychology/13face.html

Baker, D, Greenberg, C and Hemingway, C (2006) *What Happy Companies Know*, Pearson Education, Upper Saddle River, NJ

Baldwin, T and Ford, J K (1997) Transfer to training, *Personnel Psychology*, 50

Banich, M T (2004) *Cognitive Neuroscience and Neuropsychology*, Houghton Mifflin, Boston, Mass

Bardhan, A D and Kroll, C (2003) The new wave of outsourcing, Fisher Central Report no 1103, UC Berkeley, 2 November

Barletta, M (2003) *Marketing to Women*, Dearborn, Chicago

Bates, B and Cleese, J (2001) *The Human Face*, Dorling Kindersley, London

BBC (2001) *The Human Face*, dir J Erskine, perf J Cleese, VHS video

BBC (2006) Face expressions 'hereditary', 25 October [online] http://news.bbc.co.uk/1/hi/health/6055430.stm

Bedbury, S (1999) What great brands do, *Fast Company*, August/September

Begley, S (2004) How do you keep the public shopping? Just make people sad, *Wall Street Journal*, 19 March

Bennis, W and Biederman, P W (1997) *Organizing Genius: The secrets of creative collaboration*, Addison-Wesley, Reading, Mass

Berkowitz, E, Kerin, R, Hartley, S and Rudelius, W (1994) *Marketing*, Irwin, Burr Ridge, Ill

Bernbach, B (1989) *Bill Bernbach Said*, DDB Needham, New York

Bernthal, K (2006) Interview with form recruitment agency staffer, October

Bodenhausen, G, Sheppard, L and Kramer, G (1994) Negative affect and social judgment: the differential impact of anger and sadness, *European Journal of Social Psychology* 24, pp 45–62

Boyatzis, R (2006) Resonant leadership: inspiring the best in us, Nationwide Insurance Leadership Council Presentation, 17 July

Breen, B (2005) The Seoul of design, *Fast Company*, December, p 90

Brill, P and Worth, R (1997) *The Four Levers of Corporate Change*, AMACOM, New York

Broetzmann, S (2004) The conventional wisdom of customer care: fact, fiction or management myths, SOCAP Annual Conference, New York, 11 October

Buckingham, M and Coffman, C (1999) *First, Break All the Rules*, Simon & Schuster, New York

BusinessWeek (2006) Secrets of the male shopper, 4 September

Business Wire (2003) Workers have strong emotional connection to their work experience, but it's mostly negative new study finds, 28 January

Byrne, J (1998) How Jack Welch runs GE, *BusinessWeek*, 8 June

Carey, D C and Ogden, D (2004) *The Human Side of M & A: How CEOs leverage the most important asset in deal making*, Oxford University Press, New York

Carleton, R, Klein, K and Lineberry, C S (2004) *Achieving Post-Merger Success*, Pfeiffer, San Francisco, Calif

Carr, C (1997) Choice, in *Chance and Organizational Change: Practical insights from evolution for business leaders and thinkers*, AMACOM, New York

Caterpillar Inc (2006) Caterpillar Inc.'s Cat U named best overall corporate university, 29 December [online] www.cat.com/cda/components/fullArticle?ids=207849

Center for American Progress (2007) Outsourcing statistics in perspective, April [online] www.americanprogress.org

Chicago Tribune (2006) Most execs overpaid, fund managers say, 2 July (S5), pp 1, 4

Childre, L L and Cryer, B (2000) *From Chaos to Coherence: The power to change performance,* Planetary Publications, Boulder Creek, Colo

Chitwood, R (1996) *World Class Selling,* Best Sellers Publishing, Minneapolis, Minn

Clancy, H (2005) E-tail therapy, *Entrepreneur*, January

Coe, J (2003) *The Fundamentals of Business-to-Business Sales and Marketing*, McGraw-Hill, New York

Collins, J (2001) *Good to Great*, HarperCollins, New York

Compton, R J (2003) The interface between emotion and attention, *Behavioral and Cognitive Neuroscience Review* 2(2), pp 115–29

Conniff, R (2005) *The Ape in the Corner Office: Understanding the workplace beast in all of us,* Crown Business, New York

Cooper, R and Kleinschmidt, E (1990) *New Products: The key factors in success,* AMA, Chicago

Cornelius, R R (1996) *The Science of Emotion*, Prentice Hall, Upper Saddle River, NJ

Crawford, B (2006) By the board, *QSR Magazine*, January, pp 17–18

Cummins, H J (2005) Generations collide, *Minneapolis Star-Tribune*, 27 November

Darwin, C (1998) *The Expression of the Emotions in Man and Animals*, Oxford UP, Oxford

Davenport, T H and Beck, J C (2001) *The Attention Economy*, Harvard Business School Press, Boston, Mass

Davis, A, Pereira, J and Bulkeley, W M (2002) Silent signals, *Wall Street Journal,* 15 August, pp A1, A6

Davis, K (1996) *Getting into Your Customer's Head*, Random House, New York

Daykin, T (2006) Big goes small, *Minneapolis Star-Tribune,* 5 August, pp D1, D4

De Koning, G M J (2004) Evaluating employee performance, *Gallup Management Journal*, 9 December

De Koning, G M J (2005) Building your 'bench strength', *Gallup Management Journal,* 10 March

Desatnick, R L and Detzel, D H (1993) *Managing to Keep the Customer*, Jossey-Bass, San Francisco, Calif

Drucker, P F (2006) What executives should remember, *Harvard Business Review,* February, pp 145–52

Duck, J D (1993) Managing change: the art of balancing, *Harvard Business Review*, November/December, pp 109–118.

Du Plessis, E (2005) *The Advertised Mind*, Millward Brown, Sterling, VA/Kogan Page, London

Dunbar, R (1996) *Grooming Gossip and the Evolution of Language*, Faber and Faber, London

Dunham, R (2004) Read his lips – and smirk, *BusinessWeek.com*, 19 October

Dychtwald, K, Erickson, T and Morison, B (2004) It's time to retire retirement, *Harvard Business Review*, March

Economist (2006) Happiness (and how to measure it), 23 December

Ekman, P (1992) *Telling Lies*, W W Norton, New York

Ekman, P (2003) *Emotions Revealed*, Times Books, New York

Elliott, S (2006) Advertiser-agency relationships turn a bit brighter, *New York Times*, 6 November, p 8

Expansion Management (2005) Poor interpersonal skills doom many new hires, November

Feldman, M (2004) What' ya know? *National Public Radio*, 24 July

Fisher, R and Shapiro, D (2005) *Beyond Reason: Using emotions as you negotiate*, Viking, New York

Fishman, C (2001) But wait, you promised…, *Fast Company*, April

Florida, R (2002) *The Rise of the Creative Class*, Basic Books, New York

Forelle, C and Bandler, J (2006) The perfect payday, *Wall Street Journal*, 18 March, pp A1, A5

Frijda, N, Kuipers, P and ter Schure, E (1989) Relations among emotions, appraisal, and emotional action readiness, *Journal of Personality and Social Psychology* 57, pp 212–28

Frost, P (2003) Jumping ship statistic, in *Toxic Emotions at Work*, Harvard Business School Press, Boston, Mass

Garfield, B (2003) *And Now a Few Words from Me*, McGraw-Hill, New York

Gates, B (2007) A robot in every home, *Scientific American*, January, pp 58–65

Gerber, R (2005) Why can't women be leaders, too? *Gallup Management Journal*, 13 October

Gitomer, J (1998) *Customer Satisfaction Is Worthless*, Bard Press, Austin, Texas

Gitomer, J (2003) *The Sales Bible*, Wiley, New York

Gladwell, M (2002) The naked face, *New Yorker*, 5 August, pp 38–49

Gladwell, M (2005) *Blink: The power of thinking without thinking*, Little, Brown, New York

Gobé, M (2001) *Emotional Branding*, Allworth Press, New York

Goldberg, C (2005) Empathy may begin at the neurons, *International Herald Tribune*, 15 December

Goleman, D (1995) *Emotional Intelligence*, Bantam, New York

Goleman, D (2000) *Working With Emotional Intelligence*, Bantam, New York

Goleman, D, Boyatzis, R and McKee, A (2002) *Primal Leadership*, Harvard Business School Press, Boston, Mass

Grantham, C and Carr, J (2002) *Consumer Evolution*, Wiley, New York

Greenleaf, R K, Beazley, H, Beggs, J and Spears, L C (2003) *The Servant-Leader Within*, Paulist Press, Mahwah, NJ

Hawkins, J and Blakeslee, S (2004) *On Intelligence*, Times Books, New York

Heide, C P (1998) *Dartnell's 30th Sales Force Compensation Survey*, Dartnell Corporation, Chicago

Heil, G, Parker, T and Stephens, D C (1999) *One Size Fits One*, Wiley, New York

Heil, G, Parker, T and Tate, R (1995) *Leadership and the Customer Revolution*, Van Nostrand Reinhold, New York

Helliker, K (2006) This is your brain on a strong brand: MRIs show even insurers can excite, *Wall Street Journal*, 28 November [online] http://online.wsj.com/article_print/SB116468747325534284.html

Higham, P (2000) in Consumers Under Higham's Watchful Eye; Retailing One-on-One: Wal-Mart's Internet Role Taking Cautious Steps, *Advertising Age*, 09 Oct 2000, accessed 27 May 2008 <http://www.accessmylibrary.com/comsite5/bin/aml_landing_tt. pl?page=aml_article_print&item_id=0286–28440875&purchase_ type=ITM&action=print>.

Hine, T (1995) *The Total Package*, Little, Brown, Boston, Mass

Hitchcock, D (1994) *Asian Values and the United States: How much conflict?* Center for Strategic and International Studies, November

Howard, P J (2000) *The Owner's Manual for the Brain*, Bard, Atlanta, Ga

Howard, T (2005) Marketers aim for 'engaged' consumers, *USA Today*, 20 July

HR Focus (2005) Issue 82.8 (August)

Huntington, S (1997) *The Clash of Civilizations and the Remaking of the World Order*, Touchstone, New York

Hymowitz, C (2006) Women swell ranks as middle managers, but are scarce at top, *Wall Street Journal*, 24 July, p B1

Jarrett, M (2003) The seven myths of change management, *Business Strategy Review*, 14

Jeffrey, S (nd) The effect of tangible rewards on perceived organizational support, University of Waterloo, Waterloo, Ontario

Jones, D (2004) When you're smiling, are you seething inside? *USA Today*, 12 April

Jones, D (2005) Besides being lonely at the top, it can be 'disengaging' as well, *USA Today*, 21 June

Kahneman, D (2005) What were they thinking? *Gallup Management Journal*,13 January

Kanter, R M (1977) *Men and Women of the Corporation*, Basic Books, New York

Kaplan, A (2006) These days, the store of your dreams may be in somebody's basement, *St Paul Pioneer Press*, 13 October, pp E1, 13

Khurana, R (2002) *Searching for a Corporate Savior*, Princeton UP, Princeton, NJ

Klein, S (2002) *The Science of Happiness*, Marlowe & Co, New York

Kotkin, J (1999) Main Street 2020: retail's future in the age of e-commerce, Gensler Associates and La Jolla Institute Joint Report

Kotler, P (1973–4) Atmospherics as a marketing tool, *Journal of Retailing* **49**(4), pp 48–61

Kotler, P (1994) *Marketing Management*, Prentice Hall, Englewood Cliffs, NJ

Kouzes, J and Posner, B (eds) (2004) A prescription for leading in cynical times, *Ivey Business Journal*, July/August

Lakoff, G and Johnson, M (2003) *Metaphors We Live By*, University of Chicago Press, Chicago

Lauer, H (2005) *Quirk's*, July/August

Lawrence, P R and Nohria, N (2002) *Driven: How human nature shapes our choices*, Jossey-Bass, San Francisco, Calif

LeDoux, J (1994) Emotion, memory and the brain, *Scientific American*, June, pp 50–57

LeDoux, J (2003) Management wisdom from a neuroscientist, *Gallup Management Journal*, 11 December

Lehrer, J (2006) The reinvention of the self, *Seed*, February/March

Leitch, W (2004) Group thinker: you can make a living from focus groups – if you tell them what they want to hear, *New York*, 16 June

Lerner, J S, Small, D A and Loewenstein, G (2004) Heart strings and purse strings, *Psychological Science* **15**(5)

Loewenstein, G and Lerner, J (2003) The role of affect in decision making, in *Handbook of Affective Science*, ed R Davidson, K Scherer and H Goldsmith, Oxford University Press, New York

Lord of the Wind Films *(2004) What the Bleep Do We Know?* dir W Arntz, M Vincente and B Chasse, perf. M Matlin, DVD

Lowenstein, R. (2001) Exuberance is rational, *New York Times Magazine*, 11 February

MacIntyre, John (2005) Prime numbers, *Profit*, 24.4:13

Mackie, D and Worth, L (1989) Processing deficits and the mediation of positive affect in persuasion, *Journal of Personality and Social Psychology* 57, pp 27–40

Madique, M and Zirger, B J (1998) A study of success and failure in product innovation, *IEEE Transactions on Engineering Management,* November, pp 192–203

Mahrabian, A (1981) *Silent Messages*, Wadsworth, Belmont, Calif

Manning, B (2006) Measure engagement, not satisfaction, iMediaconnection.com, 13 July [online] www.imediaconnection.com/content/10381.asp

Marcus, G E (2002) *The Sentimental Citizen*, Pennsylvania State University Press, University Park, Pa

Marriott, M (2005) Amanda says: You Don't Sound Like Mommy, *New York Times*, 25 August

Mateja, J (2006) Ford helping heftier people fasten their (longer) seat belts, *Chicago Tribune*, 4 July (S3), pp 1, 6

McEwen, W J (2004) Why satisfaction isn't satisfying, *Gallup Management Journal*, November

McGregor, J (2004) Face-off, *Fast Company*, October, p 36

McNeill, D (1998) *The Face: A natural history*, Little, Brown, Boston, Mass

Medgadget.com (2006) Bandwidth of the human eye, 28 July [online] www.medgadget.com/archives/2006/07/the_bandwidth_o.html

Miller, J P (2006) A hint of restraint, *Chicago Tribune*, 2 July (S5), pp 1, 2

Minneapolis/St Paul Business Journal (2005) 5 August

Morris, J et al (2002) The power of affect: predicting intention, *Journal of Advertising Research*, May/June

Mullet, G (2003) Data abuse, *Quirk's,* February

Nelson, E and Ellison, S (2005) In a shift, marketers beef up ad spending inside stores, *Wall Street Journal*, 21 September

Nicholson, N (1998) How hardwired is human behavior? *Harvard Business Review,* July–August

Nokia, The Guest Journey

Norman, D (2004) *Emotional Design*, Basic Books, New York

O'Brien, T (2005) Spinning frenzy: P.R.'s bad press, *New York Times*, 13 February

O'Donnell, J (2004) How recruiters catch a rascal, *USA Today*, 26 August, p 3B

O'Shaughnessy, J (2003) *The Marketing Power of Emotion*, Oxford University Press, New York

Oprah Magazine (2002) The professor of truth, January, p 167

Ortony, A, Clore, G R and Collins, A (1988) *The Cognitive Structure of Emotions*, Cambridge UP, Cambridge, UK

Ortony, A, Norman, D A and Revelle, R (2004) Effective functioning: a three level model of affect, motivation, cognition, and behavior, unpublished paper

Owen, N and Miller, A (2004) *The Five Most Dangerous Issues Facing Sales Directors Today*, and *How to Guarantee a Permanent Improvement in Sales Results*, Trainique LTD and Think Training Inc

Peters, T (2000) Design as advantage no. 1, *Design Management Journal*, Winter

Peters, T (2003) *Re-Imagine*, Dorling Kindersley, London

Phillips, K (2006) *American Theocracy*, Viking, New York

Pine, J II (2004) Generating demand through marketing experiences, personal lecture notes, Carlson School of Management, University of Minnesota, 29 October

Pine, J II, and Gilmore, J H (1998) Welcome to the experience economy, *Harvard Business Review*, July

Pink, D (2005) *A Whole New Mind*, Riverhead, New York

Pinker, S (2003) *The Blank Slate*, Penguin, New York

Plutchik, R (1990) *The Emotions*, University Press of America, New York

Pooler, J (2003) *Why We Shop: Emotional rewards and retail strategies*, Praeger, Westport, Conn

Postma, P (2005) *The Ultimate Marketing Machine*, Het Spectrum, Amsterdam

Quaid, L (2006) Beer sales pop, *St Paul Pioneer Press*, 19 August, p C1

Rackham, N (1989) *Major Account Sales Strategy*, McGraw-Hill, New York

Raghunathan, R and Pham, M (1999) All negative moods are not equal: motivational influences of anxiety and sadness on decision making, *Organizational Behavior and Human Decision Processes* 79, pp 56–77

Rapaille, C (2006) *The Culture Code*, Broadway Books, New York

Ravindran, P (2005) Mergers and machismo – are take over chiefs acting rationally? *Business Line*, 14 June

Reilly, T (2002) *Value Added Selling*, McGraw-Hill, New York

Reis, L and Reis, A (2004) *The Origin of Brands*, Collins, New York

Rigby, D K, Reichheld, F and Dawson, C (2003) Winning customer loyalty is the key to a winning CRM strategy, *Ivey Business Journal*, March/April

Roseman, I, Antoniou, A and Jose, P (1996) Appraisal determinants of emotion: constructing a more accurate and comprehensive theory, *Cognition and Emotion* 10(3), pp 247–77

Sack, M (2003) Sex, lies and the Internet, *Quirk's*, January

Schermerhorn, J R, Hunt, J G and Osborn, R N (1999) *Organizational Behavior*, 7th edn, Wiley, New York

Schmidt, F L, and Hunter, J E (1998) The validity and utility of selection methods in personnel psychology: practical and theoretical implications of 85 years of research findings, *Psychological Bulletin* 124(2), pp 262–74

Schmitt, B H (1999) *Experiential Marketing*, Free Press, New York

Schwartz, T (2000) How do you feel? *Fast Company*, June

Seligman, M E (2002) *Authentic Happiness*, Free Press, New York

Sharpe, R (2000) As leaders, women rule, *BusinessWeek*, 20 November

Shin, A (2006) What customers say and how they say it, *Washington Post*, 18 October

Silverstein, M J and Fiske, N (2005) *Trading Up: Why consumers want new luxury goods – and how companies create them*, Penguin, New York

Slywotzky, A and Morrison, D J (2002) *The Profit Zone*, Three Rivers Press, New York

Smith, C and Ellsworth, P (1985) Patterns of cognitive appraisal in emotion, *Journal of Personality and Social Psychology* 48, pp 813–38

Spillman, M (2006) Cracking the engagement code, *iMediaconnection.com*, 26 July [online] www.imediaconnection.com/content/10518.asp

Steel, J (1998) *Truth, Lies & Advertising*, Wiley, New York

Stevens, M (2005) *Your Marketing Sucks*, Three Rivers Press, New York

Stock, H J (2005) Getting emotional about sales, *Bank Investment Consultant*, January, pp 32–33

Straits, D (2006) Employer hot buttons [online] http://careerbuilder.com Path: Advice & Resources; Career Advice; Employer Hot Buttons.

Strategy+Business (2006) Best business books 2006, Winter

Sullivan, L (1998) *Hey Whipple, Squeeze This*, Wiley, New York

Sutherland, M and Sylvester, A K (2000) *Advertising and the Mind of the Consumer*, Allen & Unwin, Sydney, Australia

Sway, R (2005) *DDI's State of the Industry Report*, Atlanta, Ga, 14 October

TD (2005) Workforce performance is top HR priority, International Association for Human Resource Information Management & Knowledge Fusion, July, p 16

Thottam, J (2005) Happiness variance: thank God it's Monday, *Time*, 17 January

Tiedens, L and Linton, S (2001) Judgment under emotional certainty and uncertainty: the effects of specific emotions on information processing, *Journal of Personality and Social Psychology* 81, pp 973–88

Tierney, J (2004) Political points: of smiles and sneers, *New York Times*, 18 July

Toffler, A (1970) *Future Shock*, Bantam, New York

Torday, D (2003) How to read your wife's face, *Esquire*, April, p 90

Wahrman, H, Fusso, T and Serrins, R (2003) Behavioral economics and consumer market research, LIMRA Marketing Research Conference on Behavioral Economics, May

Wartik, N (2004) Hard wired for prejudice? Experts examine human response to outsiders, *New York Times*, 20 April

WCCO (2006) Women get paternal clues in men's faces, 11 May [online] http://wcco.com/national/topstories_story_130125914.html

Welch, J (2001) *Straight from the Gut,* Warner, New York

Wellman, D (2002) Wal-Mart is not about price, *Frozen Food Age* **50**(6)

White, E (2006) For relevance, firms revamp worker reviews, *Wall Street Journal,* 17 July, pp B1, B5

Wolfe, D and Snyder, R E (2003) *Ageless Marketing,* Dearborn, Chicago

World Almanac & Book of Facts 2005, World Almanac Books, New York

Wright, R (1995) *The Moral Animal*, Vintage, New York

Wundt, W (1897/1998) *Outlines of Psychology*, Thoemmes Continuum, Bristol

Zajonc, R (1980) Preferences need no inferences, *American Psychologist,* February

Zaltman, G (1996) Metaphorically speaking, *Marketing Research* **8**(2)

Zaltman, G (2003) *How Customers Think*, Harvard Business School Press, Boston, Mass

Zaslow, J (2006) Happiness Inc, *Wall Street Journal,* 18 March

Zeitlin, D M and Westwood, R A (1986) Measuring emotional response, *Journal of Advertising Research,* October/November, pp 34–44

Zimmermann, M (1986) Neurophysiology of sensory system, in *Fundamentals of Sensory Physiology*, ed R F Schmidt, Springer-Verlag, New York

Credits and permissions

Introduction

Pg 1, StockXCHNG/Bartlomiej Fulanty; Pg 2, cover of *Blink* by Malcolm Gladwell provided by Little, Brown & Co (© 2005); Pg 5, StockXCHNG/Florian Martin; Pg 7 (Figure 0.1), StockXCHNG/Paul Williamson; Pg 10, provided by Whirlpool Corporation.

Chapter 1

Pg 13, istock photo; Pg 22, Library of Congress, Prints & Photographs Division, NYWT&S Collection, [Reproduction Number: LC-USZ62–126207]; Pg 26 (Figure 1.3), StockXCHNG/Anna H.G.; Pg 28, StockXCHNG/Hannah Boettcher; Pg 31, StockXCHNG/Luciano Tirabassi.

Chapter 2

Pg 39, StockXCHNG; Pg 41, Stock/XCHNG/John Evans; Pg 45, StockXCHNG/Katherine de Vera; Pg 49, StockXCHNG/Emilia Stasiak; Pg 58, StockXCHNG/Henry Smaal.

Chapter 3

Pg 75, StockXCHNG/Charles Sotello; Pg 78, StockXCHNG/Tim Van Damme; Pg 85, StockXCHNG/Benjamin Earwicker; Pg 86, StockXCHNG/Boris Gaasbeek; Pg 93, StockXCHNG/Maurice Beer; Pg 94, StockXCHNG/Stuart Bell; Pg 95, Courtesy of Dogfish Head Brewery.

Chapter 4

Pg 97, istock photo; Pg 99, Stock XCHNG/Marcin Bertowski; Pg 106 (Figure 4.4), Center for Strategic and International Studies, Asian Values and the United States: *How Much Conflict*, Hitchcock, David I., 1994, pg. 54; Pg 111, StockXCHNG/Tom De Bruin; Pg 116 (Figure 4.10), book by StockXCHNG/Robert Aichinger, model by StockXCHNG/Afonso Lima; Pg 117, Courtesy of Pinnacle Foods.

Chapter 5

Pg 129, StockXCHNG/Patrick Nejhuis; Pg 134, StockXCHNG/Brian S.; Pg 135, courtesy of IKEA UK; Pg 137 (a) (Figure 5.1), courtesy of BMW USA; Pg 137 (b) (Figure 5.2), courtesy of MGA Entertainment; Pg 138, courtesy of Whirlpool Corporation; Pg 141, courtesy of ING; Pg 143, StockXCHNG/Jess Rafin; Pg 144, StockXCHNG/Rurik Tullio.

Chapter 6

Pg 157, StockXCHNG/Evgenij Fursai; Pg 160, StockXCHNG/Carlos Zaragosa; Pg 162, StockXCHNG/Richard Simpson; Pg 164, StockXCHNG/Davide Gulielmo; Pg 175, StockXCHNG/Sanja Gjenero; Pg 181, StockXCHNG/Cecilia Alegro; Pg 184, StockXCHNG/Diego Midrano; Pg 187, StockXCHNG/Sanja Gjenero.

Chapter 7

Pg 193, StockXCHNG/Mark Brennan; Pg 197, StockXCHNG/Maryann Cummings; Pg 200, StockXCHNG/John Moore; Pg 209 (a) (Figure 7.4), From *Major Account Sales Strategy* by Neil Rackham, used with permission of Hutwaite (©1989); Pg 209 (b) (Figure 7.5), StockXCHNG/Ramon Gonzales, StockXCHNG/Christy Thompson; Pg 211, Courtesy of The SCOOTER Store; Pg 213, StockXCHNG/J.W.M. Pap; Pg 216 (Figure 7.8), From *Major Account Sales Strategy* by Neil Rackham, used with permission of Hutwaite (© 1989); Pg 210, StockXCHNG/Tory Byrne; Pg 222 (a) (Figure 7.10), reproduced with the permission of Nikki Owen, author of *The Five Most Dangerous Issues Facing Sales Directors Today*; Pg 222 (b) (Figure 7.11), from *Major Account Sales Strategy* by Neil Rackham, used with permission of Hutwaite (©1989).

Chapter 8

Pg 233, StockXCHNG/Martin Luckner; Pg 239, StockXCHNG/Rodolfo Clix; Pg 244, StockXCHNG/Michele Lukowski; Pg 248, StockXCHNG/Phil Feer; Pg 250, StockXCHNG/Elena Buetler; Pg 251, StockXCHNG/Eduardo Oride; Pg 252, StockXCHNG/Constantin Kammerer.

Chapter 9

Pg 255, istock photo; Pg 257, StockXCHNG/Mike Esprit; Pg 261, Cover of *Straight from the Gut* by Jack Welch care of Little, Brown and Co.; Pg 270, StockXCHNG/Constantin Kammerer; Pg 273 (a), StockXCHNG/Simon Stratford; Pg 273 (b), StockXCHNG/with kind permission of www.tomtown.net/Eveline Holland; Pg 277, StockXCHNG/Kristen Price; Pg 282, StockXCHNG/Constantin Kammerer; Pg 284, StockXCHNG/Constantin Kammerer, StockXCHNG/Kathryn Mcallum and StockXCHNG/Carl Dwyer.

Chapter 10

Pg 289, StockXCHNG/Niclas Ericsson; Pg 293, StockXCHNG/Constantin Kammerer; Pg 294, StockXCHNG/Elena Buetler; Pg 297, StockXCHNG/ Ahmed Al-Shukaili; Pg 304 (a) StockXCHNG/unknown, (b) StockXCHNG/ Constantin Kammerer, (c) StockXCHNG/Isaac Joo; Pg 308, Performance Solutions.

*All other images are property of Sensory Logic, Inc or StockXCHNG.

Index